Authoritarian Legali

Can authoritarian regimes use democratic institutions to strengthen and solidify their rule? The Chinese government has legislated some of the most protective workplace laws in the world and opened up the judicial system to adjudicate workplace conflict, emboldening China's workers to use these laws. This book examines these patterns of legal mobilization, showing which workers are likely to avail themselves of these new protections and find them effective. Gallagher finds that workers with high levels of education are far more likely to claim these new rights and be satisfied with the results. However, many others, left disappointed with the large gap between law on the books and law in reality, reject the courtroom for the streets. Using workers' narratives, surveys, and case studies of protests, Gallagher argues that China's half-hearted attempt at rule of law construction undermines the stability of authoritarian rule. New workplace rights fuel workers' rising expectations, but a dysfunctional legal system drives many workers to more extreme options, including strikes, demonstrations, and violence.

Mary E. Gallagher is a professor of political science at the University of Michigan, Ann Arbor, where she is also the director of the Kenneth G. Lieberthal and Richard H. Rogel Center for Chinese Studies. She is also the author or editor of several books, including *Chinese Justice: Civil Dispute Resolution in Contemporary China* (Cambridge 2011) and *Contemporary Chinese Politics: New Sources, Methods, and Field Strategies* (Cambridge 2010).

Authoritarian Legality in China

Law, Workers, and the State

MARY E. GALLAGHER
University of Michigan, Ann Arbor

CAMBRIDGE
UNIVERSITY PRESS

CAMBRIDGE
UNIVERSITY PRESS

University Printing House, Cambridge CB2 8BS, United Kingdom

One Liberty Plaza, 20th Floor, New York, NY 10006, USA

477 Williamstown Road, Port Melbourne, VIC 3207, Australia

4843/24, 2nd Floor, Ansari Road, Daryaganj, Delhi – 110002, India

79 Anson Road, #06–04/06, Singapore 079906

Cambridge University Press is part of the University of Cambridge.

It furthers the University's mission by disseminating knowledge in the pursuit of education, learning and research at the highest international levels of excellence.

www.cambridge.org
Information on this title: www.cambridge.org/9781107083776
DOI: 10.1017/9781316018194

© Mary E. Gallagher 2017

This publication is in copyright. Subject to statutory exception and to the provisions of relevant collective licensing agreements, no reproduction of any part may take place without the written permission of Cambridge University Press.

First published 2017

Printed in the United Kingdom by Clays, St Ives plc

A catalogue record for this publication is available from the British Library.

Library of Congress Cataloging-in-Publication data
Names: Gallagher, Mary Elizabeth, 1969– author.
Title: Authoritarian legality in China : law, workers, and the state / Mary E. Gallagher.
Description: New York : Cambridge University Press, 2017. |
Includes bibliographical references and index.
Identifiers: LCCN 2017011178| ISBN 9781107083776 (hardback) |
ISBN 9781107444485 (paperback)
Subjects: LCSH: Labor laws and legislation – China. | Labor policy – China. |
Employee rights – China. | Authoritarianism – China. | BISAC: POLITICAL SCIENCE / Government / International.
Classification: LCC KNQ1274 .G35 2017 | DDC 344.5101–dc23
LC record available at https://lccn.loc.gov/2017011178

ISBN 978-1-107-08377-6 Hardback
ISBN 978-1-107-44448-5 Paperback

Additional resources for this publication at www.cambridge.org/Gallagher

Cambridge University Press has no responsibility for the persistence or accuracy of URLs for external or third-party internet websites referred to in this publication, and does not guarantee that any content on such websites is, or will remain, accurate or appropriate.

TO MY FAMILY

Contents

List of Figures, Tables, and Charts		*page* ix
Acknowledgments		xi
List of Abbreviations		xvii
1	Authoritarian Legality at Work: The Workplace and China's Urbanization	1
2	A Theory of Authoritarian Legality	21
3	Fire Alarms and Firefighters: Institutional Reforms and Legal Mobilization at the Chinese Workplace	52
4	By the Book: Learning and the Law	112
5	Great Expectations: The Disparate Effects of Legal Mobilization	149
6	The Limits of Authoritarian Legality	191
Epilogue: Requiem for the Labor Contract Law?		216
Bibliography		229
Index		247

Figures, Tables, and Charts

FIGURES

3.1	Labor Dispute Resolution Process	page 86
5.1	Labor Dispute "Pyramid"	155

TABLES

3.1	Summary of Institutional Reforms and Effects	54
3.2	Awareness of Labor Law	95
3.3	Workers with Social Insurance, 2005 and 2010	97
4.1	Legal Knowledge	120
4.2	Determinants of Legal Knowledge	121
4.3	Propensity to Pursue Grievance	124
4.4	Propensity to Choose Litigation	126
4.5	Determinants of Effectiveness of Litigation	127
5.1	Likelihood of Experiencing a Workplace Problem	154
5.2	Generational Characteristics	177
5.3	Bivariate Analysis of Age, Education, and Employment	178
5.4	Age and Effectiveness	179

CHARTS

2.1	OECD Employment Protection Index, 2013	28
3.2	Workforce Employed with Formal Labor Contracts	65
3.3	Trade Union Membership Compared to Employment in the State Sector	74

3.4	"Law as a Weapon" Mentions in the People's Daily, 1949–2011	82
3.5	Country Ranking for "Laws Are Publicized and Accessible"	83
3.6	Labor Disputes, 2001–2012	89
3.7	Arbitrated Labor Disputes by Province, 2004–2011	90
3.8	Collective Disputes as a Proportion of All Arbitrated Disputes, 1995–2012	93
3.9	Strikes, 2011–2016	107
4.1	Med-High Labor Law Knowledge by Education Level	120
5.1	Which Resolution Methods Are You Willing to Use?	157
5.2	Which Method Is Most Effective?	158
5.3	Satisfaction with Dispute Resolution	180
5.4	Labor Dispute Resolution Patterns	180

Acknowledgments

In September 2003, I arrived in Shanghai as a Fulbright Scholar to begin a project on the legal mobilization of Chinese workers. Almost as soon as I arrived, I began to hear about plans to revise the 1995 Labor Law, which was the foundational law that facilitated workers' access to the legal system to protect their rights, by drafting a new law on labor contracts. As my project proceeded, the draft Labor Contract Law (LCL) was released to intense debate and controversy as activists rejoiced in the state's embrace of more protective laws while some economists and businesspeople warned that the law would adversely affect the Chinese economy and investment. The tumult over the law's drafting was nothing compared to the law's implementation during the 2008 Global Financial Crisis when disputes skyrocketed and large-scale strikes shook developmental zones all along China's coast. As this book was being finished, China's Finance Minister Lou Jiwei called out the Labor Contract Law in particular for its negative effects on the slowing Chinese economy. Significant revision of the law began to look extremely likely. Some economists even called for its repeal.

This sketch of the legislative progression of the LCL is one way of explaining why this project took so long and evolved in different directions as time passed. It also exemplifies the opportunities and pitfalls of studying contemporary political and social issues in China today. The speed and intensity of change yields enormously interesting social phenomena that need to be studied and understood, for their effects are felt far beyond the Chinese context. At the same time, there is no perfect time to end the story, as the story does not end. Books, on the other hand, have to be finished. I could not have predicted that the LCL would be so consequential when I began this study in 2003 nor that the same law would be in danger of significant revision, even repeal, as the study ended. This book can provide only a snapshot of an incredibly important and consequential decade or so when the Chinese state embraced notions of "rule of law" and encouraged Chinese workers to make use of these laws to protect themselves against the onslaught of economic reform and liberalization. I was lucky to start this project at the same time, but things will go on from here. My study ends by necessity now, at a moment in time when China's commitments to workplace rights and to the notion of 'rule of law' are in great doubt. While the fate of the LCL still swings in the balance of China's economic slowdown and intra-elite conflict, the government's enthusiasm for legal solutions to labor conflict has also waned.

This project enjoyed great support and encouragement from many institutions and individuals. For financial support, I would like to thank the National Science Foundation Law and Social Science Program, the Fulbright US Scholar program run by the Council for the International Exchange of Scholars, the US–China Legal Cooperation Fund and, at the University of Michigan, the Center for Political Studies at the Institute of Social Research, the Department of Political Science, and the Lieberthal-Rogel Center for Chinese Studies. In addition, I would like to thank the institutions in China that facilitated my research or worked with me on collaborative projects, including the Research Center on Contemporary China at Peking University, the Institute of Labor Economics at the Chinese Academy of Social Sciences, the East China University of Politics and Law, and Shanghai Jiaotong University's School of Law. I would also like to thank the National Committee on US–China Relations for involving me in their projects in China, especially the project on US–China Labor Cooperation and Jan Berris and Shenyu Belsky.

Over the years I gave talks at many universities and institutes in China and elsewhere at which I received excellent feedback, criticism, and suggestions. I would like to thank those institutions and the people involved for the generous experiences, including Stanford Peking University Center and Center for East Asian Studies, the Fairbank Center at Harvard University, SAIS–John Hopkins University, Wisconsin Law School and Department of Political Science, Berkeley Boalt School of Law and Department of Political Science, Emory University, US-China Institute at USC, Columbia University Center for Chinese Law, University of Iowa, Sloan School of Business at MIT, University of Washington and the National Bureau for Asian Research, Yale University School of Law, Brown University, Cornell University School of Industrial and Labor Relations and Government Department, the University of Pennsylvania Center for East Asian Studies, Keio University, Peking University, Shanghai Academy of Social Sciences, Fudan University Department of Political Science and Department of Economics, NYU Asian Law Institute, University of Texas Center for East Asian Studies, Western Michigan University, Duke University Department of Political Science, University of Chicago Center for East Asian Studies, and the Chinese Academy of Social Sciences.

In addition to this institutional support, many colleagues and friends gave their time, encouragement, and advice. At Michigan, Yuen Yuen Ang, Jenna Bednar, Pam Brandwein, Christian De Pee, Anna Gryzmala-Busse, Don Herzog, Jon Hanson, Allen Hicken, Nico Howson, John Jackson, Don Kinder, Jennet Kirkpatrick, Anna Kirkland, Ken Lieberthal, Pauline Jones, Rob Mickey, Larry Root, Arlene Saxonhouse, and Mark West. I would also like to thank the many people who commented or discussed this project in various fora, including Bill Alford, Cai Yongshun, Teri Caraway, Allen Carlson, Anita Chan, Chen Feng, Linda Cook, Don Clarke, Josh Cohen, Sean Cooney, Geoff Crothall, Jacques DeLisle, Bruce Dickson, Cindy Estlund, Mark Frazier, Eli Friedman, Steve Goldstein, Kathy Hendley, Sarosh Kuruvilla, Pierre Landry, Ching Kwan Lee, Li Chunyun, Li Lianjiang, Michael Li, Ben Liebman, Liu Mingwei, Liu Sida, Rick Locke, Melanie Manion, Ethan Michelson, Carl Minzner, Kevin O'Brien, Jean Oi, Albert Park, Margaret Pearson, Elizabeth Perry, Tim Pringle, Tom Remington, Gay Seidman, Kellee Tsai, Benjamin Van Rooij, Tang Wenfang, Andy Walder, Margaret Woo, Teresa Wright, Zhong Yang, and David Zweig. Undoubtedly, I have omitted many others who asked questions, gave advice, and otherwise contributed to my thinking on these issues. For those contributions, I am very grateful.

I would like to thank my many former and current students who have worked on this project with me. Some were co-authors on side projects and papers. Others toiled in relative obscurity before moving on to bigger and better things. They include Juan Chen, Lyric Chen, Patricia Chen, Victoria Chonn Ching, Courtney Henderson, Adrienne Lagman, Yawen Lei, Tian Tian Liu, Danie Stockmann, Bing Sun, Mike Thompson, Jason Tower, Huong Trieu, Yuhua Wang, Yujeong Yang, Qingjie Zeng, Jia'an Zhang, and Wen Zhang. Mike Thompson deserves extra thanks for copyediting and suggestions on cheesy subtitles. An article with Yujeong Yang in *Law and Social Inquiry* discusses some of the results in Chapters 4 and 5. Yujeong deserves extra thanks for her help and assistance.

Three people said something to me, during a talk or in a conversation, that had a lasting impact on how my thinking evolved. In each case, they said something in a very matter of fact way, which probably meant that I should have already known what they were saying, but didn't. So thank you for relieving me of my ignorance. Yuhua Wang noted that my portrayal of evaluation of the law as split between positive evaluation of their ability to use it and negative evaluation of the institution itself was basically the same thing as internal/external efficacy in American political behavior. Peter Lorentzen remarked during a talk that my description of labor dispute resolution in China was "a fire alarm system" and directed me to the literature on congressional oversight. Yawen Lei pointed out to me that the World Justice Project had actually measured China's success in legal dissemination, and directed me to that comparative measure of "rule of law" achievements.

This project would not have been possible without the help of many individuals in China, including many people whose names do not appear anywhere in this book. Colleagues at ECUPL were enormously generous with their time and knowledge. They welcomed me into their community despite the political sensitivity of the issue and always helped me improve the project as much as possible. Professor Dong Baohua facilitated my work on legal aid plaintiffs in 2004–2005 and allowed me to make follow-up visits many years after our first collaboration. I learned an enormous amount from him on the nature of Chinese labor law and certainly absorbed a healthy dose of his skepticism toward how legal protections work in practice. Also at ECUPL I thank Professor Li Lingyun, Qiu Jie, Haifan Zhao, Dong Runqing, Ding Zaifeng, Qian Fei, Lv Yin, Zhu Dongli, Zhou Kaichang, Xu Minglang, and Tang Laoshi. Song Jing deserves special mention for her irrepressible spirit and commitment to the project and to me! At Peking University's Research Center on Contemporary China, Shen Mingming, Yan Jie, Liu Jinyun, and Chai Jingjing developed the 2005 Labor Law Mobilization Survey, which allowed this study to examine these issues from a broader perspective. The Institute of Population and Labor Economics at the Chinese Association of Social Sciences invited me to participate in the 2010 China Urban Labor Force Survey with Albert Park, John Giles, Wang Meiyan, Yang Du, Cai Fang, and others. Without this collaboration, I would not have been able to study the impact of the Labor Contract Law on China's workers and labor markets. Other people who have helped me enormously over the years include Jiang Junlu, Wang Jianjun, Wang Kan, Sun Zhongwei, Cheng Yanyuan, Chang Kai, Lin Jia, Ye Jingyi, Zhou Changzheng, Feng Tongqing, Dai Jianzhong, Wang Quanxing, Shi Meixia, Duan Yi, among others. There are plenty of healthy disagreements within this network of labor law and labor relations scholars. I benefitted immensely from their debates and discussions.

As part of the preparation of the manuscript, Margaret Levi, then at the University of Washington, Seattle, organized a book workshop when I had barely finished writing the core chapters of the book. The participants of that workshop gave me very thorough and excellent advice on each chapter, in some cases complete with powerpoint advice on how to improve my arguments. It was a remarkable experience to have and helped enormously as I finished the manuscript. In addition to Margaret, I'd like to thank Michael McCann, Susan Whiting, Xiao Ma, Daniel Yoo, and Tania Melo for the detailed feedback. Lew Bateman and Robert Dreesen were both, in turn, supportive and responsive editors on the project at Cambridge University Press. Kathy Thelen and Erik Wibbels continued to support the project after Margaret stepped down as series editor.

An acknowledgments section is not complete without recognition of family members and friends who tolerated my strange interests in Chinese employment law and the manufacturing origins of their clothes and toys. My children, Magda, Elinor, and Liam, lived in China during long stints of fieldwork, leaving behind bucolic Ann Arbor for bustling Shanghai where the food was better if not the traffic. My mother, Munsey Alston, lived with us while the bulk of the manuscript was finished, taking up the slack in childcare and housework duties. She escaped by entering the Peace Corps in Swaziland, which might indicate the heavy burden that we imposed on her. My husband, Ken, with his own interests in the vagaries of Chinese law and workplace practices, not only tolerated the project but encouraged me to complete it, including by adding another year of living in Shanghai to our family's general frenetic pace. In Ann Arbor, I was also lucky to live and work in a supportive community of friends, family, and colleagues that made it easy to work when necessary but also provided many other opportunities to have a fun and fulfilling life.

Abbreviations

ACFTU	All China Federation of Trade Unions
CASS	Chinese Academy of Social Science
CCP	Chinese Communist Party
CLB	China Labor Bulletin
CULS	China Urban Labor Force Survey
ECUPL	East China University of Politics and Law
EEOC	Equal Employment Opportunity Commission
EPL	Employment Promotion Law of 2008
FIE	Foreign-Invested Enterprise
GFTU	Guangdong Federation of Trade Unions
HFTU	Hunan Federation of Trade Unions
ILO	International Labor Organization
LAC	Labor Arbitration Committee
LDMAL	Labor Dispute Mediation and Arbitration Law of 2008
LCL	Labor Contract Law of 2008
LLMS	Labor Law Mobilization Survey
MOHRSS	Ministry of Human Resources and Social Security
NGO	Non-Governmental Organization
NPC	National People's Congress
OECD	The Organization of Economic Co-operation and Development
RCCC	Research Center on Contemporary China (Peking University)

RMB	Renminbi (Chinese Yuan)
SCNPC	Standing Committee of the National People's Congress
SMTU	Shanghai Municipal Trade Union
WJP	World Justice Project

1

Authoritarian Legality at Work

The Workplace and China's Urbanization

500 million people have already left their rural hometowns for Chinese cities; when they do so they are looking for work. How work is structured has implications far beyond the Chinese workplace; workplace institutions directly influence the pace and nature of China's urbanization. This book is about the Chinese state's project to develop legal institutions to manage workplace relations. My motivation in writing about these topics and studying them for many years is the connection that the specialized institutions that regulate and manage China's labor markets have to the larger challenges of China's dual transition: from socialism to capitalism and from agriculture to industry. Labor institutions, as vehicles to structure labor markets and the workplace, are inseparable from these two transitions and the massive and unprecedentedly rapid urbanization that has accompanied them.

The development of "rule of law" at the workplace was a necessary part of China's transition to a market economy as the government radically restructured how people related to the workplace, moving from administrative management under the planned economy to the contractual relations of a market economy, which then allowed private and foreign firms to employ Chinese workers and state sector firms to end their cradle-to-grave employment relationship with their workers. The establishment of this contractual notion of employment also necessitated legal and administrative changes. The state had to regulate labor markets by legislating labor laws and related regulations that set legal minimum standards; it had to implement and enforce these standards to ensure employer compliance; finally, it had to take on the role of a third-party arbiter of the unavoidable disputes that arise from contracts between workers and firms. This book examines these interactions between the state, in its roles as legislator, enforcer, and arbiter, and workers as they make claims against employers for breach of the law.

During the first three decades of China's reforms, workplace institutions were bifurcated, dividing up workers based on their *hukou* status.[1] Urban citizens received social benefits and welfare from their places of work, but these benefits were dependent on their possession of urban, local *hukou*. Rural migrant workers were usually excluded from these social benefits, even if they were long-term residents in an urban area and employed by an urban firm (Solinger 1999; Zhang 2001; Wang 2005; Chan 2010). Instead, they were granted user rights over collectively-owned rural land in their hometowns. This division between workers – the granting of social security to urban, local workers and of land security to rural migrant workers – ensured a pattern of urbanization that was partial and temporary. Not only was it inadequate in meeting some of the basic needs of migrants, it also severely restrained labor mobility, exacerbated inequality, and encouraged social discrimination and mistreatment of rural citizens in cities (World Bank 2014).

China's central government has now rejected this pattern of urbanization, ostensibly moving toward a development model that is more inclusive, equitable, and sustainable. In order to leave this prior system of the bifurcated workplace and spatially-determined, differential citizenship rights behind, the new process of urbanization in China must include provision of formal employment (and with it participation in the urban welfare state) for rural migrants in exchange for the abrogation of their user rights over rural land. The workplace has a key role, not only in the payment of wages but also in the dispersal of social insurance. It is the linchpin of an urbanization scheme that exchanges rural security through land for urban security through employment. It is the central node of a strategy to move from industrialization via a temporary, migratory workforce to industrialization via a permanently urbanized population. The workplace is the setting in which the state transforms rural people into urban citizens.

Rising expectations for security through state-sponsored social welfare may be a natural consequence of urbanization, but in the Chinese context, this expectation is compounded by the lack of private rural land

---

[1] In the Chinese context, with its residential registration system (*hukou*), every citizen is tied to a specific place (a city for urban citizens, a county for rural citizens) and to a type of production (agricultural for rural vs. non-agricultural for most urban citizens).

ownership. Once peasants leave the countryside for employment, they risk losing their land security totally. Much of the social welfare provided by the Chinese state to its urban residents is attached to employment, and this protection via the workplace is key to urbanization and rural land reform because migrants will not willingly give up rural land security without it. In 2014, the Central Committee of the CCP and the State Council jointly issued a plan for a National New Type of Urbanization, 2014–2020 (*guojia xinxing chengzhenhua guihua*). This six-year plan for "state-led urbanization" (Ong 2014) proposes to increase the permanent urban population from 54 percent of the total population to 60 percent while increasing the number of permanent urban residents with urban *hukou* from 35 percent of the total population to 45 percent. Under this plan, over 100 million rural residents would be given legal status to reside in urban areas permanently and have full access to urban social welfare benefits (Yang 2014). But this assumes that these migrants will enter into formal labor contracts with their urban employers. Without formal employment, these urbanizing rural citizens will continue to be excluded from the most consequential urban social welfare, such as pensions, medical insurance, unemployment insurance, and occupational injury and disease insurance.[2]

This opening chapter situates the rest of the book in this larger context of urbanization. I lay out the key challenges that face the Chinese government in its ambitious plans to urbanize the majority of China's population by 2050 and show how each of these challenges are linked to the workplace reforms and legislative changes studied in this book. These challenges include: the need to adjust to China's changing demographic structure, the need to convince rural residents to give up land security for the allure of urban residency and employment, and the need to reform the *hukou* system to end systematic discrimination against rural migrants in the cities. While the first challenge is mostly a straightforward adjustment to China's rapid demographic shift toward an aging population, the other two challenges are legacies of the socialist era institutions of collective rural land ownership, which substituted for rural social welfare, and *hukou*, which bifurcated society and constrained migrant workers' opportunities to urbanize legally and permanently.

---

[2] There are other types of urban social welfare, including the minimum income guarantee (dibao) and urban resident social insurance. However, these programs provide only the most basic support.

MOTIVATING PUZZLE

These macro issues of China's development trajectory explain the existence of the motivating puzzle of this book: why did the Chinese government legislate high labor standards and encourage its citizens to not only know about them but to actively press for their implementation and enforcement? The period under study in this book was a moment in time when the interests of workers and the central Chinese government converged over core workplace issues while firms and local governments were reluctant or unable to adjust. While workers' interests in better conditions and more stable employment are naturally related to their own subordinate status in the employment relationship, the central state has far more strategic and long-term needs to change China's development model away from its reliance on low-cost, low-skill, low-tech manufacturing employing an exploited migratory workforce. This model also included an exclusionary welfare state that covered an aging and less productive urban workforce while excluding millions of young, healthy rural workers. These necessary changes are not the romantic political ideologies of a workers' party, whatever the origins of the CCP in working class politics. These are instead the challenges of an ambitious middle-income nation confronting the exhaustion of its previous developmental model.

As Chapter 3 details, in order to reach these goals, the government now promotes both higher labor standards and more inclusive protection in a bid to bring more workers into the formal sector. The 2008 Labor Contract Law targets the issue of formality most directly by dramatically increasing the incentives to sign contracts and the penalties for failure to do so. Formalization of employment relations is the first step toward better protection of all workers and more inclusion of rural migrants in particular. The pathway to a more stable pattern of urbanization is via these reforms to the labor market and also through another major and related institutional reform: rural land rights and the exchange of land security for employment security and concomitant social insurance. Like other East Asian development states, China's evolving welfare state is a *productive* one – with most social benefits tied to work (Holliday 2000; Frazier 2010; Mok and Hudson 2014).

The legislation of high standards and the formal expansion of social welfare programs to rural migrants are only the first steps. Enforcement of and compliance with these new standards by local governments and employers is far from guaranteed. China, like many developing countries, has a large gap between what is formally promised in law and what is actually delivered on the ground. Enforcement and compliance mechanisms are key to how the ratcheting up of standards and inclusive policies play out. In subsequent chapters, I show that the Chinese government has very deliberately chosen methods of enforcement and compliance that are suboptimal for compliance but both politically rational and market conforming. With the exception of occasional top-down campaigns to target severe problems (such as wage arrears), the Chinese state has delegated enforcement of these new labor protections to workers themselves. Through the media and propaganda system, the state has propagated knowledge and awareness of workplace rights in order to facilitate bottom-up legal mobilization. Through the dispute resolution system, workers are tasked with their own rights protection, a role that many have taken on with alacrity.

Through restrictions on organization and selective repression of civil society, however, this bottom-up mobilization is individualized and fragmented. Many collective disputes are divided up into individual complaints; labor non-governmental organizations (NGOs) and "rights-defense" lawyers are constrained by the political environment; and the official trade union, the All-China Federation of Trade Unions (ACFTU), continues to serve as a junior partner of the government in resolving labor disputes. These constraints in the enforcement model lead to suboptimal outcomes for compliance as detailed in Chapters 4 and 5. The heavy reliance on workers themselves benefits workers with the skills and education to make use of the law. Compliance improvements accrue to the higher rungs of the labor market. Restrictions on organization and bargaining impede other workers, especially those with fewer skills and resources, to harness their collective power. The political threat from labor is reduced, but better compliance is sacrificed. The suboptimal outcomes for compliance and the frustrating and often ineffective road of legal mobilization also leaves many workers disenchanted and increasingly prone to search out more extreme methods of resolution, including strikes, demonstrations, and violence. As the concluding chapter details, in lieu of allowing for more effective organization and representation by workers or trade unions, the government must now manage this emergent intensification of labor conflict and instability directly.

Given what we know about the Chinese state – both its ambitions and its fears – it is perhaps not surprising that the current dilemma is a result of its "overresponsiveness" (Liebman 2014, 103). The crux of the matter is that workplace reforms and improvements are not merely tactical responses to the grievances of a marginalized working class; they are strategic levers for the state to push the Chinese economy toward a new development model and a new, more lasting path of urbanization. For workers, however, the government's attention to these issues has been emboldening. Through the promulgation and heavy promotion of new legal rights at the workplace, the government has raised expectations of workers and enlarged the political space for rights' mobilization. At the same time, organization and representation structures have hardly budged; the monopoly role of the official ACFTU is still firmly entrenched, suffocating to workers and labor activists outside the system. It is to labor's benefit that the government needs these changes to manage its larger developmental challenges because they have been pursued despite the political risks. Without these reforms and improvements, the following three challenges will severely affect China's ability to move beyond the current development model. There should be no mistaking the convergence of interests between the central government and workers as anything but an alliance of convenience.

THE DEMOGRAPHIC CHALLENGE: CHINA'S FADING DEMOGRAPHIC DIVIDEND

Many factors led to China's growth miracle that began in the 1980s and has now been sustained for three decades. While there is a long-running debate about the contribution of top-down decisions (policy making by China's leaders) versus bottom-up action (market making by China's farmers, entrepreneurs, and local officials), it is indisputable that China's demographic structure was extremely favorable, though absolutely temporary. At the onset of reforms, China's working-age population was much larger than the proportion of older and younger residents. This was attributable to declining birth rates, which had started to occur even before the onset of the strict one-child policy in the late 1970s, and declining child mortality rates during the Maoist period. This "demographic dividend" paid off as a relatively young workforce became more productive and had fewer dependents to support (Feng 2011; Song, Garnaut, and Cai 2014).

This demographic structure has evolved as the workforce has aged, fertility rates have reached non-replacement levels, and the average life span of China's population has lengthened. By 2050, 33 percent of the population will be over sixty years old, making China's demographic structure look more like some of the advanced industrialized countries of Europe (Development Research Center of the State Council and World

Bank, 2013, 276). The size of the working population has already begun to decline, squeezed at both ends as women have fewer children and older people live longer. The World Bank estimates that by 2030 China's old-age dependency ratio (the proportion of those over sixty-five to those of working age) will resemble that of Norway and the Netherlands (Development Research Center of the State Council and World Bank, 2013, 16).

China's demographic dividend went beyond simple demographics, however. It was also significantly enhanced by the institutional structure of the household registration system and the barriers on permanent migration of rural citizens to China's cities. Once the barriers to temporary migration were relaxed in the early reform period, these policies ensured that a young rural workforce was available for urban employment while still being almost totally excluded from social welfare benefits via the urban workplace and labor protections via the evolving labor legislation. The lack of social welfare and access to public goods such as health care and public education for migrants' children ensured that most migrant workers were only temporary residents in their cities of work (Golley and Meng 2011). They would either voluntarily return to their hometowns as they aged or they would constantly seek out new employment at higher wages, giving up security for higher returns. Their status as temporary workers also made it easier to justify their exclusion from legal protections and contractual benefits that should have been extended to the workforce as part of the implementation of the 1995 Labor Law. Migrants' inability to build secure, complete lives in cities made this "demographic dividend" particularly beneficial to employers who were able to hold down their labor costs considerably through the cyclical employment of young rural migrants.

In 2004, however, coastal Chinese manufacturing centers began to report labor shortages as factories struggled to attract enough young migrant workers onto their production lines. Various explanations exist for what now is a persistent problem for manufacturing firms across the country: a dearth of entry-level workers into the monotonous jobs that fueled China's rise as an industrial powerhouse producing ever larger amounts of the world's electronics, automobiles, and household items. Some economists argue that China has reached the Lewis turning point, when the absolute supply of rural labor dwindles and drives up wages in the low-skilled urban sector (Garnaut and Song 2006; Du and Wang 2010; Meng 2012). As Arthur Lewis argued, this point is critical for the path of industrialization of developing countries and helps explain the non-linear nature of wage increases as agricultural labor moves into manufacturing and service sectors (Lewis 1954). Compounded by the broader demographic shift of the declining working age population, this turning point requires that China do more to boost the productivity of current workers as it can no longer rely on simply increasing cheap labor inputs from the farm. Many other economists, however, disagree, arguing instead that the labor shortages in the cities and development zones are the result of the institutional barriers to permanent migration and citizenship. For example, Golley and Meng estimate that if the institutional restrictions of *hukou* were significantly relaxed, China's migrant labor supply would double from 150 million migrants to 300 million (Golley and Meng 2011). Migrants would also be far more likely to reside more permanently in the regions where they have found employment. Surveys of migrants certainly support these claims. Most migrants report that they are very interested in long-term, permanent migration to urban areas. Many migrants also say that the major barriers to this goal relate back to the *hukou* system (Knight and Yueh 2008).

Although the debate over the proportional impact of straight demographics versus institutional barriers continues, both problems make changes to the Chinese workplace absolutely essential for the longer-term viability of a *new* China model of development. At the workplace, this model of development differs from the older one in key characteristics: the workforce profile is older and more stable; quality and training matters more than quantity and low cost; rural workers are less migratory and shifting to locate permanently in urban areas. The division and separation between migrants' work and their home lives, especially the raising and educating of their children, diminishes. As Chapter 3 details, China's central government has pursued legislative and policy changes to work toward this development model. Employment security has been enhanced by the new protections of the 2008 Labor Contract Law, with the hope that companies will be more likely to invest in the skills and training of a more stable workforce. The 2011 Social Insurance Law and the broader policy changes to the hukou restrictions also aspire to integrate migrants into urban social insurance programs, improve the portability of social insurance benefits, and expand their access to other urban public goods, including legal residency and public education for their children.

As this book amply demonstrates, achieving these goals will be extraordinarily difficult because they threaten to disrupt the structures that have benefitted powerful actors in China's economy and place considerable new burdens on local governments to serve their entire populations, not only those with long-term local residency rights. Moreover, the enforcement mechanisms that the state has deployed thus far have been insufficient to compel compliance. Restrictions on collective organization of workers, repression of civil society organizations that advocate for workers' rights, and a dispute resolution system that is individualizing have minimized the power of these new protections and welfare entitlements.

THE SECURITY CHALLENGE: EXCHANGING LAND FOR WORK

The two leading causes of social unrest in China are labor disputes and rural land disputes (Li, Chen, and Zhang 2015). These disputes are usually analyzed and considered as discrete problems, each related to the respective dysfunctions of the urban workplace and rural local governments. However, the two are closely intertwined. The declining access to land security among rural residents drives the increasing demands and expectations of rural migrant workers. As access to land security decreases, demands for social security climb. Farmers pushed out of villages by land expropriation must seek out jobs and employment security in cities to replace what they have lost in their hometowns.

Since the 2011 Social Insurance Law, migrants' access to urban social insurance has improved gradually from very low levels of participation to moderately low levels of participation. Migrants' complaints about social insurance arrears and demands for enhanced compliance with social insurance laws among migrants have greatly increased over the past five to ten years. Social insurance is now one of the leading causes of labor disputes and strikes (Li, Chen, and Zhang 2015, 256). In 2014, over 50,000 workers of a large shoe manufacturer in Guangdong went on strike to demand that their Taiwanese employer pay social insurance arrears going back several years. Other recent large strikes in Guangdong, Jiangsu, and Heilongjiang have also involved demands for social protection (China Labour Bulletin 2015).

At the same time that social insurance disputes have rocked large urban employers, rural villagers have struggled to retain their land or to improve their compensation packages from local governments attempting to take their land for commercial development. Violent clashes have occurred with some frequency (Erie 2012; He 2014; Ong 2014; Hornby 2015). The root of the rural land problem lies in the collective land ownership system, which privileges local governments with the power to expropriate land, and the fiscal system, which since 1994 has centralized tax revenue at the central government level while leaving local governments with not only a smaller proportion of tax revenue but also more unfunded mandates to provide public goods to local residents. The fiscal constraints tightened over the 1990s, but became even tighter for local governments after the central government cancelled the agricultural tax in 2006. Many onlookers heralded this historic move as a key sign that the administration of Hu Jintao and Wen Jiabao was serious in their bid to improve rural livelihoods, tackle rural–urban inequality, and reduce social conflict over rural taxation. However, this change had one very serious side effect. It made rural local governments much more dependent on land and real estate revenue (Whiting 2011). Local governments became more interested in "flipping" agricultural land by taking land from farmers and leasing the land-use rights to industrial and commercial developers. In the 1990s, these tactics led to the "zone fever" among local governments to reclaim agricultural land as space for industrial development through the establishment of economic development zones and attraction of foreign direct investment (Rithmire 2013). In the 2000s, local governments, especially in suburban areas, began to look more to commercial development as an engine of income and tax revenue by building real estate developments for both commercial and residential use. The infamous "ghost cities" of recent years are one consequence (Sorace and Hurst 2016). The drive for land development reflects the fiscal and budgetary incentives of local governments rather than consumer demand. Luxurious shopping malls, ornate high-end apartment complexes, and magnificent government offices also demonstrate modernity to visiting higher-ups and potential investors.

The creation of a new class of "landless peasants" is another consequence of the land dependence of local governments. Ong estimates that from 1987 to 2010 over fifty-two million peasants lost their access to collectively owned land. Land loss also drives migration to cities, but without the fallback security of rural land, more and more Chinese peasants must look to the state for social welfare and long-term security. While previously failure to participate in social insurance was often on the part of both employers and migrant workers, more migrant workers are beginning to claim their rights to state schemes for social insurance. The swift uptick in social insurance disputes among migrant workers indicates this growing demand. If the expropriation and commercialization of rural land are to continue, which it should as a function of rapid urbanization and because of fiscal dependency on land revenue, the responsibility of urban workplaces to meet the social security demands of migrant workers will also only intensify. While land and labor disputes are discrete problems that do not overlap directly, their dual rise is inextricably linked. As land security diminishes, the urban workplace becomes even more important – not just as the place to earn a wage, but also a place to earn state-sponsored welfare.

THE EQUALITY CHALLENGE: MIGRANT WORKERS AS URBAN CITIZENS

The challenges of China's ambitious urbanization scheme are not solely regarding the relationship between the state and its rural citizens. Urbanization is also leading to greater contention between urban and rural citizens as migration to urban areas puts pressure on scarce resources and increases competition for jobs and public goods. Urban citizens have long enjoyed policies favoring them, from social insurance to public education to access to quality health care (Solinger 1999; Zhang 2001; Tang and Yang 2008; Wallace 2014). Local governments have also been accustomed to the notion that they are responsible for local legal residents, but much less so for the legions of rural migrants who toiled in their midst, often doing the dirtiest and most dangerous of jobs without the benefits of local citizenship. The goals of China's new urbanization schema include the undoing of this urban bias and a more equitable distribution of resources, not only between rural and urban citizens, but also between legal local urban residents and their migrant neighbors. Achieving a more equitable distribution requires that the relative benefits of urban residency decline and that these scarce benefits be divided up more equally between urban residents and newly urbanizing migrants.

While the Chinese media and public opinion have been generally sympathetic toward the plight of migrants as a marginalized and exploited sector of society, this sympathy can dry up when policies change that directly impact the lives of urban residents. For example, in 2013, Beijing and Shanghai residents very vocally opposed a central government plan to allow the children of migrant workers to take the university entrance exam in those cities. Competition into the most elite universities in China is intense, with many of the most prestigious universities located in those two cities. Local residents receive preferential admission policies for schools in the same city. Beijing and Shanghai high school students can gain entrance to the best schools with lower scores than their provincial compatriots. Local residents rightly feared that a large influx of new students, perhaps with greater determination to achieve high scores and escape rural poverty, would reduce the educational opportunities of their own children. In the end, while many second and third tier cities did open up their exam system to migrant children, Beijing and Shanghai continued to strictly limit access (Fu 2013; Luo and Jin 2013).

There is a direct line between the controversy over educational access and the role of the workplace in structuring urbanization. While labor market segmentation through the *hukou* reduced direct competition between local residents and migrants for jobs, the new plan for urbanization links migration to formal employment. Competition for employment will intensify as urbanization speeds up (Knight and Yueh 2008). Employment competition then extends to competition over formal employment status, wages, social insurance, and finally to the public goods that come with long-term urban residency – education, housing, and access to medical care. In changing the rules of public goods distribution, the central government has begun to threaten the traditional pattern of urbanization that encouraged adult migrants to come to cities as temporary sojourners, often divided from other family members, with a return to rural hometowns as the only safety net in the event of injury, sickness, and even old age. As many critics of the current situation point out, access to urban public goods for migrant workers is still quite constrained. Progress is slow, for example, in their access to formal employment through contracts and to social insurance for pensions and medical as I detail in subsequent chapters. Moreover, sectors with very large numbers of migrant workers such as construction and low-level services have far worse compliance than manufacturing. However, progress is slow because local governments *and* local residents alike often oppose central government edicts to grant migrant workers access to the benefits of urban life.

WORKPLACE RIGHTS AND THE CHALLENGES OF URBANIZATION

Urbanization in China will be difficult to achieve without the gradual dissolution of the household registration system. As a system that some have likened to a form of apartheid, the separation of the population into rural and urban populations and the allotment of employment, social welfare, and many other benefits has unfairly benefitted a proportionately small urban minority while excluding hundreds of millions of rural citizens (Chan and Buckingham 2008). As migration-for-work accelerated in the 1990s, the number of people residing in urban areas and working in non-agricultural jobs rose rapidly so that by 2015, more than half of the Chinese population was ostensibly urban. And yet, due to *hukou* restrictions, only about 36 percent of the population has legal rights to reside permanently in their cities of employment. Over 260 million people live in cities without the long-term right to do so (World Bank 2014, 5).

As much *hukou*-related research has shown, reforms to the *hukou* system have been painfully slow. Although the central government announced its intention in 2001 and many times since to gradually end the rural-urban division of *hukou*, the reforms have been constrained at every step by the politics of deeply entrenched urban bias and redistribution of scarce resources (Wang 2005; Chan and Buckingham 2008; Whyte 2010). And yet it is essential to the Chinese economy that these changes be made. The demographic future of most Chinese cities is bleak without an influx of younger workers from the countryside who can pay into the social insurance accounts to support retirees. Labor mobility and decreased segmentation of labor markets will benefit the economy and enhance productivity. While this will increase the competitive pressure on urban workers, it will benefit rural citizens who have been excluded from many jobs because of their *hukou* status. Allowing migrating rural citizens to become full urban citizens may also alleviate the intense social conflict over rural land rights. Finally, these changes may at last begin to bring down China's high rates of inequality and the scourge of social discrimination against rural people.

The workplace rights and protections extended in China's new labor laws are the focus of this book and they are directly connected to these issues as well. In a sense these new laws and regulations are substituting for more substantial *hukou* reforms by broadening protection to all workers, encouraging formal employment status for migrants, and changing social insurance policies to increase migrant participation. While these reforms cannot replace more fundamental changes to the *hukou* system, they have led to the relative decline in the value of an urban *hukou* by making formal urban employment and participation in social insurance core workplace rights for migrants and urbanites alike. In doing so, these workplace changes have the potential to change the nature of China's urbanization.

As subsequent chapters detail, however, the enforcement model that the government has deployed to reach these goals is woefully inadequate for the task. By leaving the tasks of enforcement and compliance to workers themselves, the government has encouraged the mobilization of workers from the bottom to put pressure on recalcitrant local officials and employers. This model *has* had some effect, with greater rates of formalization and expanded participation on social insurance. However, the benefits of these new protections tend to compel compliance at the high end of the labor market, leaving many frustrated and dissatisfied with the large gap between the promise of the law and its realization on the ground.

Data and Methodology

This book is based on a decade of research that combines in-depth qualitative research at a legal aid center in Shanghai, data from two multi-city surveys of labor and employment issues, follow-up interviews with survey respondents with labor dispute experience, interviews with Shanghai enterprise managers in the aftermath of the Labor Contract Law of 2008, and multi-year visits to the field to interview officials, academics, lawyers, NGO leaders, and trade union officials. I was also a regular participant in conferences and workshops on labor issues in China and Hong Kong where key cases, events, and laws were extensively discussed and analyzed. In the following paragraphs, I lay out how these data were collected and combined, my strategies to exploit different types of data to "triangulate" gaps or selection problems, and the limitations of the data used.

The East China University of Politics and Law (ECUPL) Legal Aid Center for Workers was established in 2001 under the jurisdiction of the university, a well-known law school in central Shanghai. While a Fulbright research scholar at ECUPL, I began a multi-year collaboration with the Center to study case outcomes and to analyze how legal aid recipients experienced the process and outcomes of legal mobilization. From 2004 to 2005, a student volunteer at the center and I collected forty-nine case histories from the first two years of the center's operation. We then conducted forty-six in-depth interviews with the litigants (three litigants refused to be interviewed at length but their case documents were included in some analysis). During the spring of 2013, I returned to the center to conduct ten additional interviews with recent litigants and to collect case narratives and documents. In the interim, I returned to the Center on a yearly or twice yearly basis and regularly interviewed the director, the practicing lawyers, and student volunteers. The ECUPL Center closed in early 2016 after litigating nearly 500 labor disputes and offering consultation to thousands of workers. I discuss the center's evolution and eventual closure in greater depth in Chapter 6.

These case narratives, which include the litigant interviews and the official case documents, form the core of the book. The in-depth interviews allowed me to ask detailed questions about the litigant's dispute experience from beginning to end. This gave me key insights into how people mobilized the law, where they sought out help and information, and how law was only one of many pathways available for restitution. The interviews also explored the litigant's subjective understandings of the legal process and evaluation of key administrative and judicial institutions. The case histories included written documents, such as the original complaint, court and arbitration decisions, correspondence between the litigant and the employer about the dispute, and the legal aid litigator's final assessment of the case and the outcome. Key arguments about mobilization, legal consciousness, and access to justice are formed through my interpretations of the case narratives. That being said, this select group of legal aid recipients in Shanghai is never considered to be a representative sample of the population – of the country, or even of Shanghai, one of the wealthiest and most developed cities in China. This cohort of legal aid plaintiffs is unusual in at least two important respects: first, their access to legal aid is very unusual. Most workers with workplace grievances cannot find adequate, affordable legal assistance, though they almost always have ample access to legal information via the media. Second, these litigants had already very deliberately chosen the law as a viable pathway for dispute resolution. They may have unobservable characteristics that made them more litigious or more trusting in the law than other aggrieved workers.

To compensate for these deficits, I participated in two multi-city surveys of labor and employment issues. The 2005 Labor Law Mobilization Survey, funded by the National Science Foundation, and administrated by the Research Center on Contemporary China (RCCC) at Peking University, is a household survey of over 4,000 respondents in four cities: Wuxi, Jiangsu (in the Yangtze River Delta near Shanghai), Foshan, Guangdong (in the Pearl River Delta near Hong Kong), Shenyang, Liaoning Province (in China's northeastern "rustbelt"), and Chongqing (a provincial level city in China's southwest). This survey investigated the labor and employment situations of the respondents, asked questions about past experiences with workplace grievances, measured the respondent's knowledge of existing labor protections, and asked about expected behavior using a hypothetical vignette of a workplace problem. Eighty-two respondents of the LLMS reported taking formal action to resolve a workplace grievance, so in order to compare the experiences of the ECUPL legal aid recipients to those of the general disputing population, we conducted twenty-six follow-up interviews with these disputants.

During this period of intensive, qualitative fieldwork, the legislative framework structuring workplace rights began to change rapidly. At the end of my first extended period of fieldwork in 2005, I participated in workshops and discussions regarding the draft legislation for a new law on labor contracts. The draft law was eventually passed in 2007 along with two other important laws: one on employment discrimination (the Employment Promotion Law) and another on dispute resolution (the Labor Dispute Mediation and Arbitration Law). In 2010, China's legislature passed the Social Insurance Law. I was then invited to participate in the third wave of the China Urban Labor Force Survey (CULS), a survey conducted by the Institute of Population and Labor Economics (IPLE) at the Chinese Academy of Social Sciences (CASS). This third wave (the earlier waves were in 2001 and 2005) added new sections on labor disputes, labor contracts, and awareness of workplace rights. Like the LLMS, the CULS 2010 is a multi-city household survey. The cities include Shanghai, Guangzhou (in the Pearl River Delta), Shenyang, Liaoning (in the northeast), Wuhan, Hubei (in central China), Fuzhou, Fujian (in southeastern coastal China) and Xian, Shaanxi (in the northwest). The 2010 CULS allowed us to understand how the legislative changes of 2008 were beginning to affect the Chinese workplace and also to study a group of disputants from the general population in the aftermath of the 2008 Labor Contract Law.

In 2010, two of my doctoral students interviewed a selection of human resource managers from Shanghai companies, both state-owned and foreign, to qualitatively assess company reactions to the new laws and the rising tide of labor disputes that were occurring across the country. I also visited legal aid NGOs operating in other cities, including Beijing, Nanjing, Shenzhen, and Guangzhou. In 2012–2013 while a visiting scholar at the Koguan School of Law at Shanghai Jiaotong University, I completed follow-up case studies of legal aid recipients, and took part in many workshops and discussions on recent strike waves, revisions to the 2008 Labor Contract Law, and social stability and governance in China. During this entire period, from 2004 to 2015, I participated actively in the professional network of government and trade union officials, labor law scholars, activists and cause lawyers, and other academics by attending conferences, workshops and seminars on pressing issues or legislation. These venues were key opportunities for data collection through the speeches and papers of key actors in these important debates. I relied on these statements and discussions at conferences as well as written statements and documents to make empirical claims about government policy, NGO activity, and so forth.

Although the book ends with a rather pessimistic assessment of the current state of rule of law initiatives in the realm of labor and employment, this is based on data that, if anything, could be criticized for suffering from "best case" selection bias. In terms of the qualitative data, I largely collected data on legal aid from Shanghai, one of China's most developed cities, and from a legal aid center that was highly professionalized with an excellent reputation among local judicial professionals, including judges and lawyers. Shanghai's legal system is also very developed with adequate resources and high capacity. This is not representative of the legal aid resources in most other cities. In Chapter 6, I examine the role of labor NGOs in facilitating collective legal disputes. Here I draw on the network of labor activists who are mainly located in Guangdong Province (with strong ties to academics in Beijing and elsewhere). The strong civil society characteristics of the Pearl River Delta, however, are also not apparent in other parts of China. Moreover, the large-scale crackdown on labor activism since 2015 has had a chilling effect on even Guangdong's vibrant community. Finally, in terms of the survey data used to buttress my main points and to provide a wider view of trends, these surveys are multi-city surveys, varied by region but in all cases "tier one or two" cities, (most are provincial status cities or provincial capitals). They represent key regional differences between cities at the same level, but they are not nationally representative and, as such, probably give a more optimistic picture of compliance and enforcement than would be the case in a national sample of all Chinese cities.

Roadmap

The organization of this book follows the thread of "legality" through the different processes important to legal mobilization around workplace rights. Chapter 2 situates the Chinese government's deployment of rule of law in the wider debate on autocratic institutions. In this chapter I argue that China's use of legal institutions to structure the workplace and labor markets has a functional logic relevant to the current challenges of the Chinese system. Empowering workers with highly protective rights creates bottom-up pressure on local governments and firms to improve enforcement and compliance with central laws. It also builds "hierarchical trust" between citizens and the central state, whose benevolent laws are thwarted by corrupt local officials. Under some conditions, autocrats have incentives to build institutions that empower citizens.

Chapter 3 examines the institutional context of rights mobilization, focusing on three crucial institutions that shape rights consciousness and mobilization: the legislative framework of China's labor laws; the legal dissemination campaigns that educate citizens about rights; and the dispute resolution system set up to resolve labor grievances. I argue for a constitutive interpretation of law in its ability to shape rights consciousness. By examining the trajectory of the legal framework and mobilization trends during a period of activist lawmaking, I show how workers' mobilization and dispute behavior have in turn shaped law making.

Chapters 4 and 5 examine patterns of legal mobilization and its consequences. In Chapter 4, I investigate the role of education and legal awareness in bringing people to the law. Workers with high levels of formal education are more likely to invoke the formal legal system to protect workplace rights. They are also more likely to be satisfied with the results. This argument is intuitive, as law requires skills and resources to be used effectively. However, I also find that many less-educated workers exploit the ample publicly available information about labor laws to "self-educate," becoming knowledgeable about their workplace rights and more confident in their abilities to protect themselves.

Chapter 5 also examines patterns of legal mobilization by leveraging differences in the populations studied. First, I examine what kinds of workers are inclined to make use of law by examining differences between those who pursued legal resolution and those who did not. I then examine how the presence of legal representation can positively affect not only substantive outcomes, but also subjective experiences of the legal process. While access to legal representation is extremely limited, workers lucky enough to attain it report more positive impressions of the legal system and more inclination to make use of these institutions again. Finally, within the group of legal aid recipients in Shanghai, I examine how different generations of workers understood and experienced their workplace dispute. Older workers of the socialist era (those who entered the workplace during the "iron rice bowl" era) face a number of obstacles to mobilize the law effectively. While some of the obstacles are attributable to the typical variables of education and awareness, the switch to law and contractual obligations fundamentally undermined their claims to employment security and, by extension, social benefits of the state-owned workplace. Younger workers of the reform era (those who entered the workplace under the labor contract system) are more confident in their abilities but they also have quite different expectations of the workplace and its obligations.

In Chapter 6, I explore the limitations of China's authoritarian legality, focusing on the relationship between the labor law system as set out in Chapter 3 with the trend of rising labor unrest, which began in earnest in 2008 with the Labor Contract Law and the onset of the Global Financial Crisis. Labor disputes doubled nationally that year with workers responding to the economic instability and the law's new protections with a wave of lawsuits against employers. In the years following, labor disputes continued at a high rate while strikes and demonstrations also increased as workers' bargaining power expanded in response to widening labor shortages and the economic boom that followed the government's investment program following the crisis. In response to the rising tide of lawsuits and strikes, the state's role in resolution changed substantially after a concerted effort to reduce lawsuits and channel as many disputes as possible to state-led mediation. Under the ideological goal of "harmonious society," the state sought to reach mediated (not litigated) resolution, thwart collective action and organization, and retain significant state discretionary power over social conflict. The state's "turn against law" (Minzner 2011) however, was matched by a growing number of workers and labor activists who resisted the atomizing and fragmenting dispute resolution system, attempting to maintain their collective power by extra-legal action such as strikes, demonstrations, and informal collective bargaining with management. This nascent social movement attempts to not only leverage the rights given by the state's legislation, but to harness collective grievances and interests despite the state's opposition. These dynamics between a stability-obsessed state and a disenchanted but empowered workforce reveal the limitations of the current labor law system.

Chapter 6 focuses on three limitations: one, a mode of compliance that relies on individualized legal mobilization will produce suboptimal outcomes. Compliance will be uneven and will tend to accrue to the higher end of the labor market. Second, there continues to be no effective institutional mechanisms to resolve conflicts that go beyond the legal minimal standards. As workers' bargaining power has increased, they are demanding better conditions and higher wages. When these demands are already above the legal standards set out in the laws, the current system is ineffective. Third, for workers who are caught between the two dynamics of collective mobilization and individualized legal resolution, the legal process is ill-equipped to defuse conflict. Channeling collective unrest through the individualistic resolution system increases workers' disappointments and frustrations. The incentive structure that leads local governments to prioritize "stability above all" creates escalation dynamics that encourage extreme behavior and violence. In the absence of further institutional reform, the state's reactive approach is likely to exacerbate conflict rather than reduce it.

In the epilogue, Chapter 7, I briefly relate these issues to the debate in 2015–2016 to revise and weaken the Labor Contract Law in the wake of a significant deceleration in Chinese economic growth. This debate and the eventual expected revision of the LCL may mark the end of this experimental period with state-sponsored rights mobilization. The goals of a changed development model and rapid urbanization will remain, however.

2

A Theory of Authoritarian Legality

> The Dictator lives continuously under the Sword of Damocles and equally continuously worries about the thickness of the thread.
> – Gordon Tullock, *On Autocracy*

Luo Guomin was a quiet, deliberate man who spoke in a dispassionate voice about his work injury and subsequent lawsuit. He was a 1982 technical school graduate in engineering who was allocated a job at a research and development institute inside a well-known Shanghai SOE that produced name brand footwear. As a younger member of the socialist generation, Luo was hired into the old system of allocated positions, permanent employment, and enterprise-based benefits – socialist China's "iron rice bowl." Promoted to deputy director of the general office ten years after starting in the company, Luo was doing well. Married with a six-year old daughter, his technical education set him apart from less educated staff around him. This path of relative stability and advancement ended in 1992, when he was just over thirty years old. While checking on new equipment in one of the factory's workshops, his left arm was pulled into a machine and crushed from the elbow down. The subsequent amputation and recovery lasted more than a year, leaving him deeply depressed about his future.

As Luo finished his recuperation and recovery, the local Shanghai government evaluated his injury as level three in seriousness, declaring him unfit for work. Luo and his company's leaders negotiated a generous salary and benefit package as long-term compensation for his injury, which was attributed to faulty equipment. As a permanent employee in the research arm of a state company, Luo eventually reached an agreement that granted him wages and subsidies equaling 150 percent of his salary. By 2002 when the dispute began, he was receiving about 1900 RMB per month ($229), 15 percent higher than the average Shanghai wage for SOE employees. For Luo the compensation was never enough to assuage his sense of loss and anger that the accident had cost him his future, but it did provide a stable income and security. "I was trained as an engineer! I had the ability to be promoted, everything was ahead of me."

Luo's employment stability and advancement prior to his injury and his generous benefit package following the injury are representative of the benefits that the socialist system offered to urban residents, especially those employed by large SOEs in major cities. Even before the dispute began in 2002, however, this foundation of security and protection was crumbling. His misfortune coincided with the onset of SOE restructuring and reform in Shanghai and China more broadly. From the mid-1990s to the early 2000s, tens of millions of state enterprise workers were laid off or had their employment terms changed from "permanent worker" to "contract employee." Others were left destitute as their employers went bankrupt and disappeared. Luo's relative security was shattered in June of 2002 when the company suddenly cancelled the 1994 agreement and lowered his monthly compensation by 40 percent in line with the current legal minimum. The company carried a heavy debt load and had changed management. In documents submitted to the court, they argued that in the new context of the market economy they were no longer in a good economic position to pay compensation that was far above what the law required. Luo faced the possibility of a large decline in his monthly income. In his first documents presented to labor arbitration, he maligned the heavier burden on his wife "to act as both father and mother" to their school-age daughter. Referring to himself as a "useless person," he despaired at his inability to properly provide for his family. More importantly, in private Luo worried that this initial reduction marked the beginning of the enterprise's attempts to be rid of burdensome employees; many colleagues had already been laid off or pushed out entirely. Luo resolved to fight back.

Luo's path to the courts and his transformation from a moralizing petitioner to a "little legal expert" embody key themes in this book. The microcosm of his experience, while intensely personal and specific to his particular dispute over a severe occupational injury, uncovers important generalities of legal mobilization and citizens' experiences of the state's authoritarian legality. First, Luo's dispute experience is indicative of the widening public space for workplace disputes to be heard and processed and of the significant expansion of state-sanctioned public knowledge and awareness of workplace rights. China's authoritarian legality is more than the instrumental deployment of legalized repression. Legal reforms in the labor realm and waves of legal dissemination campaigns since the 1990s have drawn in citizens as active participants of a "rights defense movement." The "rights defense" practiced by individual citizens, activist lawyers, and civil society has its roots in the state's own recourse to law as a tool of governance during market reform (Fu and Cullen 2008; Fu and Cullen 2011; Benney 2013). Even though the state under the Hu Jintao administration (2003–2013) retreated from its earlier enthusiastic promotion of "rights awareness" and encouragement of citizen's own right defense (Minzner 2011), the seeds of China's rights defense movement are in the state's own turn toward legality during the early reform period. In 2014, President Xi Jinping's revival of rule of law rhetoric seemed to signal the state's continued commitment to legality as a source of authoritarian stability (Yang 2014) though this has not materialized on the ground. Chapter 3 lays out this interaction between the changing institutional context and workers' legal mobilization, showing how iterative waves of protective legislation encouraged bottom-up attempts at right-protection.

Second, Luo's standing as a permanent worker from the old system of lifetime employment and his relatively high educational background underscores two critical variables that affect how individuals experience the authoritarian state's embrace of legality: generation and education. Luo was embedded in a socialist workplace system that was deliberately and totally dismantled by the reformist state's recourse to the new discourses of capitalism and the market economy: rule of law, contract relations, and legal rights and responsibilities. His educational background facilitates his metamorphosis from a moralistic petitioner who invokes the language of socialism, obligation, and ethics to a feisty litigant who invokes the language of contract terms, evidence, and legality. Chapters 4 and 5 examine these patterns of mobilization and the differential effects of education, legal awareness, experience, and political generation.

Third, Luo's transformation is made possible by his unusual access to high-quality legal assistance, underlining the importance of complementary institutions that provide representation to disputing workers. As this book demonstrates, access to adequate legal representation is not at all the norm; it is the great exception. The experiences of legal aid plaintiffs detailed here are unusual – not because they always end happily on the side of justice, many do not, but rather because access to adequate representation improves a citizen's experience of law no matter what the outcome. As I discuss in Chapter 6, the lack of adequate representation and the political strictures on collective organization fundamentally impede China's authoritarian legality as a mode of effective governance. In so much as legal experience exposes the inequities and flaws of the legal system, the state's encouragement of individualized legal mobilization as a legitimate and safe channel for social grievances and conflict may further erode legitimacy of the system.

As Luo began his long road to justice, his first reaction was to invoke his status as a permanent worker for a socialist firm. He began to protest and petition at government offices around the city. He sat for hours in his firm's corporate headquarters waiting room until the company nervously sent in trade union officials who tried to persuade Luo not to "stir up trouble." They offered him cash compensation if he would give up his claims, but he refused and went further up the petitioning chain. Luo tried his luck at the municipal city hall, the Shanghai Disabled Persons Society, and the Labor Bureau. But no one would offer him concrete help or advice. The city government redirected him back to his workplace. The Disabled Persons Association could not determine what his legal rights were. The Labor Bureau told him that he had to proceed through the labor dispute resolution system. "Everything was very vague."

Luo consulted a lawyer friend who encouraged him to "use the law as a weapon." His friend would not take the case himself, commenting to Luo that it was too much time and not enough money. But he encouraged Luo to do it on his own. With this meager advice, Luo turned to the legal system for the first time. He drafted the initial application to the government-run Labor Arbitration Committee (LAC) himself, still in the mode of the state sector worker who sacrificed his health and well-being to the company. In his application, he entreated the LAC to rule on his behalf because of his fallen position in society, his position as a "master" of the factory, and the potential detrimental effects of his misfortune on his daughter's education, which might cause her to drift like a "wayward lamb." Luo's appeal was couched in the language of morality and fairness not in codes, regulations, or contracts.

Luo's moralistic appeals, heartfelt language, and expressive descriptions of his family's hardships earned him nothing. He lost the case in arbitration, which ruled fully in support of the company's right to change the original compensation package.

In seeking out professional legal help after his arbitration defeat, Luo began to research and study the law. He consulted with a famous labor lawyer who advertised in a local newspaper. A visit to their office furnished him with some free advice about the importance of evidence and the need to document the process through which his original 1994 settlement was determined. Luo collected evidence with the help of his colleagues. Luo reached out to two retired colleagues, including the former trade union chairman, who then agreed to serve as his witnesses. Luo finally recognized that the critical issue of the case was not the degree of his personal hardship or the ethical obligations of his employer but simply whether or not the 1994 settlement was a unilateral change in company policy or a negotiated contractual agreement between two equal parties. Was it a policy or a contract?[1]

Luo's lawyer friend then decided to take the case for him at a reduced fee of RMB 2000 (USD$245). At his court appeal, Luo was impressed with the judge who seemed to be an expert in labor disputes. When the judge offered the opportunity to mediate a compromise, the company offered RMB 10,000 (USD$1234) but Luo refused, increasingly confident that the law would rule in his favor. He told the court stenographer that he would only accept RMB 60–70,000 (USD$7407–8641) – nothing less for mediation.[2] Although the man ridiculed him, telling him that he was crazy and will never get that much, Luo reported that he was confident and not intimidated by his reaction. "If I hadn't already gone this far and learned so much, I would have been frightened out of my mind."

Luo's court case benefited from a knowledgeable and sympathetic judge who informed Shanghai TV about the compelling case replete with a life-changing injury and a family wracked by economic hardship and health issues. Luo believed that the judge revealed the case to the media before the decision was made in order to gain the power and support of the media and public opinion.[3] This support allowed her to rule in the way that she wanted to rule, which was to support Luo.

Luo was totally successful at court. The court ruled that the 1994 settlement, as a contractual agreement between two equal parties, was still in force and that the company could not change the agreement unilaterally. Luo's compensation returned to its original levels and the filing fees were paid by the defendant. When the enterprise appealed the ruling to the intermediate court and the case attracted even more media attention, a well-known university-based Legal Aid Center offered free assistance to Luo to fight the appeal. Luo noted that this further helped his case as

---

[1] If the agreement is interpreted as a contractual change in his employment, the company cannot unilaterally make changes according to Article 17 of the National Labor Law.
[2] During SOE restructurings and related labor disputes, it was not unusual for the company to offer larger sums of money during mediation to "buy out" the employee's job tenure.
[3] On the role of the media in influencing court decisions, see Liebman (Liebman 2011b).

the student assistants and the litigator appeared early to court, helping him with legal procedures and regulations and improving his confidence. They also passionately announced at the opening of the hearing that their representation was pro-bono on behalf of the university. For Luo, "this was very important and moving to hear in the courtroom." The second appeal also fully supported Luo, rejecting the company's appeal entirely.

Luo realized that his legal problems may not end with this second victory. The company's fortunes could further decline, leading to bankruptcy and the end of their support. But he spoke enthusiastically about his plans and strategies for the future. While the company continued to ask him to sign a labor contract and formalize their long relationship, he refused, suspecting that any contract would be used to reduce his long-term security. He collected materials related to the sale of the company's property and watched carefully for signs that company leaders were taking advantage of the restructuring process to make profits of their own and to strip assets from the public sector to line their own pockets. He was confident in his own abilities and of the courts to help common people like him. He recognized that the laws don't work well and are routinely ignored. Noting the abysmal conditions of migrant workers in private companies, Luo said, "I'd heard from friends and relatives that labor law was 'too black.' The law is only enforced if something bad happens or someone reports a violation." But Luo's confidence was partly from the belief that he had **become** that sort of person – someone who would speak up and take notice of legal violations. He became someone who learned to use the law to protect himself.

In the interim between Luo's injury in 1992 and his dispute a decade later, workplaces in China were undergoing massive transformation and change. New legislation and regulations were developed as the burgeoning private and foreign-invested sectors created new opportunities for employment and for employment grievances. Within the planned economy, state and collective enterprises were moving away from the tinkering reforms of the 1980s to full-blown privatization and corporate restructuring. In all sectors of the economy, internal migration of rural residents to China's coastal cities was reshaping labor markets.

In 1995 the Standing Committee of the National People's Congress passed the first national Labor Law in PRC history. This law marked an important milestone in China's move away from a planned economy and state socialism that had included expectations of lifetime employment and extensive welfare benefits. However, this "iron rice bowl" employment system only covered a relatively small proportion of the entire workforce (about 20 percent) – people with urban residency employed in the dominant public sector – enterprises owned by the state or collectives. For this minority group of entitled citizens – people like Luo Guomin – the switch to labor law, contract labor relations, and contribution-led social insurance was a step down in their privileges as the state moved away from promises of lifetime employment security and began to rely more heavily on labor market mechanisms to reward outcomes and reduce enterprise burdens. For other sectors of the labor market, however, younger urban residents employed in the new private and foreign sectors and rural migrant workers, the development of Chinese labor law since the 1995 Law has meant increased state protection, enhanced workplace rights, and gradual inclusion into social insurance policies. If we examine the 1995 Labor Law only in an abstract sense, it was clearly an attempt by the state to protect workers and regulate labor markets with standards that are relatively high compared to other developing and developed economies. If we examine the law in the political and social context of 1995 China, however, the shift to law had a bifurcated effect. It was a radical diminution of socialist workplace rights and privileges that accrued to the urban working classes by dint of their importance to the socialist project, industrialization, and their connections to the Communist Party. At the same time, for rural migrant workers leaving subsistence agriculture in the hope of finding temporary but still long-term work in the industrial, commercial, or service sectors of urban China, the promise of the law was substantial. It provided minimal working standards, standards on minimum wages, and social insurance in the event of workplace injury. For one group it was the death knell of socialist labor relations; for another it held out the possibility of equal treatment and inclusion into welfare and insurance schemes that had heretofore excluded them.

As detailed in subsequent chapters, in the two decades since the 1995 law, the Chinese central government has moved even further toward high standards for workplace protections, including higher minimum wages and new restrictions on short-term contracts in favor of long-term employment security. The state has developed extensive social insurance programs that cover an expanding proportion of employees. Informal employment has been targeted and reduced, though it continues to be a significant problem at the lower end of the labor market.[4] The OECD Employment Protection Index finds that China's protections for

---

[4] Informal employment is defined as workers without written labor contracts. The reduction in informal employment since the 2008 Labor Contract Law does not mean that

CHART 2.1. OECD Employment Protection Index, 2013.

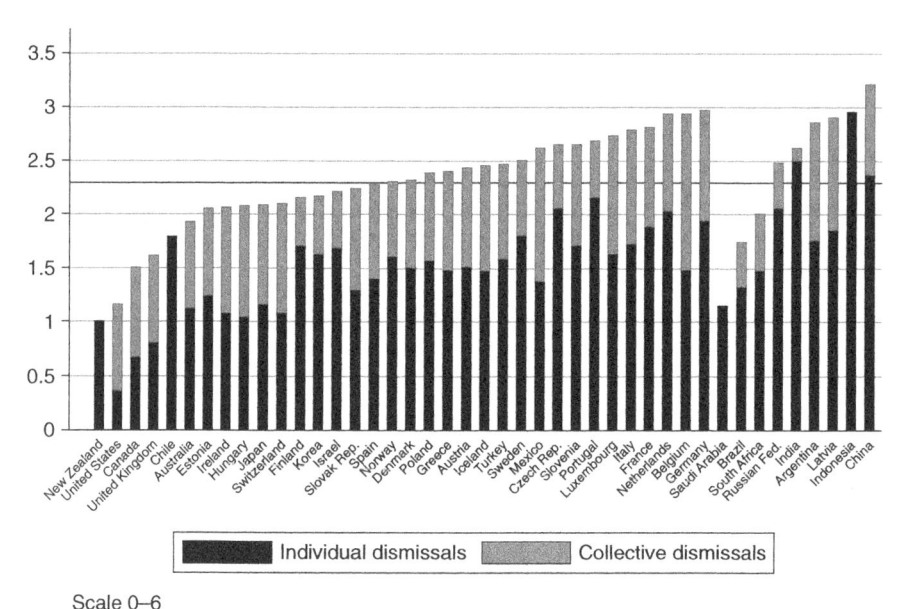

Scale 0–6
Solid line shows OECD average for employment protection

individual and collective dismissals are among the highest in the world, significantly higher than the OECD average and above highly protective countries such as Germany (Venn 2009). (See Chart 2.1.) Over time, China's employment protection levels have increased and more workers have moved from the informal sector to the formal sector, with related increases in the proportion of workers with social insurance and written labor contracts. While inclusion of migrants has been slow and uneven, it continues even as protections have climbed higher.

The regime not only legislated high standards, it also heavily advertised and promoted them. Through "legal dissemination" campaigns at the workplace, at schools, and most importantly via the state-run media, the government ensured that people became more aware of these guarantees. While ineffective enforcement of workplace rights is endemic in China, as it is in many developing countries, Chinese workers know a significant amount about their workplace rights through these state-led education campaigns. Beginning in 1986, the government moved to not only

---

precarious work overall has declined. In fact, since the passage of the LCL, many workers are now employed through subcontracting arrangements with reduced employment security and generally lower wages and benefits.

rebuild its legal system, but also to inform and educate Chinese citizens about their "legal rights and interests." The campaign is part empowerment and consciousness raising – extorting citizens to use the law to protect themselves as the state withdraws socialist protection and part social control – educating citizens about their legal obligations and responsibilities. Legal dissemination campaigns have been a major feature of China's legal reforms since the 1980s.

In addition to high legal standards on the books and heavy promotion of these rights in the media, the Chinese state developed a system of labor dispute resolution that empowered individual workers to seek restitution of workplace grievances via a formal process of voluntary mediation, compulsory but not binding arbitration, and court litigation. First put into place in 1993 for state sector employees as restructuring began to increase the likelihood of disputes, the process was codified in the 1995 Labor Law for all workers, and refined in the 2008 Law on the Mediation and Arbitration of Labor Disputes. The number of disputes has climbed precipitously over the years since 1995, especially during periods of economic strain and after new legislation. In 2008 disputes doubled nationally as the Labor Contract Law went into effect and the economy suffered the effects of the global financial crisis. The dispute resolution process, as detailed in Chapter 3, is flawed and rife with problems of access, expense, duration, and lack of capacity and training. Many aggrieved workers also suspect that arbitrators, as employees of the local labor bureau, are biased toward employers. However, in comparison to the previous modes of dispute resolution that left the aggrieved worker caught in administrative processes that empowered the firm and were reined in by few formal legal or administrative rules, the movement to an external and formalized system of dispute resolution granted workers more space to press their claims and greater access to more autonomous administrative or judicial actors to deliberate on the merits of their claims. An important caveat is that this empowerment of individual workers to file disputes has not translated to greater collective or organized power. China's dispute resolution process is overwhelmingly individualized by design; enlarged political space for individual workers is only in the context of Party-State control over collective labor organization via the All-China Federation of Trade Unions. The state's empowerment of labor and its expansion of workplace rights have never extended to notions of freedom of association or competition for the right to represent Chinese workers.

Taken as a whole, China's labor market institutions include high legal standards, state-initiated education and propaganda campaigns to educate workers about their workplace rights, and administrative and legal channels for third party dispute resolution. While the laws severed the ties of permanent employment enjoyed by urban workers in the socialist period, high legal standards and ambitious social insurance programs have dramatically increased the state's obligations to workers and increased expectations about workplace conditions, employment security, and social welfare entitlements. In the context of weak and ineffectual implementation and enforcement of these new standards by local governments, the gaps between "law on the books" and "law in practice" and between the aspirations of the central government and the capacity and will of local governments have been dramatically and publicly exposed. These gaps have opened up considerable political space for rights-claiming behavior and social contention around workplace issues.

TOWARD A THEORY OF AUTHORITARIAN LEGALITY

As an authoritarian regime, focused on staying in power and maintaining control, the Chinese state's behavior described above in general (and in detail in subsequent chapters) is puzzling. Why do authoritarian regimes pass legislation to grant citizens more rights and to increase the responsibility of the government in granting and protecting those rights? Why would an authoritarian regime encourage social mobilization around rights and risk the possibility that such mobilization will spin out of control, leading to new demands or widespread instability? Why do some autocracies need or desire mass support even when an "electoral connection" between the rulers and the ruled does not exist? Can a single-party authoritarian regime use "rule of law" and other institutions associated with democracy to rule more effectively, increasing the chances of its political survival?

China's adoption of authoritarian legality is a state-led move, the instrumental adoption of rule of law from the beginning of the reform period to improve governance and structure newly permitted market institutions. As such, it is bounded, limited, and unstable. As Stern describes in her study of environmental law, the Chinese state's self-conscious adoption of legality is full of "political ambivalence" (Stern 2014), or what Wang terms "partial" rule of law (Wang 2014). However, it is also consequential. The half-heartedness is a sign of the state's trepidation, but the lack of full commitment does not mean that the consequences of a limited and bounded rule of law are unimportant. Authoritarian legality has "functions" that assist the Chinese Communist Party (CCP) in its move from a revolutionary party to a ruling one. However, there are also dysfunctional unintended consequences brought forth because of the inherent contradictions created by the incomplete adoption of "rule of law" principles and institutions. This chapter theorizes the nature of authoritarian legality, showing both why authoritarian states are attracted to the allure of rule of law, but also how it produces consequences that undermine its long-term stability as a mode of authoritarian governance.

China's embrace of quasi-democratic institutions, such as "rule of law," elections, and a more active and consequential legislative system is not unique. There has been renewed attention and interest in comparative politics on autocratic borrowing of institutions that are normally associated with democracies for sometime (Diamond 2002; Levitsky and Way 2002; Schedler 2006). However, much of the analytic focus has been on the elite political dynamics that emerge as politics becomes more institutionalized. These "quasi-democratic" institutions become arenas for power-sharing, cooptation, and credible commitments between rulers and elites. General theories of authoritarian political survival and more detailed studies of authoritarian institutions have both tended to downplay how dictatorships cultivate mass support to survive, focusing instead on intra-elite strategic interactions and repressive tactics to limit the challenge of mass revolution.[5] We have overlooked regime–mass connections that are outside the electoral connections inherent only in "competitive authoritarianism." Rather than a story of elite cooptation and mass repression, which is common in the comparative literature, the PRC leadership has at times moved to bolster mass support and mass legal mobilization as a means to restrain and threaten local elites.

China's autocratic ruling party, the Chinese Communist Party (CCP), uses rule of law (including law-making and law-enforcement) not only to make bargains and commitments to elite supporters of the regime, *but also to manage principal–agent problems between levels of government, to cultivate mass support, and to exploit and reshape social cleavages*. My analysis of the deployment of rule of law by the CCP exposes a strategy for durable authoritarianism that relies on rights-giving legislation and regime-initiated social mobilization to divide and rule. This framework can be defined as a "high standards, self-enforcement" model that creates space for bottom-up mobilization as workers exploit the gap between law on the books and law in reality. In the absence of strong proactive

---

[5] But see Hess 2013; Kim and Gandhi 2010; Trejo 2012 for attention to mass mobilization and cooptation.

state enforcement of these standards, workers must mobilize their own resources to protect their rights. This model has functional value to the ruling CCP for three reasons: first, it alleviates principal–agent problems between central and local officials; second, it builds hierarchical trust and legitimacy that benefits the central government; third, the mobilization that occurs is market-conforming and politically constrained.

Principal–Agent Problems and Diverging Incentives

Bottom-up legal mobilization creates upward pressure on powerful local actors (officials and firms) to enforce and comply with central laws and regulations. In the context of a centralized political system that retains lawmaking power to the central government while delegating significant political and economic responsibilities to lower levels, local agents of the central government are incentivized via the cadre evaluation system and political competition with the leaders of other localities for promotion and appointments to privilege economic growth, investment inflows, and employment (Li and Zhou 2005; Whiting 2006; Landry 2008). Indeed, the incentive structure of the cadre evaluation system, with its heavy emphasis on economic growth and investment, encourages collusion between local governments and firms to evade central policies and legislation that negatively affect growth (Wang 2014; Ang 2016). When strict implementation and enforcement of central laws conflict with the incentives of the promotion system, they are sacrificed. But this gap between standards and reality also expands space in the political system for social mobilization. Thus, bottom-up, individualized legal mobilization is a substitute for top-down local government enforcement and regulation. It is a compliance model dependent on worker complaints and grievances. As the goals of the central government have increasingly diverged from the professional and personal incentives of local officials, bottom-up mobilization has become more important as a tool for policy implementation. In addition to high standards, the government promotes legal awareness and rights consciousness among workers via campaigns and the media, and it builds formal legal institutions to process disputes and social conflict out in the open, external to the firm. This institutional context is a critical precondition of social mobilization. The regime's "activation" of lower level social forces begins with these policies.

The decentralized and fragmented nature of China's political system conflicts with a centralized system of lawmaking. While China's political system is at times likened to federalism, it is *de jure* a unified and centralized political system that delegates significant economic and political responsibility to lower levels of government (Montinola, Qian, and Weingast 1995). Without any constitutional division of powers, the powers that have accrued to lower levels have occurred because of the central government's preference for decentralized governance, greater local autonomy, and competition between regions. While there is space for local legislation and standard setting according to local conditions (for example, the minimum wage), legislative autonomy is much more constrained in this centralized model. Instead of legislative variation via different standard setting, China's variation is more apparent in the realms of implementation and enforcement (Paler 2005; Rooij 2006).

While decentralization allows localities to adjust central legislation to its own conditions, diverging goals between the central and local levels make it more likely that implementation and enforcement of central laws will be actively ignored when they cut against local interests. As the central state's ambitions have moved away from a singular focus on economic growth to more complex goals of reducing inequality, solving environmental pollution and food safety crises, and boosting urbanization of rural citizens, local governments remain focused on economic targets and revenue, which are still the main criteria for evaluation and promotion. Revenue and economic growth are also important for wealth accumulation of local officials and to fund local budgetary needs. As goals diverge, the central government is faced with more extreme difficulties in managing its agents at lower levels of government. Reliance on bottom-up mobilization has become more important as a result.

Building Hierarchical Trust

Second, "high standards, self-enforcement" is a reflection of the central government's instrumental use of law as a tool for building "hierarchical trust" (L. Li 2013; Li 2016; Tang 2016) High standards allow the central government to accrue popular legitimacy, while attributing enforcement failures to local governments. Centrally-encouraged bottom-up mobilization as a substitute for local, top-down enforcement is a tool to enhance the central government's ability to foster compliance of lower level government officials with its new edicts and goals. The structure of central legislation and local implementation, combined with high standards set by the central government, allows the central government to take credit for good legislation while shifting blame to lower levels for bad enforcement. While many scholars have noted that Chinese citizens tend to hold higher levels of trust in the central government than in local governments, the reverse of patterns observed in most democracies, we do not have a good understanding of how this "hierarchical trust" is built and sustained (Li 2013). Nor do we understand the dynamics by which this trust could be undermined or implode.

As O'Brien and Li (2006) show in their analysis of rightful resistance, the central government's use of law has opened the political opportunity structure to allow for citizens to claim rights that are promised by the central state, but not delivered by localities. Protective and inclusive labor standards, even if only as aspirational goals, draw a portrait of a central government that is benevolent though distant. The central state's role in designing protective legislation is burnished by the legal dissemination campaigns, which broadcast the benevolent laws and protections emanating from the center. At the same time, lax enforcement and sporadic workplace scandals and disasters become the responsibility of the local governments that are tasked with enforcing the law. Individual citizens who take up legal "weapons" to protect themselves hope that higher levels of government have bequeathed these weapons with state power and authority. Hierarchical trust is built and reproduced by the interaction between individuals and the law. However, as I show in subsequent chapters, this trust can also be undermined via the process of legal mobilization, which exposes the systematic flaws of the dispute resolution process in stark relief. While the regime has encouraged legal mobilization, it is not clear that it actually contributes to greater state legitimacy or citizen confidence in their government as more people engage the system directly rather than just hearing about its accomplishments from afar.

Market Conforming, Politically Constrained

Third, the consequences of authoritarian legality at the Chinese workplace are both market-conforming and politically constrained. Due to the overwhelming reliance on individualized legal mobilization, China's labor protections have divergent effects, determined by one's ability to utilize these institutions effectively and on one's expectations and entitlements under the old system. Emphasis on legality and contractual relations distributes the benefits of "rule of law" unequally across the population. The empirical patterns of legal mobilization and varied perceptions of justice explored in Chapters 4 and 5 reflect this divergent impact of law and "rights giving." In chapter four, I discuss the importance of education and know-how in the process of mobilization. In the new legalized environment of the workplace, new divisions and inequalities appear. While the new laws promise greater contractual protection to all workers, in practice their inclusiveness is tempered by the reality of who is more able to make sense of the law and make use of the law effectively. The enhanced protections and inclusiveness of the 2008 Labor Contract Law are accruing to those with the skills and education necessary to mobilize the law in a system that does not allow collective representation to protect those lower down.

For migrant workers, the inclusiveness of the 1995 Law began a process that still is unfolding today, the gradual dissolution of residential status-related (*hukou*) discrimination and the possibility of more inclusive, fair, and open labor markets, while the adoption of legality diminished the entitlements of those who benefited most from the socialist system. In Chapter 5, I show that the state's deployment of legal labor rights redefined and utterly recast the relationship between socialist workers and the state. By granting legal rights, it stripped away socialist entitlements. This generational cohort lost out while new entrants into the labor markets, such as younger workers and migrant workers, were socialized into a new language of contractual employment and labor market competition. The Party-State's social contract was rewritten via the power of "rights-giving" laws that, in essence, gave new rights to a disempowered social group (migrants) while simultaneously removing the state's obligations under socialism to its urban labor aristocracy. In doing so, the state used law to remake and redefine social cleavages. Different generations judge the law differently dependent on where they come from and what their expectations are. The legal protections of the 1995 Labor Law stripped an earlier generation of socialist workers of their rights and privileges as an entitled class.

The market-conforming dimensions of China's authoritarian legality are reinforced by the marked restrictions on collective representation and organization, which prevent the individualized legal mobilization studied here from coalescing into a larger social movement for labor rights. This mode of popular mobilization should be seen as part of a continuum of CCP policymaking that activates individuals while maintaining strict control of collective action and organization outside the CCP. China's reliance on individualized legal mobilization fulfills the state's goal to mitigate some of the ill effects of the reform era on employment security and working conditions. Informal and formal barriers to collective mobilization remain, enhancing the regime's stability and reducing the likelihood of a political challenge from aggrieved workers. While mass mobilization of the Maoist Era is no longer possible or desirable, individualized legal mobilization does play a critical role in bottom-up implementation of laws and regulations. While the legalistic aspect of workers' mobilization is new and a product of the reform era's emphasis on law, the campaigns of "legal dissemination" and the unleashing of populist grievances against powerful actors, like firms and local governments, do have precedents in earlier eras (Heilmann and Perry 2011). This type of mobilization may be effective in increasing the law's responsiveness while limiting political challenges from organized interests.

China's individualistic approach has ramifications for access to justice, as the benefits of these institutions accrue to those with more political, economic, and social resources. Even compared to other countries that also place more emphasis on individual labor relations, China's system is particularly individualistic, reliant on citizen action often with little assistance from government agencies or civic associations. To exaggerate only slightly, individual workers are expected to sound the fire alarm, find water to put out the fire, and then put the fire out on their own. The labor bureaucracy and courts at the local level are necessary institutions in the dispute resolution process, but they are mostly reactive to worker complaints. Government passivity is matched by weak civil society associations that are often unable to aggregate worker grievances or mobilize collectively for workers' interests. The weakness of intermediary associations that might advocate for individuals with grievances further accentuates existing patterns of inequality in compliance. Fire-alarm mechanisms reinforce market inequalities, advantageous to some workers over others, affecting some firms more than others. In this way, they reinforce inequities of economic and political resources rather than mitigating them.

CHINA'S AUTHORITARIAN LEGALITY IN COMPARATIVE PERSPECTIVE

The nature of China's authoritarian legality is important to our understanding of three theoretical debates in comparative politics. The first debate is the most general and overarching: how do authoritarian rulers survive in office? It concerns the very nature of autocratic rule and political survival. Posited as broad comparative theory that can explain the nature of political survival and performance across regimes, these theories aspire to explain regime survival through the strategic calculations of the ruler and the nature of the political institutions that constrain him.

I argue that these ambitious theories "of everything" do not get us very far in understanding why some autocratic leaders choose constraints and policies that empower people who have no formal role in the selection or survival of leaders.

Second, how do nominally democratic institutions function in autocracies? These mid-level theories examine the structural and coalitional factors that explain why some autocracies adopt political institutions that appear to constrain their rule. Much of this literature focuses on the role of institutions that are normally associated with democracy (legislatures, elections, and courts) in illiberal contexts. My emphasis on rule of law and mass empowerment is different from the general tendency in the literature to focus on elite dynamics and strategic interactions between dictators and their supporters (who are also their potential challengers). I show that while the Chinese case has been more or less marginalized in the comparative debates, this has been for superficial reasons that make cross-national comparison with China more difficult. The CCP's political choices over the reform period are consistent with many of the comparative theories of authoritarian rule. However, the Chinese case also reveals that autocrats, in the context of political uncertainty, do not restrict their attempts at cooptation and inclusion to elites, but also seek out mass-based policies that not only effectively create or reshape social cleavages but also constrain and impede the power of elites who might threaten their rule.

Finally, I turn to the debates in the China field on the nature of Chinese governance. China specialists are divided about the durability of the Chinese state and the relative weight of the contribution of institutional reforms versus the historical legacies of CCP adaptation, flexibility, and pragmatism in explaining China's autocratic success thus far. While much of the empirical research on reform China has focused on institutional changes to the political system, such as grassroots elections, retirement rules, and legislative change, many others have noted the importance of Maoist legacies (Heilmann and Perry 2011), informal institutions (K. S. Tsai 2006; L. L. Tsai 2007), and "rule by law" tactics of the Party-State that reference earlier modes of Chinese rule (Pan 2003; Liebman 2011a). This school of "sustained resilience" is doubtful that China's development path is moving toward a liberal future. Those who emphasize the formal institutional changes that have occurred over the last thirty years, including "rule of law," legislative activism, judicial professionalism, and the expansion of civil society, posit the likelihood of "delayed convergence" with the traditional expectations of modernization – that an increasingly wealthy and urbanized China is also likely to be increasingly democratic (Nathan 2003, 2009; Liu and Chen 2012).

My analysis of legal reforms in the labor realm does not dismiss the importance of new rules and the new "rights-giving" activity of China's lawmakers; despite their genesis from the top, their role in fomenting social mobilization from below is a critical part of the labor story and of the rights-defense movement of labor activists. Emphasizing the process of legal mobilization as a form of political participation, I show that the state's deployment of law increases expectations and fosters new challenges to China's political system. I also do not ignore the important legacies sustained since the Maoist period that root individualized legal mobilization, ironically perhaps, in the Maoist traditions of mass mobilization and campaigns against unjust local agents, bureaucrats, and company managers. Most fundamentally, I argue that the half-hearted and half-way adoption of legality undermines the state's goals of improved governance by exposing the gaps between law on the books and law in reality, by mobilizing individual workers to protect themselves, and then depriving labor, the weaker side in the employment relationship, of effective representation and the ability to harness its collective power. The genius of the Chinese state has been its ability to utilize both its Maoist legacies and the borrowed institutions of democracy to sustain a Communist regime that seems anachronistic and out of sync with its dynamic society. However, this book questions the long-term sustainability of this eclectic mix. The borrowed legality of the labor realm with its heavy reliance on individual rights protection and legal mobilization with inadequate legal representation jeopardizes both possibilities – autocratic resilience or democratic convergence.

China and General Theories of Authoritarianism

The key distinction between authoritarian regimes and democratic ones is that the former lacks formal mechanisms or institutions for the transfer of power between rulers. A small number of single-party regimes now do a fairly good job in institutionalizing transfers of power between individual party leaders, such as what now happens in China every five years.[6] This is no small feat compared to the Maoist period or to other autocracies where the death of leaders or political crises leads quickly to instability. It remains the case, however, that the only way for the CCP, as the

---

[6] Membership of the Politburo changes at every CCP Party Congress, held every five years. Leadership of the CCP and the government change every two terms, or every ten years.

ruling party, to lose power would be through some kind of unplanned, uninstitutionalized transition: for example, a peaceful or violent revolution similar to what occurred across the former Soviet Union and its satellite regimes in East and Central Europe nearly three decades ago or a top-down liberalization that occurred over a longer period of time in South Korea and Taiwan.

This uncertainty of political transition is a fundamental characteristic of authoritarian regimes. In terms of what sets apart dictatorship from democracy, uncertainty is more critical than access to repression, as democratic regimes have deployed repressive tactics against domestic opponents with some frequency. The rule of a dictator could last for decades or a fortnight. Even strong dictators that face little overt opposition understand the fragility of their position. This problem is not the same as Wintrobe's (2000) "dictator's dilemma"; rather this uncertainty of rule is a precondition of his dilemma. For Wintrobe, the dictator's dilemma is a vicious circle between repression and information. A dictator is unsure about his standing among the population, so he uses repression to enforce compliance. In resorting to repression, he reduces the likelihood that he will be able to gain accurate information about what his "subjects" really think. Paying important sectors of society off, buying loyalty, is also an option for many autocratic rulers. Therefore, in reality, we see autocracies using both repression and buying loyalty to reduce the likelihood of a political challenge. But given the uncertainty about political transitions in general, and the lack of accurate information about the level of mass or elite support, attempts to buy loyalty are no guarantee. The more fundamental dilemma of autocratic leaders is the uncertainty under which they rule. Democratic leaders are faced with electoral uncertainty – whether they will win re-election or not, but autocrats are worried, in a much more constant way, about the uncertainty and fragility of their day-to-day survival. While autocrats occasionally leave office after a humiliating election, they face the possibility of losing office (and often their lives) in any number of ways – military coups, mass insurrection, assassination, intra-party revolt, etc. The inability to discern between who offers support and who quietly plans insurrection complicates the behavior of autocratic leaders. While we might expect dictators to repress, because repression is a key tool of non-representative government by definition, given these uncertainties, autocrats might also be more responsive than their narrow base of support indicates.

Most general theories of regime survival do not sufficiently acknowledge the effect of autocratic uncertainty. It has the potential to make the behavior of autocrats more varied and complex than assumptions based on the narrow preferences of a dictatorial leader (Gallagher and Hanson 2015). The selectorate theory (Bueno de Mesquita 2003) is an ambitious attempt to design a model that explains the behavior of rulers in general, across regimes and across the dictatorship/democracy divide. The theory connects a regime's institutions for selecting rulers to the policy choices rulers make and their prospects for survival. It describes these selection institutions in the most skeletal terms possible. In their formal model only three actors are included: the members of the selectorate (S), a ruler, and a challenger. The rest of the populace (the "disenfranchised") are citizens of the country but not members of the selectorate. The members of the selectorate are a subset of the population "whose endowments include the qualities or characteristics institutionally required to choose the government's leadership and necessary for gaining access to private benefits doled out by the government's leadership." The winning coalition (W) is a subset of the selectorate, defined as the necessary subset of S to keep the leader in power. Its size is determined by the institutional arrangements of the country, but which must be necessarily large "enough" to endow the ruler with political power necessary to rule over the selectorate and the disenfranchised. The mix of public/private goods depends on the institutional rules of the country and the size of W/S. When W is larger, the ruler has an incentive to provide more public goods, but when it is small, the ruler is likely to distribute private goods to the important few who support him, impoverishing the disenfranchised.

The original theory in *Logic of Political Survival* (2003) did not acknowledge any important role of the disenfranchised in the political calculus of the ruler or of members of the selectorate. Political competition and intrigue occurred between elites. Later iterations of the theory argued that leaders take into account revolutionary threats from the disenfranchised through repression or broader distribution of public goods. But the model's constraints do not allow regimes to do both at the same time – repress opposition while strategically distributing public goods to coopt potentially revolutionary citizens. Even after taking into account revolutionary threats from the disenfranchised in BDM and Smith (De Mesquita and Smith 2008; Smith 2009; De Mesquita and Smith 2010), the theory cannot explain why some autocratic regimes, such as China's, have moved to substantively expand public goods provisions to a broader population, including members of the disenfranchised who are defined as having no role in the selection or survival of leaders.

While the selectorate theory is extremely ambitious in its scope – claiming to provide a unified theory of regime survival with similar treatment of both democracies and autocracies, the theory relies on notions of selection that only work in regimes with formalized political institutions to signal support of or opposition to the ruling regime. Under the conditions of authoritarian uncertainty, is it possible to make analytic distinctions between selectorate members and non-members? The means by which an autocrat might be removed from office by a member of the elite (a palace coup) might differ from a peasant uprising, but the dictator clearly has incentives to pay attention to the possibility of support from a plethora of elite and non-elite actors. A smart dictator would curry support, play off possible supporters against each other, and use repression sparingly. Autocrats rule in a condition of uncertainty with myriad threats from multiple actors, real or imagined. Strategic behavior often involves placating different subsets of society, but it can also involve policies of divide and rule, of empowerment of some and the demobilization of others.

Acemoglu and Robinson (2006) also attempt to provide an overarching theory that explains why some nations prosper and become democratic and others do not. In *Economic Origins of Dictatorship and Democracy*, they present a model of non-democratic rule that also builds from theories of voting in democracies. They assume that in autocracies, there is some discernible part of the population with "political rights" to select and support the dictator.[7] But the definition of a dictatorship is the very opposite: political rights either do not exist or are routinely violated. Amid authoritarian uncertainty, not only is the dictator insecure (and probably paranoid), so is everyone else, rich and poor alike. Support for the dictator does not happen through formal political institutions of selection, but rather is made and remade every day through the everyday politics of dictatorship. Uncertainty and insecurity can make dictatorships intensely repressive. It can also make them extremely responsive to societal demands.

One common flaw of these overarching theories is their tendency to simplify conflict as dyadic – between the leader and his supporters (or challengers) as is done in Logic of Political Survival (Bueno de Mesquita 2003) or between rich and poor in the redistributionist theories of Acemoglu and Robinson (2006) and Boix (2003). As I analyze here in the Chinese state's deployment of rule of law, autocratic leaders have strong incentives to develop policies that play off social groups against each other

---

[7] They write: "in democracy, the preferences of all citizens matter in the determination of the political outcomes. In nondemocracy, this is not the case because only a subset of the people, an elite, has political rights" (Acemoglu and Robinson 2006, 118).

and that use cooptation of one group to weaken or threaten another (Albertus 2015). These strategies are particularly important when the regime's political foundations are at risk or when principal–agent problems between central officials and their local agents are severe, as is the case today in China's fragmented system. Risk can occur because of exogenous events like a foreign threat or a natural disaster, but risks are also increased when the regime unilaterally shifts policies, needing to cultivate new support and to defray the costs of losing traditional allies. Risks to the Chinese state have grown over the reform period. In the first two decades of reform (1978–2001), the state moved gradually but aggressively away from socialist policies, allowed regional decentralization, and incentivized local governments to grow by cutting central subsidies and assistance. By focusing on growth and the expansion of markets, the central state aligned incentives with local officials who were professionally and personally rewarded for growing their local economy. In more recent years, however, the incentive structure is misaligned; the central government now attempts to mitigate the externalities of growth, to improve environmental protection, enhance food and product safety, and reduce inequality. Local officials have strong reasons to remain fixated on growth: promotion and advancement, climbing local expenditures, personal and familial interests. In the context of dysfunctional relations between the central and local governments, Beijing encourages the bottom-up legal mobilization of citizens as a check on local power and as a device to pressure local governments to implement central policy.

These general theories that attempt to predict how dictators will behave given the political constraints around them tend to over-predict repression and under-predict inclusive behavior and policies. They do a good job explaining the tinpots, but not the dictators who pursue broad developmentalist goals. In *Why Nations Fail*, Acemoglu and Robinson (Acemoglu and Robinson 2012) focus on the inclusiveness of political institutions to explain developmental outcomes. They argue that nations with inclusive institutions will tend to thrive over time by distributing freedom and choice to a larger subset of the population. Defining these institutions as political democracy, rule of law, and respect for private property, Acemoglu and Robinson cannot explain why some autocrats (by definition via exclusive institutions) pursue policies that expand public goods, develop the economy, and, via economic growth, empower those outside the regime. In short, they cannot explain why exclusive regimes adopt inclusive policies. China may be exceptional. As most social science theory is probabilistic, China may merely be an outlier, outside the normal trends for whatever reason – its large size, its long history, or its aspirations as a rising superpower. For theorists who are most interested in cross-national generalization, the failure to explain one case is hardly damning to their overall theory. A more worrisome problem is whether these theories fail to explain the broader rise of East Asia in the post WW-II period. Many of the economic powerhouses of this period are located in this region and developed most rapidly and most successfully under illiberal regimes. These were regimes that were not institutionally obliged to distribute public goods, develop the economy, or foster social welfare, but did so anyway.

China and Theories of Authoritarian Institutions

Recent research on authoritarian exploitation of "quasi-democratic" institutions is not restricted by the assumptions of general theories, which by necessity attempt to reduce the complexity of political conflict by limiting the number of relevant actors and by measuring authoritarian constituencies via size measures borrowed from analysis of democracies, no matter how inappropriate. The study of authoritarian institutions is motivated by the question of what these nominally democratic institutions *do* when embedded in an autocratic context. Scholars have examined the role of elections, legislatures, and judicial institutions (Collier and Levitsky 1997; Diamond 2002; Schedler 2006; J. Gandhi and Przeworski 2007; Ginsburg and Moustafa 2008; Jennifer Gandhi 2008; Magaloni 2008; Magaloni 2008b; Greene 2009; Levitsky 2010). Many of these institutions have democratic roots and should be seen as attempts by authoritarian leaders to borrow the institutions of democracy – not to liberalize or open up politics, but as mechanisms to improve the stability and governing capacity of the regime. It is democracy in the service of authoritarianism.

This literature began with the recognition after the third wave of democratization in the 1980s and 1990s that many regimes with electoral institutions were not exactly thriving democracies. In many cases, authoritarian leaders were re-establishing themselves back into power or taking power anew from failed transitions, but continuing to use democratic institutions that bequeathed a sense of mass legitimation. Studies of "competitive authoritarianism," "electoral authoritarianism," and "hybrid regimes" multiplied as comparativists adjusted to the new reality that the dividing line between regime types had grown less distinct as autocracies grew more adept at selectively borrowing democratic institutions to bolster their own rule. Much of this work has focused on the role of elections in authoritarian regimes and the related role of political parties (Gandhi and Lust-Okar 2009).

Gandhi (2008) and Gandhi and Przeworski's work (2007) on legislatures in authoritarian regimes show that regimes with legislatures enjoy longer tenures and higher rates of economic growth. Their research finds that autocrats who institutionalize via parties and legislatures receive significant benefits. They hypothesize that the existence of these institutions provides opportunities to broaden support and coopt potential opposition leaders via political office. "For the dictator, opposition demands and concessions made within a closed forum such as a legislature or a party are better than their expression on the street" (Gandhi 2008, 11). Gandhi and Przeworski emphasize the external conflicts that can be smoothed out and regularized via these institutions. Magaloni presents an alternative explanation for the existence of these institutions, with a focus on the internal regime dynamics. Dictators use institutions such as political parties, legislatures, and other offices to compensate insiders and to provide a credible commitment that power will be shared (Magaloni 2008). These "democratic" institutions are much less important for democratic functions; but they are critical to the dictator's ability to assuage elites who might otherwise be encouraged to rebel. Boix and Svolik (2013) also emphasize the importance of power-sharing to explain the authoritarian deployment of democratic institutions.

Research focused on judicial institutions also focuses on elite dynamics when explaining the development of legal institutions in autocracies. Moustafa argues that Egypt under Mubarak created constitutional courts and a more independent judiciary as a mechanism to convince foreign investors that Egypt was a safe place for their capital (Moustafa 2009). Similarly in China, Wang finds that localities with mobile capital are more likely to build efficient courts (Wang 2014). Rajah in her work on Singapore argues that high ranking in rule of law indexes is critically important to Singapore's international legitimacy as a safe place for global capital, despite its illiberal use of legality to control political dissent and restrict civil freedoms (Rajah 2012).

Much of the comparative literature on modern authoritarianism has tended to emphasize interactions between the state and societal elites, often the nascent or recently legalized opposition parties within the recently opened political space of these institutions. This elite focus is in the substantive work on institutions such as elections and legislatures in autocracies and also in the theoretical treatments of authoritarianism that usually frame strategic interactions between a dictator and some subset of elite actors who support or defy the dictator. While work on electoral/competitive authoritarianism recognizes the significance of citizens as voters (Magaloni 2008; Greene 2009; Blaydes 2010), in analyses of single-party authoritarianism, non-elites are less critical except as a revolutionary threat under some limited conditions. In some cases, non-elites are almost completely left out of the picture.

The Chinese case, as a single-party regime with no legal opposition to the Chinese Communist Party and no national-level competitive elections, remains largely outside these debates. Although like most modern autocracies, China's ruling regime has been very active in developing political institutions that borrow from democracy and include social actors into politics, including new elites (private entrepreneurs) and non-elites (workers), the lack of any legal political opposition or even autonomous social groups in China makes analysis more insular and less comparative. Although we know that single-party regimes are more stable and tend to grow faster than other types of authoritarian regimes (Magaloni and Kricheli 2010), the Chinese state's seemingly successful mix of limited inclusion on the Party's terms (no organized opposition to party rule) has ironically limited study of its particular type of authoritarianism.

Within the China field, however, there is a growing body of work that demonstrates the particular mix of responsiveness and repression that defines the regime and is often linked to populist tendencies that go back at least to the Mao Era (Gallagher 2005; Heilmann and Perry 2011; Liebman 2011a; Dickson 2016; Tang 2016). Unlike much of the literature in other parts of the world that link populism or clientelism to electoral politics under authoritarianism, these studies demonstrate the ability of the regime to harness other institutions to build connections between "the masses" and the CCP. Manion's research on local people's congresses shows that these institutions do little to allow formal participation in policymaking, but they do serve as pork-delivering devices to local citizens (Manion 2014, 2015). Both Tang (2016) and Lorenzten (2013) argue that many of the contentious protests that rock Chinese society are in fact tolerated and used by the regime to collect information and build support for higher levels that solve problems caused by corrupt local officials. Liebman's study of Chinese courts also shows how judicial institutions can be used by the regime to generate mass support though often violating important legal norms (Liebman 2011a). China's authoritarianism is built on carefully calibrated encouragement of what Tang calls "regime-inspired contentious politics" (Tang 2016, 100) and what Xi Chen labels China's "contentious authoritarianism" (Chen 2010).

The Chinese case remains outside the core discussions of competitive authoritarianism because the regime has rejected any toleration of opposition forces. Outside the realm of political science, however, China's authoritarian resilience is of great interest to the world at large. Its economic success and relative political stability are the envy of developing countries around the world. Its development model and its political system pose the first real challenge to the liberal West since the end of the Cold War. With the collapse of communism in the late 1980s and the transition of many economies to neo-liberal reform, deregulation, and democratic politics, there has been little sense of alternative paths even as markets and democracy have not always borne out their promise in many transitional or developing states. The Chinese case, while often marginal in comparative politics, has come to represent in the larger public sphere the key potential challenge – not only to American foreign policy and to the international system that was set up to benefit the US and its allies in the post-WW II world – but also the challenge to the ideological supremacy of competitive multi-party democracy and free market capitalism. If China proves successful over time or has even proved success thus far, it shows a different path forward for many developing nations that have struggled to grow out of poverty traps, post-colonial conflict, and predatory rule.

China and the Resilience Debate

Scholars of Chinese politics have spent considerable time describing, analyzing, and theorizing the nature of Chinese authoritarian resilience. Two major, but contradictory, themes emerge from the literature. The first, in the seminal piece by Nathan (2003) but carried through in many other studies, is the "concept of institutionalization," which Nathan defines as the creation of formal and informal structures to constrain and guide the state's behavior. Nathan's key examples draw from institutions that structure elite conflict and competition – such as the institutionalization of retirement norms and leadership transition – and institutions that are more inclusive and society-oriented (what he calls "input institutions"), such as mechanisms for political participation, open government, and dispute resolution mechanisms that encourage citizens to take their grievances to the state for processing.

The second, put forth by Sebastian Heilmann and Elizabeth Perry, is that of flexibility and pragmatism, or what they term – "guerrilla policy style" (Heilmann and Perry 2011). In direct contrast to Nathan's focus on predictability, norms, constraints, Perry and Heilmann define Chinese governance style as "a change-oriented 'push-and-seize'" style that contrasts with the stability-oriented "anticipate-and-regulate" norm of modern constitutional government and rule-of-law polities (which typically aspire to a predictable environment where political leaders are held accountable for their actions" (Heilmann and Perry 2011, 13). As Perry and Heilmann describe it, the underinstitutionalization of politics is critical to this policy style, which relies on power, flexibility, discretion, and subterfuge to get things done.

How can we reconcile these two apparently contradictory explanations for Chinese authoritarian survival? The examination of authoritarian legality here shows the attraction of formal institutions to autocrats. Institutionalization brings the allure of constraints and rules on others while continued state-led control over deployment of these institutions provides opportunity for discretion and flexibility. As seen above, China's leaders tactics are not unique; building institutions can be seen as a hedging strategy by the ruling elite to provide greater structure to politics, avenues for elite cooptation, and stages for making commitments to supporters. And yet autocrats also need to find ways to maintain flexibility, preserving their own freedom of movement when it is required. The question is not then institutions OR flexibility, but rather how flexibility and discretionary power are built into the governing institutions of autocracies.

In comparison to the pre-reform period or even the last two decades of the twentieth century, the Chinese political system is much more institutionalized, formalized, and transparent than it was previously. Nathan is surely correct in highlighting the huge importance of, for example, the retirement rules for government officials and the ten-year (two-term) limits on the President and the Premier. At the same time, Perry and Heilmann's analysis of the CCP's distinctive policy style captures the myriad ways in which the party avoids the strictures of institutionalization and rule-bound governance. This is one of the privileges (and dilemmas) of single-party regimes. It makes the rules; it does not necessarily bind itself to those rules. In doing so, it enhances its own flexibility, but it may also fail to convince (to provide credible commitments) its supporters within the regime and its citizen-subjects that the rules will be honored. Authoritarian legality as an instrumental play for power and political stability is ultimately contradictory; as such "rule of law" in autocracies is bounded, limited, and unstable.

In my examination of authoritarian legality, I examine this dual process of institutionalization, "rule of law building," with the regime's attempts to maintain and even enhance flexibility and discretion. While not a comprehensive treatment of China's legal realms, this examination of labor and employment law captures the triangular relationship between the state, capital, and citizens. By examining the legal realm surrounding labor and workplace issues, we can observe most directly how the regime balances the multiple challenges and dangers of new institutions that give individuals rights, create political and economic obligations on the state, require regulation of private actors, and foster disputes and social conflict over redistribution. Conclusions drawn from my analysis of labor and employment law are not necessarily generalizable to other legal realms, but this arena of the workplace is an integral place to view how the state's laws and policymaking affect the distribution of power and resources in society.

While China's use of democratic institutions to manage social change and hold on to political control is well-recognized in studies of grassroots elections and the system of peoples' congresses (Melanie Manion 1996; Cho 2006; L. L. Tsai 2007; Yan 2011; Kamo and Takeuchi 2013; M. Manion 2014), research on the development of rule of law in China and, in particular, Chinese citizens' engagement with the law from this perspective came later. In the early reform period, development of rule of law in China was primarily linked to economic reforms, especially how law fostered China's ability to attract foreign direct investment and trade.[8] However, the use of law to mobilize the masses is not a new phenomenon in the PRC. Going back to the 1950 Marriage Law, Diamant shows the agency of rural women in using the law to challenge traditional family relations (Diamant 2000). Studies of veterans, workers, and homeowners have all shown how aggrieved citizens appropriate new laws and policies to challenge the state and powerful elites (Lee 2002; Diamant, Lubman, and O'Brien 2010; S. Whiting 2011; Erie 2012). I show that the Chinese state has built legal institutions and sanctioned legal mobilization of workers to exploit social cleavages, foster mass support, and improve governance through bottom-up mobilization of workers against "the middle" of the power structure – local officials and firms. Bottom-up mobilization of workers aids the central state in its attempts to improve governance by putting pressure on local leaders who are most responsible

---

[8] For example, The China Quarterly, the preeminent journal on modern China, hosted a special issue on the Chinese legal system in 2007 that primarily dealt with economic law. See Clarke 2007.

for the implementation and enforcement of law. Legal mobilization of workers functions as a "fire-alarm" system of regulation, with worker-led lawsuits substituting for effective government regulation and enforcement of labor laws and standards (McCubbins and Schwartz 1984). As with Nathan's analysis for other parts of the political system, the regime has paid ample attention to the strengthening and development of legal institutions – passing protective labor laws, using campaigns to boost awareness of laws, and designing grievance processing systems to manage the inevitable conflict that arises from contractual arrangements.

Flexibility and state discretion have not been abandoned, however. The model of "high standards, self enforcement" ensures significant room for the state to act, react, or ignore. First, the state's delegation of law enforcement to individual workers who must then engage in their own "rights defense" minimizes the effects of these protections even as it exalts the righteous behavior of individuals. The state's dependence on worker action ensures that a very large number of infractions and violations will never be punished. Workers who are unaware of their legal protections or dependent on employment for basic subsistence will be far less likely to alert the state to violations, no matter how egregious. On the other hand, the high standards in the laws creates space at the top of the labor market – for more highly educated and skilled employees to make demands for protection. Finally, high standards create space for the state to engage in selective enforcement that might target certain types of firms or certain issues during enforcement campaigns.

The Chinese state also uses the legal system instrumentally to exploit social and class cleavages to bolster its own rule. This bottom-up mobilization of workers has empowered a new generation of migrant workers from the countryside while a doctrine of contractual labor relations stripped socialist workers of their previous entitlements under the "iron rice bowl." The deployment of law to structure labor relations in the 1990s was empowering to new generations of workers as they entered the workforce under the market economy. But law did not empower socialist workers; rather it diminished and narrowed their claims.

This divisive nature of law is not just important at the moment of transition from one economic system (the plan) to another (the market). Law's power continues to accrue to some workers over others. In practice, legal mobilization tends to benefit those with the skills, know-how, and education to use the law effectively. These social divisions, across generations and across different kinds of workers, diminish the threat of legal mobilization to the state. Especially in the context of limited collective representation of labor, legal mobilization pushes forward limited social change while reinforcing new patterns of market inequality.

Authoritarian legality is necessarily constrained by the state's focus on law as an instrumental tool for social stability and political survival. Substantive outcomes are easier to control and to dictate within dispute resolution procedures that emphasize discretion, flexibility, and extra-legal settlement. This cycle of mobilization and state-led resolution is a dysfunctional dynamic that exposes the limitations of democratic institutions in authoritarian regimes. The state's response to the unprecedented mobilization after the 2008 Labor Contract Law has been, at least in part, a repudiation of the state's own legality project. The social mobilization around China's newly enshrined labor rights exceeded the bounded legality of the autocratic state. In particular, the state continues to halt the mutation of individual legal mobilization into sustained collective action and independent worker organization.

In order to explain why democratic institutions test the patience of their authoritarian creators, we need to understand the dynamics that they foster. Why are they so frequently deployed by autocrats only to be nipped in the bud when they blossom? As the following chapters will demonstrate, the Chinese state is caught in a dilemma of its own making. As a developmentalist state, its ambitious goals of economic growth and power are unattainable without a workforce that is well-educated and equally ambitious. As China reaches the limits of its reformist development model with its dependence on export-oriented, labor-intensive industrialization and high levels of state investment, the upgrading of skills and expansion of higher education have become top goals of China's developmental state. One of the noted characteristics of the new generation of migrant workers is their higher level of education and their heightened expectations for the future (ACFTU 2010; SFTU 2010; Pun and Chan 2013; Siu 2015). Like its East Asian neighbors, the Chinese state's focus on industrialization *as* development has fostered certain commitments to state investment in primary education and skills training. Increasingly, with its sight now on a transition to a new development model, state investment goes to skills upgrading and the rapid expansion of secondary and post-secondary education. Urbanization and inclusion of migrants are also part of this rebalancing away from export dependency and reliance on government investment for growth. Better-educated citizens, it is hoped, will help China realize its long-term goals for "wealth and power." But higher levels of education also affect how citizens perceive and use the political institutions at their disposal. Autocrats build democratic institutions for instrumental reasons to stay in power. In the rapid growth industrializing autocracies of East Asia, "benevolent" dictators similarly educated their populations to man the world's factories. China, as one of the most successful converts to this model, reflects these development dynamics of ambition and climbing the technological ladder away from the labor-intensive floor to the high tech clouds. Its ambition and its higher expectations are also reflected in its citizens as they engage these institutions to advance their rights and interests.

3

Fire Alarms and Firefighters

Institutional Reforms and Legal Mobilization at the Chinese Workplace

> When I petitioned in Beijing and Shanghai, I brought a whole collection of labor laws and regulations and took them out for the officials to see, to show that the company's behavior is clearly illegal. Then I said, "I didn't make these laws up, so why aren't they being implemented?"
>
> (SH2004049)

It is difficult to overemphasize the radical nature of China's shift from socialist employment relations to its current system of labor and employment law.[1] The move toward legal protection at the workplace is rooted in the transition to capitalism, with the construction of labor markets and the contract as the embodiment of the employment relationship. Beginning in the mid-1980s, the rights and responsibilities of both employers and employees began to be structured by law and guaranteed in the individual labor contract. This legislative framework accounts for both the impressive rights consciousness and rights mobilization of workers and for the highly individualized system of labor regulation and protection, which yields unimpressive levels of labor law enforcement and subpar labor conditions at many Chinese workplaces. This framework broke both with socialist norms of employment and traditional Chinese cultural expectations about collective well-being and paternalistic relationships between laborers and bosses.

In this chapter, I first trace this institutional trajectory over time as it evolved in concert with rising workers' rights consciousness and

---

[1] In China, "labor law" (劳动法) refers to laws governing the relationship between individual employees and employers as well as laws governing collective relationships via trade unions.

mobilization. This includes attention to three separate but related institutions: the legislative framework for workplace rights; legal dissemination campaigns, which spread legal awareness and education to the general population; and the labor dispute resolution system, which serves as the primary mechanism for workplace rights' enforcement. I then turn to the consequences of these institutional reforms by examining broad trends in workers' legal mobilization, firm compliance, and government enforcement. I depict an interaction between "rights giving" by the state and "rights protection" by individuals. As China's labor standards have become more protective and inclusive over time, workers have reacted to these protections by claiming rights and bringing their grievances to the dispute resolution system. The government has constructed a system of labor law enforcement and firm compliance that is both *reactive* to individual legal mobilization and *dependent* on the rights consciousness of workers. As a system of law enforcement, it is suboptimal in the sense that enforcement and compliance are only partial and tend to accrue to workers with higher skills and education. The heavy reliance on individual rights and the tight restrictions on collective mobilization reflect the political preferences of an insecure autocracy.

In connecting these institutional reforms to changes on the ground, I argue that these institutional changes have dramatically contributed to workers' awareness about workplace rights and led to a very large increase in labor disputes nationally, but also have intentionally prevented the expansion of rights mobilization to collectivities of workers and subordinated pro-active state enforcement of rights in favor of far greater reliance on reactive worker mobilization. Firm compliance reflects these trends as well, with intensified workplace conflict, increased firm sensitivity to the threat of lawsuits, and enhanced compliance at the higher end of the labor market, both in terms of the kinds of workplaces that are most affected and the types of workers who are most likely to enjoy these protections. Chapters 4 and 5 go into individual level analysis more deeply and focus more on workers' subjective experiences of and judgments about the legal system.

The chapter proceeds in three parts. Below I sketch out this constitutive theory of authoritarian legality to explain the build out of legal institutions by an autocratic state, which has, in turn, shaped workers' legal mobilization. I also briefly compare the construction of workplace rights and legal mobilization in China to earlier periods in the United States when workers' rights were often constrained and limited by the competing rights of firm (property) owners. This comparison emphasizes the rising

TABLE 3.1. *Summary of Institutional Reforms and Effects*

Institutional Reform	EFFECTS		
	Workers' Mobilization	Firm Compliance	Government Enforcement
Legislative framework	– Expanded mobilization of migrant workers – Curtailed entitlements of urban state workers – Individualized	– Some improvement in formal employment and social insurance coverage – Evasion of law via outsourcing increased	– Labor inspection decentralized and reactive
Legal dissemination campaigns	– Increased awareness of legal rights – Encouraged workers to use law as protective "weapon"	– Greater awareness of employees drives compliance – Firm responsiveness to worker grievances and media attention	– Increased pressure from below to improve enforcement – Sporadic campaigns in reaction to "hot button" issues
Labor dispute resolution system	– Rapid increase in labor disputes by lowering barriers, streamlining path to courts – Collective mobilization restricted – Mediatory solutions encouraged, esp. post-2008	– Fear of worker-initiated disputes increased – Suboptimal compliance	– Worker-initiated "fire-alarms" emphasized over "police patrols"

rights consciousness of Chinese workers as a by-product of these institutional reforms, which share some similarities to "rights revolutions" in other countries. But, as with the experience in the United States, a legislative and judicial emphasis on individual rights can also limit and constrain social movements. In the second section, I lay out the three institutional changes put into place to transform relations at the workplace: the legislative framework, legal dissemination campaigns, and the labor dispute resolution system. Finally, I relate these institutional changes to trends on the ground, examining workers' legal mobilization, firm compliance with new labor laws, and government enforcement of the rights that it has granted. Table 3.1 summarizes the chapter's main points.

I. A CONSTITUTIVE THEORY OF LEGAL MOBILIZATION

The limitations of China's enforcement model, which grants expansive rights that are weakly protected, should not detract from the importance of the institutional changes or the significance of workers' enthusiastic embrace of rights-protection. My theoretical perspective on rights' mobilization in China rejects culturalist and materialist perspectives of Chinese rights consciousness, which tend, from different directions, to discount the importance of the institutional changes that have taken place and interpret rights mobilization as a rhetorical device through which workers strategically "parrot" the state's discourse (Perry 2008, 47). These interpretations not only strip rights mobilization of its significance and importance while removing agency from those that invoke rights, they also underestimate the importance of the state's own turn toward rights as a substitution for other kinds of social guarantees and protection. The focus on individual rights and the reliance on individual rights' mobilization for enforcement is a move by the state to absolve itself of duties to enforce the rights that it has legislated, either through a system of collective enforcement via trade unions and collective bargaining or pro-active state enforcement through labor inspection. In this move, the Chinese state is treading a familiar liberal path away from class-based interest articulation and collective representation toward individualized rights. I argue for a perspective on Chinese rights mobilization that takes law as constitutive of social reality, underlining the important choices made in Chinese labor legislation to strip away socialist entitlements from the entrenched urban labor elite, choosing to empower specific notions of workplace rights but not others, and to build an enforcement system that is reliant on individual rights consciousness and mobilization as well as conforming to market principles. In this story, law is not revolutionary but it is transformative; it can bequeath rights and bring about movements of rights mobilization, but it also rules out other kinds of empowerment and reinforces the inequalities inherent in capitalist labor markets.[2]

Elizabeth Perry's work on Chinese "rules consciousness" is the most articulate version of the historical paradigm (Perry 2008, 2010), which prioritizes the cultural consistency of protest repertoires through the Imperial, revolutionary, and reform periods. In her argument, the

---

[2] For a critique of the rights revolution at the American workplace see Lichtenstein 2003.

rise of "rights consciousness" rhetoric from Chinese peasants, workers, and other aggrieved groups is attributable to their strategic use of state-sanctioned language to press for their social and economic interests. It is deeply bound to the historical relationship between the ruler and the ruled, with mutual expectations for the ruler to provide social and economic protections to those below. Such "rules consciousness," it is argued, reflects the state's own shift to law from class struggle and other socialist discourses rather than a true sense of rights emanating from natural law or religious principles that Perry attributes to Anglo-American rights discourse. In China, rights' claims are newly packaged and seem akin to similar "rights revolution" in other contexts, but they are actually part of a cultural tradition of state hierarchy and subject subordination (not citizen empowerment) that goes back centuries. While China's protest tradition is alive and well, this newest round of contestation is not qualitatively different from earlier struggles: the dominated use the language of the state to seek its benevolence and protection, but their goals, limited in their nature to social and economic needs, do not challenge the state's right to rule or the system itself.

Perry's construction of "rules consciousness" argues against the more mainstream interpretation of rights discourse in contemporary China as something new and different, linked to the reform era's developmentalist ideology and the actual development that it has spawned, which unleashed typical processes of modernization – urbanization, rising levels of education, and a burgeoning middle class. The mainstream interpretation evokes a "modernization theory" assumption that development and its corollary trends are leading to new conceptions of citizenship rights and new demands for political participation and rights (Y. Liu and Chen 2012). Perry's rules consciousness argues for a much more conservative interpretation of "rights talk" by ordinary Chinese. The language of rights is, in her interpretation, a superficial veneer on traditional demands for state benevolence.

A similarly skeptical interpretation of legality and workers' rights rhetoric can be seen in C.K. Lee's analysis of the two most marginalized sectors of the Chinese workplace: the state enterprise workers of China's rustbelt, who faced long-term unemployment and deprivation as the state sector shrank dramatically in the early part of this century due to restructuring and privatization and the migrant workers of southern China's manufacturing enclaves, who faced abysmal working conditions and little state protection as they toiled making goods for the rest of the

I. A Constitutive Theory of Legal Mobilization 57

world during China's export boom (Lee 2007). While the groups differ markedly in other aspects of their framing and mobilization strategies, both groups embrace law and notions of rights as symbolic resources in their fight against corrupt local governments and abusive managers. These marginalized groups adopt "the language of legality and citizenship as a tactic, not out of as sense of empowerment or entitlement" (Lee 2007, 117). In this Marxist paradigm, law is a reflection of the social and economic forces that dominate the Chinese workplace. Local officials are embedded in relationships with enterprise owners (or SOE managers in the rustbelt) of mutual self-interest and enrichment. Under this system of "decentralized legal authoritarianism," law fails to deliver on its promise and initial enthusiasm for the law is later re-directed toward protest. Law represents the hegemony of China's state capitalism and the fusion of power between the economic and political elite. As with Perry's interpretation, it is used as a rhetorical device, but as a subaltern critique against a powerful state, not as the claims of emergent citizens.

The approach outlined here does not contest some observations and arguments presented both in Perry's historical perspective and Marxist critiques of China's authoritarian legality. The culturalist stance that legality is a top-down project initiated by a reformist and ambitious state gets the basics correct. It is unlikely that worker rights' mobilization would have occurred had the state not first emphasized notions of contractual obligation and market fundamentals as new organizing principles of labor. The disappointment and frustration that Lee observes among legalistic migrants exposes the unfair attributes of the legal system that closes off access to justice for those at the bottom rungs of the labor market. However, I take law more seriously as a constitutive element of social change and transformation (McCann 1994; Ewick 1998). It is not merely a tool wielded from a domineering state from above or a weapon unleashed from unruly would-be citizens from below. The role of labor law in setting out new rights while taking away socialist entitlements is a critical element in China's reform transformation since the 1980s. By laying out here in detail the institutional elements of China's labor law regime, we gain a firmer understanding of how legislative and institutional changes have shaped workers' mobilization. By tracing these elements out over time, especially from the first 1995 National Labor law to the 2008 Labor Contract law, we also understand how legal dissemination campaigns and patterns of worker mobilization and grievances shape iterative rounds of legislation and rights-granting. Finally, by examining the dispute resolution system as the main mechanism for making legislative rights real, I show that China's workplace rights are protected by individual action, not state benevolence.

This institutional approach builds off the "rightful resistance" model of state–society relations articulated by O'Brien and Li in their studies of peasant mobilization in rural China (O'Brien and Li 2006). Rightful resistance is defined as social mobilization that invokes the "commitments" of the powerful to expose breaches of such commitments, uses formal institutions to press for protection but also pushes the limits of such institutions via mobilization and the production of protest "spectacles," cultivates popular and elite support against miscreants, and relies on divisions between the state to garner such support (O'Brien 2013; O'Brien and Deng 2015). Although the concept of rightful resistance is from the study of rural China, the genesis of resistance by villagers and workers is similarly rooted in the early reform period's invocation of "contract" as the new mode of organization to structure relationships between people and the state. In the labor realm, even more so, rights' mobilization is structured by the individual contract system. This mode of rightful resistance is not reducible to law-parroting; by interacting with the law, workers have shaped and changed legal institutions and employer compliance. I argue for an understanding of rights mobilization and rights consciousness in China that is not as tradition bound or as culturally unique as the culturalists argue nor as empty and rhetorical as the Marxists claim. Moreover, rights' mobilization is more than just a strategic ploy or rhetorical device by disadvantaged workers against powerful firms and officials. While rights mobilization often involves the deployment of existing legal protections to expose the failure of local enforcement of such protections, it has also led to changes in the existing protections and the expansion of new rights and protections.

This progressive view of rights mobilization is not to make teleological claims about the future or to link China's "rights revolution" in labor to political reform or democratization. Much of the rightful resistance literature has been criticized for what O'Brien terms "developmental thinking" – the idea that rightful resistance is a pathway toward democratization and liberal politics (O'Brien 2013). Indeed, instead what I argue in this book is that the emphasis on labor rights and the individual labor contract combined with restrictions on collective disputes, limits on civil society, and inadequate legal representation leads to suboptimal labor rights enforcement, disenchantment with legal institutions, and unequal access to justice that conforms to existing market inequalities (Gallagher

I. A Constitutive Theory of Legal Mobilization 59

2006; Michelson 2006). As I argue in the concluding chapter, these limitations on rights' mobilization in China have led to greater social instability and further inhibit possibilities for liberal political change and reform by stunting the societal offshoots of the state's rule of law project. The construction of China's illiberal rule of law contributes neither to its authoritarian resilience nor to a gradual pathway of reform and political liberalization. Unlike Perry, I do not find that these institutions are "system-supportive" but rather that they breed instability and disappointment while cutting off possibilities for improvement because such improvements require social organization and representation for aggrieved workers that the regime deems too risky.

A brief departure from China to the United States is instructive to demonstrate this constitutive interpretation of law as not only embedded in specific socio-economic and cultural contexts but also shaping that context in fundamental ways. Rights consciousness and patterns of mobilization are not only the results of long-inherited cultural attributes, but are more immediately shaped by the institutional context. Perry's critique of "rights consciousness" is built upon an East–West (mainly China–US) dichotomy that posits an individualistic "rights conscious" and anti-government American society against a "rules conscious" Chinese society that demands collective well-being and socio-economic rights from a benevolent state. In the labor realm, which encompasses both civil and political rights – the right to association in particular – and socio-economic rights, such as minimum wage laws and decent work regulations, this dichotomy falls apart. In both societies, the recourse to rights has been both "enabling and confining" (Forbath 1991). During the heyday of its rapid industrialization, the United States constructed institutions that championed both collective rights, such as the protection of collective bargaining through the National Labor Relations Act of 1935 (the Wagner Act), and individual labor standards, such as the eight-hour day and the minimum wage, in the Fair Labor Standards Act of 1939 (Estlund 2017). But workplace rights in the United States have continuously been under pressure from competing rights claims from capital as property owners and from the government's pursuit of industrial peace. Historically, the central role of the judiciary in delineating the rights of labor had an important hand in shaping how labor activists and trade unionists defined their movements and their goals (Forbath 1991; Orren 1991; Pope 1997). While weak class consciousness and the paucity of workplace rights in the United States are usually attributed to the fragmentation of the federalist political system and ethnic and racial social cleavages, the judiciary and its construction of labor law are key to understanding how American workers conceive of and articulate rights at work (Forbath 1991; Orren 1991).

In fundamental ways, the rights consciousness of American workers is weak and inextricably linked to the development of labor and employment law through our own period of rapid industrialization. For example, both the civil and socio-economic rights of American workers were historically subordinated to the rights of capital owners to autonomy and freedom of operation, rooted in the common law expectations of "master and servant" contracts. Until the 1840s, judicial decision-making cast strikes as criminal conspiracies; courts also used injunctions to limit strikes and boycotts well into the twentieth century. In describing the late nineteenth century, Wilentz notes that "the major political reality in these years was the extraordinary repression visited upon organized workers by employers' associations, with the cooperation of the courts, state legislatures, and, increasingly, the federal government" (Wilentz 1984, 15). More recently "right to work" laws in many states have further undermined the power of collective organization. As collective rights declined, however, the civil rights movement of the 1960s and the subsequent "rights revolution" opened up new avenues for workplace protection and social mobilization. In the context of "at-will" employment and the prioritization of market principles and the rise of the "fissured workplace" (Weil 2014), employment security and protection in the United States is often only available through the laws governing civil rights protection and non-discrimination. These laws were first passed to protect the collective interests of groups – first racial minorities, then extended to women, the elderly, the disabled, and sexual minorities; as such, they are intimately tied up with America's history of slavery and racial injustice. In the context of declining trade union protection, these laws promote the rights' consciousness of individuals based on identity. The American workplace exhibits a bifurcated rights consciousness that legitimizes claims based on non-discrimination and equal treatment, but subordinates class-based rights. Lichtenstein notes this enduring conflict between labor rights and human rights:

"From the early 1960s onward, the most legitimate, and in many instances the most potent, defense of American job rights would be found not through collective initiative, as codified in the Wagner Act and advanced through the trade unions, but through an individual's claim to his or her civil rights based on race, gender, age or other attribute. If a new set of work rights was to be won, the decisive battles would take place, not in the union hall or across the bargaining table, but in the legislative chambers and courts" (Lichtenstein 2003, 5).

In the enforcement of workplace rights, however, the United States looks far less individualistic than China. The legal changes in the 1930s expanded the parameters of collective enforcement via trade union legalization, collective bargaining, and the right to strike. In the post WW-II period, class action litigation and the granting of litigation rights to administrative agencies to file lawsuits on the behalf of employees, such as the Equal Employment Opportunity Commission (EEOC), expanded litigation space and state assistance for individual workers. Legislative acts protected certain groups, such as older workers, disabled workers, and women, from discrimination. Social movements around unrealized legal protections advanced both citizens' consciousness about workplace rights and company behavior (McCann 1994). Although trade union density in the private sector has declined inexorably in the last several decades, workers' rights can also be protected through the collective mobilization of social movements, civil society actors, and legal aid organizations.

The exact character of rights mobilization will be tied to the particular cultural and historical place, but also influenced by the global context. The emphasis on non-discrimination in the United States – now expanded to include many groups beyond racial minorities – is rooted in our history. The relatively high standards of the 1995 Labor Law in China are in part a link back to the principle of benevolent protection embedded in China's socialist and Confucian past (Hung 2011). The secular decline in trade union density and political influence across many countries, the individualization of rights, and the rise of managerial autonomy are part of global capital's ability to relocate and the global marketplace's emphasis on flexibility. "Rights revolutions" and global capitalism are linked together with their emphasis on individual rights and resources (Kagan, Garth, and Sarat 2002). A dichotomy that posits American "rights consciousness" and rugged individualism against Chinese "rules consciousness" and collective protections cannot account for the weakness of workplace rights in the United States that combines with strong collective institutions that enhance enforcement and implementation. This not only includes civil society actors, such as trade unions, NGOs, and legal aid organizations, but also the state itself, which can represent aggrieved workers in the battle for protection. China's legislative work over the past twenty years, on the other hand, has championed the notion of individual rights at the workplace and stripped away collective entitlements. Its enforcement and regulatory institutions are weakly constructed; the state delegates enforcement to individual workers while restricting collective institutions that might improve their results. The individualistic rights mobilization of the Chinese worker is not a cultural anomaly, but a product of a legal regime that is liberal in its economic principles and illiberal in its political restrictions.

II. THE INSTITUTIONAL CONTEXT OF CHINA'S RIGHTS CONSCIOUSNESS

The political logic of the "high standards, self enforcement" regulatory model is laid out in chapter two. This model creates a large gap between law on the books and law in reality, which provides an opportunity for social mobilization and rights-claiming behavior by Chinese workers. What produces this large gap? Why does an authoritarian regime promise what it cannot deliver in the realm of labor rights, risking greater social instability and dissatisfaction? This model is a function of two problems in the Chinese political system since reform began in 1978. First, in the context of a decentralized and fragmented political system, the government has difficulty monitoring enforcement measures of its local agents and the compliance levels of firms, especially firms in the non-state sectors. Bottom-up legal mobilization, as a fire-alarm system of regulation, is a substitute for top-down government enforcement and regulation, a compliance model that is dependent on worker complaints and grievances. It is government oversight that is indirect, decentralized, and reactive to these complaints. But why such high standards, standards that put China's labor protections on par with or above those of most developed economies? While a fire alarm model could be possible even with lower standards, China's high standards benefit the upper levels of the labor market, as these standards can encourage even relatively well-off workers to push for improved enforcement of standards. Higher standards promote the mobilization of workers who are already well above market-enforced standards in wages, conditions, and contract terms. As we see in Chapter 4 on the role of education in mobilization, bottom-up mobilization is a strategy that privileges workers with the education, awareness, and skills to claim legal protections. While it is populist in tone, in practice it can reinforce existing patterns of inequality.

But the political logic or functionalist account of the state's strategy is only part of the story. This chapter provides an analysis of the institutions that make this strategy possible: the legislative rights guaranteed in China's labor laws since 1995, the legal dissemination campaigns that have championed "rights protection" in the media and propaganda system to aggrieved workers, and the labor dispute resolution system that has provided a space for worker grievances to be heard and processed outside of the workplace. The system is constructed to encourage individual rights protection, but never to encourage collective organization independent of the CCP or to allow sustained activism. Combined with active and ongoing campaigns to popularize the law and disseminate legal rights to the population, individualized legal mobilization by workers puts pressure on powerful elites – local governments and firms – to enforce and comply with the new laws. The regime's "activation" of lower level social forces begins with these policies. This institutional context of legal mobilization is critical to situating Chinese workers' "rights consciousness" and notions of legality that are explored in the three subsequent empirical chapters, which detail mobilization trends and the state's response to the unprecedented levels of mobilization that followed the passage of the 2008 Labor Contract Law.

The Legislative Turn: Inclusive and Protective, But Individualized

China's labor legislation drafting process began with a set of conflicting crises and challenges: how to protect workers in the emerging market economy working in private, foreign, or restructured state firms? How to gradually end the socialist employment relations of state sector firms so that they could compete in a more competitive and open economic environment? Law and contracts became the tools to grant rights and protections to migrants and private sector workers while taking away security and socialist guarantees from urban state sector workers. The timing of the 1995 Labor Law, just prior to deep restructuring of the state-owned public sector, translated into an initial reduction in employment security when compared to the socialist permanent employment enjoyed by the small minority of urban workers in the public sectors (about 20 percent of the total population). Meanwhile, for migrant workers who had just begun to stream into China's coastal cities looking for work, the 1995 Labor Law held promises of protections and social welfare that had never been granted to China's rural workforce.

The legislation that followed was specifically tailored to manage these conflicts and crises. It has both empowered and constrained worker mobilization. This section details these choices and provides an overview of the progression of China's labor legislation from the drafting of the 1995

Labor Law to the 2012 revisions of the 2008 Labor Contract Law and focuses on three fundamental characteristics: inclusion, protection, and individualization. First, China's labor laws are motivated by an inclusionary impulse to broaden coverage. Unlike many developing countries that have developed exclusionary laws that tend to privilege certain sectors and workers, Chinese labor laws provide for expansion of legal protection to nearly *all* non-agricultural workers. Laws are not specifically designed to cover urban workers and they include regulatory oversight over all enterprises, domestic, foreign, and state-owned, as well as some employees of government-affiliated institutions, such as hospitals, social organizations, and schools. In 1995, this inclusionary impulse was aspirational; in practice many firms and workers were not covered, but the longer-term consequences of this inclusionary law have been transformative. The inclusionary impulse has strengthened over time with supplementary laws since 1995 increasing inclusion through stiffer penalties and restrictions on informal work. While this inclusionary impulse has had a laudatory effect on the mobilizing capacity of migrant workers, it also had a leveling effect on workers in the socialist system as these laws stripped away the privileges of those working in the public sector. Despite the ill-effects on socialist workers, the labor standards provided for in these laws are very protective, compared to other countries, and commit China to labor standards that are on par with or higher than the protections in many developed economies. Drafted mainly by state planners and labor insiders, these highly protective standards encourage mobilization at the high end of the labor market and also allow for selective enforcement of high standards for certain types of workers and firms. Finally, China's labor and employment laws are exceptionally reliant on the individual labor contract as the crux of inclusion and protection. This reliance on the individual written labor contract comes at the expense of the collective representation of workers via collective negotiations and contracts. By constructing labor relations between individuals and employers, these laws atomize and fragment workers, especially those with grievances.

Inclusive and Protective
China's labor legislation began with laws and regulations to structure the economic reforms of the 1980s. Labor legislation at the time was highly specific to the new ownership sectors, mainly foreign companies, and restructuring reforms were just beginning in the public sectors as the government gradually introduced the labor contract system in 1986 for newly hired workers (White 1987). Different standards existed for

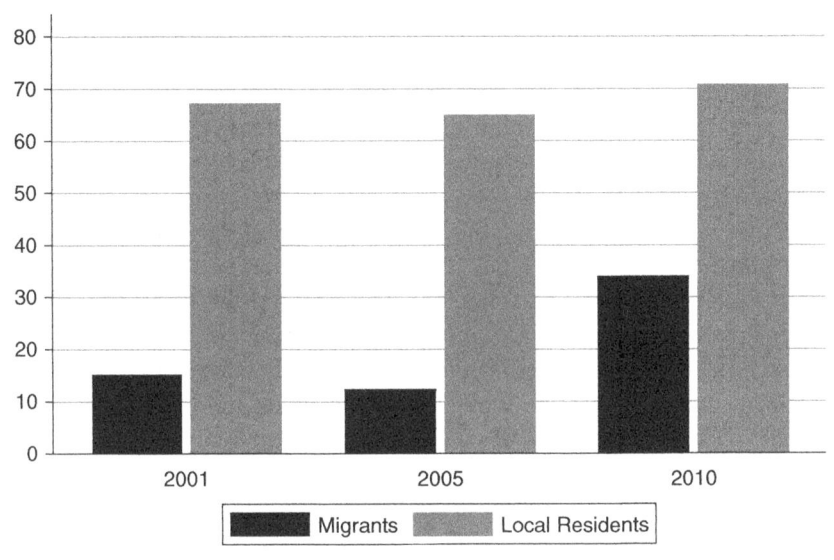

CHART 3.2. Workforce Employed with Formal Labor Contracts.
Source: CULS.

different types of firms and different types of workers, regulated by a patchwork array of administrative regulations and enterprise rules. The first national law was not passed until 1995, but it changed the landscape of labor relations in China with its ambition to be broad in coverage, shifting away from the segmented nature of labor regulation in the early reform period. Unlike the slew of laws, regulations, and circulars before it, the 1995 Labor Law was drafted to have broad application to workers regardless of firm type and worker background. This move away from ownership and worker-specific laws in principle began to expand workplace protections to workers heretofore left out of the system – most importantly, rural migrant workers who were flocking to urban areas to find work in China's burgeoning manufacturing, construction, and service industries on the coasts. The extension of the law to all types of firms and workers also meant that workers who were previously well-protected via socialist employment would now begin to lose those protections. For these workers, adoption of contractual protections could not compare to the administrative protections they enjoyed in the planned economy. Moreover, they lost the most important aspect of socialist work, permanent employment, via the 1995 Labor Law and the move to contracts.

The inclusive nature of the 1995 Labor Law moved nearly the entire non-agricultural workforce to the labor contract system, which mandated that employers sign written labor contracts with their employees. A written labor contract formally establishes "labor relations" between the firm and the employee. The existence of labor relations then qualifies the employee protection under the 1995 Labor Law and inclusion into social insurance schemes. The 1995 Labor Law declared obligations to provide social insurance for retirement, medical care, occupational injury and disease, unemployment, and maternity leave. Implementing regulations at the local level require significant contributions from employers and employees, usually estimated at around 40 percent of the wage, with about 10 percent of the total coming directly from the individual worker's wage and the remainder from the employer. In a comparative study of social insurance, Rickne finds that China's social insurance system is "one of the world's costliest in terms of the relative rise in unit labor cost stemming from contributions." In the United States, companies pay 10 percent in social insurance, in Germany, 20 percent, and Sweden, 23 percent (Rickne 2012).

Examining China's labor standards through restrictions on working hours and overtime, China's laws and regulations meet or exceed current international practices. China reduced the weekly working hours from forty-eight hours to a forty-hour week in the 1995 Labor Law and also put into place restrictive overtime regulations that limit monthly overtime to three hours per day or thirty-six hours per month. The 1995 Labor Law also instructs lower level governments to institute a minimum wage system with the actual wage set by local governments. In 2004, the Ministry of Human Resources and Social Security (MHRSS) released implementing regulations for the minimum wage system, stipulating that localities set up a standard system for the minimum wage. The law also prohibits the termination of labor contracts of pregnant or breast-feeding employees as well as employees with occupational injuries or illness. The World Bank's Doing Business Index ranks employment conditions in China as quite protective, 67 out of 100.

While the goals of the 1995 Labor Law were to increase flexibility of the public sectors and to increase protection of the other sectors, the law was far more successful in promoting flexibility and much less effective at increasing protection. At best, it promised limited employment security through individual contracts if employees were lucky enough to be offered one. At worst, it encouraged informality and short-term employment with weak or non-existent penalties for failure to conclude contracts. The law's weak framework for enforcement allowed labor markets to develop; employment became much more flexible and dynamic with vast increases in labor mobility compared to the earlier periods (Cai, Du, and Wang 2009). As the state sector restructured, employment grew quickly in the non-state sectors while informality increased as more workers were hired without contracts or benefits. Employment security declined even among workers with contracts as contract terms became shorter and employers used contract expiration to avoid long-term employment and severance obligations ("Speech Excerpts: Group Deliberation on the Draft Labor Contract Law (1)" 2005; Lin 2007; Wang 2007). The yearly increases in protests and demonstrations, signals of rising social instability, were at least partly attributed to the lack of legal protections afforded most Chinese workers.[3] As one academic expert involved in subsequent legislative publicly noted, "China's recent economic growth and success has been at the expense of its workers. They have been sacrificed" (Chang 2007). These voices strengthened and found greater reception in the Hu Jintao and Wen Jiabao administration. Alongside broader trends in the late 1990s and early 2000s of increased income inequality, rising social instability, and severe problems in workplace conditions, central government officials began to push for a renewed emphasis on labor protection and enhanced job and social security.

The drafting of the 2008 Labor Contract Law reflected this newfound interest in reducing inequality and enhancing social justice. This law pushed for new advances in inclusive labor standards and new penalties for avoiding these obligations. While the 1995 legislation was a premeditated move to "smash" the iron rice bowl, 2007 was touted as the "year of social legislation," the government's belated attempt to catch up with and mitigate some of the adverse effects of China's rapid transformation (Zhu 2007). The 2008 Labor Contract Law was the key law amid a number of new labor laws that were passed during this period. In 2007, two other major employment-related laws were passed, the Employment Promotion Law and the Labor Dispute Mediation and Arbitration Law. The Social Insurance Law, which broadened the coverage and inclusive goals of social insurance, was passed in 2010.

The move toward greater protection and enhanced enforcement was not without controversy. The legislative drafting process of the Labor Contract Law was much more contentious and participatory than the 1995 Labor Law, attracting widespread media and social attention to the

---

[3] Some of the largest labor protests in the history of the PRC occurred in the years following the massive layoffs in the state sector. For a detailed report on these protests, see Human Rights Watch 2002. See also Hurst 2012; Hurst and O'Brien 2002; Lee 2002.

debate over China's labor standards, workplace conditions, and worsening inequality. The controversy intensified once implementation of the Labor Contract Law began during the 2008 Global Financial Crisis and has continued as the impact of these laws occurs, in the context of rethinking a development model built on exports and cheap labor, and since 2014, a slowing economy. The implementation of the 2008 Labor Contract Law and other recent labor laws has been contentious and fraught with the competing concerns of the state, capital, and labor during a period of significant economic uncertainty.[4] In 2006, the National People's Congress (NPC) opened a thirty-day period of public comment on the draft labor contract law. The draft law received over 191,000 comments, a record at the time for any law since the 1954 PRC Constitution (*Xinhua News Online 2006*). Foreign business associations and chambers of commerce used the period of public comment to draft detailed criticisms and suggestions for the law. Some investors warned of "capital flight" from China because of the law's severity. Labor activists warned of widespread pressure on China to weaken the legislation in favor of global capital.[5] Contention and controversy has followed the 2008 Labor Contract from its drafting in 2006 to its implementation in 2008 during the crisis, and to its subsequent revision in December 2012 (Harper Ho and Huang 2014). Amid the economic slowdown and volatility of 2015–2016, the LCL has been singled out for its effects on the economy. Finance Minister Lou Jiwei has been its most vocal critic, singling it out for contributing to the slowdown in a private speech at Tsinghua University in 2015 before openly opposing the law during a speech to the NPC's annual meeting in 2016 (*South China Morning Post 2015*; *Xinhua News Online 2016*).

---

[4] There were calls by academics and businesspeople to repeal or revise the labor contract law after the economic crisis led to a steep drop in exports. However, the National People's Congress stated that revision or repeal was out of the question. "Economist Zhang Weiying Calls for a Decisive Halt in the Implementation of the Labor Contract Law, Says it Hurts the Interests of Workers" [jingji xuejia zhang weiying: laodong hetongfa sunhai gongren de liyi guoduan tingzhi zhixing) Caijing (online), 8 February 09; "China won't revise labor contract law amid financial crisis: lawmaker," Xinhua (online), 9 March 09.

[5] See, for example, Christine Buckley, "Foreign Investors May Quit if China Tightens Up Labor Law." The Times Online, June 19, 2006, www.business.timesonline.co.uk/tol/print.do?articleid=676240; Jiangtao Shi, "New Labor Law Would Bring Conflicts, European Firms Fear." South China Morning Post. April 22, 2006: pg 8; Toh Han Shih, "Labor Contract Law Draws Protest from Every Side." South China Morning Post. November 13, 2006: pg. 18; Geoff, Dyer, "China's Labor Debate Spurs War of Words for US Interests," The Financial Times. May 3, 2007: pg. 11; Andrew Batson, "China Toils over New Labor Law." Wall Street Journal. May 7, 2007: pg. 8.

II. The Institutional Context of China's Rights Consciousness 69

Despite the controversies that have dogged the LCL since its early drafting, the LCL also enhanced the penalties for failure to conclude written labor contracts. The lack of penalties in the 1995 Labor Law had allowed employers to evade the most basic responsibilities of "labor relations." Without evidence of labor relations, workers were often deprived of their salaries, of their rights to occupational injury and disease compensation, and of other employer-dependent forms of social welfare. The 2008 LCL provides punitive and severe liabilities for failure to conclude written labor contracts with employees. Employers that fail to do so face paying double wages for any term of employment that is completed without a written labor contract (Article 82). After one year of work without a contract, an employee earns the right to an open-ended contract. These changes dramatically increased the incentives for employers to acknowledge formal labor relations with their employees and by doing so incurring responsibilities related to social insurance payments and employment security. The law also states that the new company formed after any merger, acquisition, or division must honor all existing employment contracts (Article 34). The LCL further recognizes the notion of de facto labor relations, through which workers without written contracts could more easily prove that they were employed by providing evidence of payment, management control, etc. Finally, the LCL also addressed two common problems of migrant workers: employers' failure to pay wages and employer attempts to limit workers' mobility by taking deposits or identification cards. The LCL is much more detailed and more punitive in dealing with companies that do not pay wages in a timely manner or that attempt to restrict workers' mobility by taking their property, ID cards, or deposits.

The LCL further enhanced employment security by increasing the costs of contract expiration and limiting use of short-term contracts. The government attempted to roll back the dramatic decline in contract length and the use of contract expiration to minimize employer obligations. While Chinese labor law does not permit at-will employment, requiring cause for early termination of the labor contract, the devolution to shorter contracts after the 1995 law allowed employers to use contract expiration as a source of labor flexibility. Workers would repeatedly sign short-term contracts, perhaps one or two years, until the employer decided that they were no longer needed. At times contract expiration was used to terminate workers with long tenures, workers who had acquired occupational illnesses or disease, or to avoid entering into a non-fixed term contract after a worker gained ten years tenure and had the right, under the 1995 law, for an open term contract. Termination via contract expiration also absolved the employer from any responsibility for severance compensation. The 2008 Labor Contract Law reversed this trend toward greater flexibility with new restrictions on fixed term contracts and requirements for severance compensation upon contract expiration. According to Article 14, employers should enter into an open-ended contract after the consecutive completion of two fixed-term contracts or when an employee has ten or more years of consecutive tenure. Employers that fail to sign a written contract with an employee also should revert to an open-ended contract after one year has passed. These clauses have proven to be some of the most controversial aspects of the 2008 Labor Law, leading to the expansion of labor subcontracting and labor outsourcing as well as many practices that are flagrant violations of the law but that serve to avoid the responsibility of granting workers more security. Restrictions on fixed-term contracts were paired with new requirements that employers pay severance compensation for termination for cause, in the event of a bankruptcy or shutdown or other employer-related reasons. Severance is calculated based on work tenure with one month of salary paid for every year worked as the typical calculation method.

After the 2008 LCL, there was a pronounced increase in the use of labor subcontracting to get around the more onerous contractual requirements for regular employees. The December 2012 revisions to the 2008 Labor Contract Law responded to this trend by reinstating some restrictions that first appeared in 2006–2007 drafts of the Labor Contract Law as well as limiting the number of subcontracted workers to 10 percent of the entire workforce of an employer in the implementing regulations released by the MOHRSS in 2013. The revisions required that labor subcontracting be restricted to positions that are "temporary, auxiliary, and substitute" and provided fairly detailed definitions of what these terms mean in practice, further requiring that there be "equal pay for equal work" between regular workers and subcontracted workers. The law also increased the fines for companies that violate these clauses and fines for subcontracting firms that are not licensed. All in all, the 2012 revisions of the LCL moved considerably further in inclusiveness as the government attempted to sew up loopholes in the law.

Individualized
Despite the progression in the protections and inclusiveness of China's labor laws from 1995 to 2012, the individual labor contract remains the most important mechanism for the enjoyment of these benefits. While

legislation on individual protections and security has progressed markedly since 1995, there have been almost no improvements in the aspects of the laws that emphasize collective rights, representation, and bargaining. The individual worker's rights and obligations at the workplace are determined by the laws, which are overwhelmingly focused on individual protections, and by his/her own individual attributes, whether they are related to formal education, skills, or social status. While some aspects of treatment are determined by collective identities via local regulations, such as hukou status, there are few functioning mechanisms to aggregate the collective power of workers and to represent their collective interests. The main area where improvements and changes have occurred is in the bureaucratic power and influence of the ACFTU, which has led to improvements in individual protections, increases in union density, and a louder policy voice for labor's interests within the bureaucracy. However, even with these changes of the ACFTU, the union's role is more akin to a pro-labor government bureaucracy than a body to organize and represent the aggregated interests of workers (Taylor 2000; Taylor, Chang, and Li 2003; Pringle and Clarke 2011; Traub-Merz, International Labour Office., and Global Labour University (Germany). 2011).

While the reform-era laws and regulations detailed below attest to this individualization of the labor relationship via the labor contract system, the individualization of the worker began much earlier in the Maoist Era, with its restrictions on trade unionism, "economism," and any movement of worker organizations toward autonomy or opposition to CCP policy. Yunxiang Yan argues that the Maoist emphasis on heavy industrialization and the social and political engineering required to achieve it led to the "partial individualization" of Chinese society even before the onset of economic reform (Yan 2010, 491). The socialist state's desire for modernity required that the "masses" be remade in service of collectivized agriculture and state-led industrialization. Building off Walder's notion of "organized dependency" of the Maoist workplace, Yan describes social life as highly restricted and controlled, "whereby Chinese individuals were socio-economically dependent on their work unit or collective, politically dependent on state-sponsored management, and personally dependent on Communist cadres" (Walder 1988; Yan 2010, 491). Competing associations of family, kinship, and horizontal social networks were diminished in favor of the tie to the work unit, and by extension to the state. As Walder found in his study of "communist neo-traditionalism," vertical patron–client ties between enterprise leaders and activist workers were far more important than horizontal networks between workers via the

ACFTU, ostensibly organized at every Maoist workplace as a sign of the workers' elevated status at the workplace (Walder 1988). In practice, therefore, workers learned to cultivate ties with individual leaders as a means to better their conditions and benefits. The transition of the early reform era toward individual contract relations was easier to achieve given the lack of strong collective organization of workers and the subordinate position of the ACFTU to CCP leadership.

As Feng Chen has argued, the legislative drive for labor rights in the reform era has focused on individual rights and protections without a concomitant strengthening of collective representation and bargaining (Chen 2007). The 1995 Labor Law and 2008 Labor Contract Law both contain clauses (indeed, the 2008 law has a whole section) on collective labor relations. However, there is very little change in the collective rights guaranteed between the two laws, in stark contrast to the progression in individual labor rights from 1995 to 2008. In 2004 the Ministry of Human Resources and Social Security (MHRSS) released Provisions on Collective Contracts that provided more detail on the nature and content of collective contracts as well as the process of negotiation. Many localities also passed their own local regulations on collective contracts as well, including Henan (1999), Shaanxi (2001), Beijing (2005), and Shanghai (2007). The 2008 LCL significantly expanded legislation on collective contracts through the addition of a whole section late in the drafting process. However, this expansion did not translate into expanded rights. The 2008 Law did not expand the legal powers of the enterprise trade union though it is more precise about the role of the trade union in enterprise decision-making. Moreover, the 2008 Law did not include any new penalties or other mechanisms to entreat companies to comply with the procedures on collective contracts and collective consultation. Below I examine these two points in greater detail: the role of the ACFTU in labor relations and the formalistic push for ACFTU-led collective consultation and wage bargaining.

As a Leninist-structured "transmission belt" union, the ACFTU has become increasingly anachronistic and challenged by the realities of China's marketized, mixed economy. By law, the ACFTU is the only organization permitted to organize and represent workers in the country. The 2001 Trade Union Law (a revision of the 1992 law) emphasizes the contradiction of the trade union's basic functions. As Article 6 states, "The basic duties and functions of trade unions are to safeguard the legitimate rights and interests of workers and staff members. While protecting the overall interests of the entire Chinese people, trade unions shall represent and safeguard the legitimate rights and interests of workers and staff members." Other clauses similarly charge the union with dual responsibilities: protect the legitimate rights and interests of workers while also taking "economic development as the central task, uphold the socialist road, the people's democratic dictatorship, leadership by the Communist Party of China, and Marxist-Leninism, Mao Zedong Thought and Deng Xiaoping Theory, persevere in reform and the open policy" (Article 4). The contradictory functions of the ACFTU and its structural limitations have been noted in the literature (Chen 2003, 2007; Ngok 2008; Pringle and Clarke 2011; Traub-Merz, International Labour Office., and Global Labour University (Germany). 2011; Friedman 2014).

The structural limitations of the ACFTU are not limited to the upper level ACFTU's subordination to the CCP and the provincial, municipal, and sectoral trade union branches' subordination to the governments at their territorial level. Enterprise-level trade unions (grassroots unions) are tied closely to the company. Trade union officials often serve concurrently as middle or high-level managers. Unionization of enterprises generally is from the top-down via local ACFTU campaigns to unionize firms. As paid employees of the company, trade union representatives are not able to advocate strongly for worker issues lest they risk their own job security. The installation of managers as trade union representatives further widens the distance between an organization ostensibly created to represent workers and workers themselves.

The weak, subordinate position of the ACFTU-affiliated unions limits progress on labor law enforcement and implementation. But the existence of the ACFTU is an important symbol of the government's intolerance toward competing organizations of workers. Its presence contributes to the individualization of workers by crowding out other possibilities. This crowding out has been achieved even as employment in the public sector declined rapidly from the end of the 1990s, which is an indication that the ACFTU was targeting the non-public sectors for unionization. The government prioritized ACFTU penetration into the private and foreign sectors and also recognized the responsibility of the ACFTU to organize rural migrant workers as part of the working class since 2003 (Pringle 2013). (See Chart 3.3.)

Labor NGOs and labor activists that seek to supplant some of the duties and responsibilities of the trade union threaten the monopoly position of the ACFTU and often find themselves on the wrong side of the political system (Cheng, Ngok, and Zhuang 2010). Recent attempts by

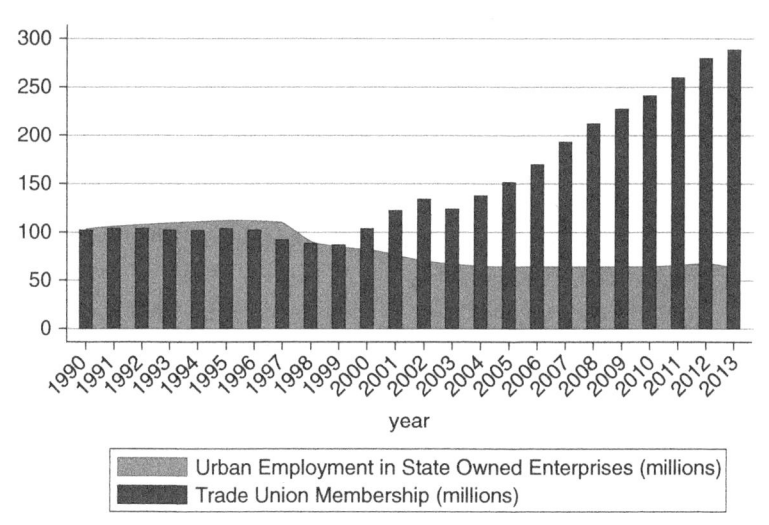

CHART 3.3. Trade Union Membership Compared to Employment in State Sector. *Source:* China Statistical Yearbook (2014).

the Guangdong branch of the ACFTU to coopt and constrain competing labor NGOs are one example. In 2012 the GFTU established the Association of Social Organizations for Worker Service to bring labor NGOs under the umbrella of the union. Labor NGOs that did not cooperate with the GFTU faced greater repression later in the year (M. Liu 2014).

The trade union did, however, play an active and important role in the drafting of the 2008 Labor Contract Law. It was the only "nongovernmental" entity to have a formal role in the drafting and it mobilized grassroots trade union cadres to send supportive comments about the draft law to the NPC during the period of public comment. While it very successfully promoted the expansion of individual rights and more severe penalties for violations in the 2008 Labor Contract Law, it did not win any major victories for its own powers and responsibilities. For example, while earlier draft versions of the LCL significantly expanded the power of the enterprise union to intervene in company decision-making, the actual law only gives the trade union the right to express opinion on company policy (Kuruvilla, Lee, and Gallagher 2011). The new section on collective contracts, which was inserted only in the final draft, lays out procedures for the conclusion of collective contracts and other types of collective agreements on working conditions, wages, health and safety, etc. These clauses provide space for the union, at various levels, to play a role

II. The Institutional Context of China's Rights Consciousness 75

in collective agreements and wage bargaining. The law also provides for collective consultation and contracts even at firms without a union presence, calling for worker representatives to conclude the agreement with "guidance" from the union at a higher level. However, compared with the clauses on collective contracts in the 1995 Labor Law, the entire section in the 2008 Labor Contract Law makes only one significant expansion by delineating the possibility of sectoral or regional collective consultation and contracts. Article 53 of the LCL reads, "industry-wide or area-wide collective contracts may be concluded between the labor union on the one hand and representatives on the side of the enterprises on the hand in industries such as construction, mining, catering services, etc., within areas below the county level."

While the allure of collective consultation and formation of collective contracts has been on the horizon since the 1995, the results so far have been very meager. At the regional or sectoral level, there are only a few studies that have found positive results and these cases are not representative, but are rather high-profile pilot cases that do not seem to have been adopted elsewhere. Liu examined sectoral-based collective bargaining in Wenling, Zhejiang and found that the agreements reached did result in higher wages and less labor conflict in that industry (M. Liu 2010). However, these processes of "bargaining" between the higher level unions, local governments, and employer associations are more accurately described as wage setting exercises with very limited input from workers and no grassroots mobilization. In these situations, the ACFTU-affiliated unions are subordinate to the local territorial governments and are not likely to press for wage demands that disrupt the local economy. While it is laudable that the government might try to anticipate wage demands of workers and bargain with employers for higher wages or regular wage increases, these exercises do not constitute genuine collective bargaining, but rather are more akin to government wage-setting during a period of rapid growth.

The government and the ACFTU have also heavily promoted enterprise-level collective consultation and collective contracts since the 2008 Labor Contract Law. Brown cites official reports that show that by 2012 over 88 percent of all enterprises nationwide had some form of labor contract (Brown 2015). However, there is little evidence that the existence of collective contracts has any beneficial effect on worker welfare (Yao and Zhong 2013). It is more likely that companies with better conditions are more likely to be chosen by the local trade union and government as targets to establish collective contracts. Most researchers describe collective consultation and the subsequent contracts as formalistic, often inserting local legal standards and minimum wages as the conditions for the collective contract (Zheng 2008; Dong and Li 2015). Worker involvement and input into the process is minimal. Another indication of the formalism of the collective contract process is that few disputes have occurred involving collective contracts. While collective disputes are an everyday occurrence at Chinese workplaces, either arbitrated disputes of groups of workers or strikes and protests at the worksite, very few of these disputes involve issues of collective contract. The rarity of finding collective contracts at the heart of disputes is a sign of their impotence (Qiu 2014).

Given the high rates of labor unrest, however, some regions have attempted to use collective labor relations to stabilize industrial relations, reduce turnover, and preemptive seasonal demands for wage increases. In 2011, Shanghai's Bureau of Human Resources and Social Security issued local regulations on handling collective disputes that might arise from collective negotiations. However, by 2014 there were no reports of such disputes occurring (Qiu 2014, 11). In 2014, Guangdong Province passed new provincial level regulations on collective contracts (Brown 2015; *Guangdong Regulations on Collective Contracts* 2014). These new regulations are the first step in making collective bargaining and contracts more than a mere formality. Yet these regulations also fall far short of their goal. First, the regulations have no mechanism to impel enterprises to agree to the bargaining process. Second, the regulations explicitly forbid industrial action (strikes or work stoppages) as a tool during the bargaining process (Article 24). In 2015, Shanghai amended its existing Collective Contract Regulations to put additional public pressure on companies to agree to collective negotiations by allowing the municipal and district level unions to issue rectification notices to companies that fail to comply. This could then be used in the Shanghai Municipal Public Credit Information Index (Baker & McKenzie 2016, 7).

Finally, with the slowdown in the economy and increased economic volatility, the national legislative future of collective bargaining and collective contracts is in doubt. The Guangdong Regulations are already a sign of pessimism because they do not push forward incentives to impel enterprises to bargain at the same time that they do not allow workers to strike. As the economy edged down in recent years, there has been less enthusiasm, even among central leaders for national labor reforms that have increased the costs of employment and reduced the flexibility of the labor markets that was achieved by the 1995 Labor Law. The possibility of a national law on collective contracts has been noted many times in the past but no longer appears on the future legislative agenda of the NPC. In March 2015, Premier Li Keqiang even left collective wage bargaining out of his annual report to the National People's Congress (NPC) after making a promise to promote it a year earlier. In April 2015, Finance Minister Lou Jiwei in a speech at Tsinghua University blamed the Labor Contract Law for making the labor market too rigid and highlighted sectoral bargaining as particularly harmful. "Promoting wage bargaining at the enterprise level is right, but promoting sectoral or regional bargaining is just too dreadful. It is exactly the problem that led to the ossification of European labor markets" (*South China Morning Post 2015*).

In a global era of declining union density, deregulation of labor markets, and increased competition for investment, China's turn toward greatly increased union density, and more protective and inclusive labor standards stand out. While the 1995 Labor Law clearly achieved a kind of deregulation and undoing of the socialist workplace, the legislative trajectory since then has not been a "race to the bottom" in labor standards. While still a far way off from realization, the relatively high standards of the 1995 Labor Law made important promises to those outside the previous system – younger urban workers and rural migrants, including employment security via the labor contract system, minimum working standards, and social insurance benefits. These promises became more attainable with the subsequent legislative advances of the 2000s, which targeted informalization and social insurance inclusion.

On collective labor rights and representation, however, China's move toward individualization is more in line with global trends that reflect the weakness of labor movements in developed and developing economies. Individual labor protections through the legal system have expanded, but collective organization and representation of workers has been strictly limited. Even the official ACFTU has mostly been successful in its role as a supporter of enhanced legislative rights for individuals. It has been far less successful in promoting collective mechanisms that go beyond formalistic promises. As part of the Party-State's bureaucracy tasked with managing industrial relations, the ACFTU has improved its standing and has more responsibility and pressure to achieve social stability. As a trade union tasked with representing workers' interests, it remains limited by its structural dependence on the state and its subordinate position within growth-promoting local governments.

Legal Dissemination Campaigns: Control and Mobilization

The codified high standards of the 1995 Labor Law and 2008 Laws would have been meaningless had workers remained unaware of them. The rights granted in these laws are contingent on individuals taking action to ensure their enforcement. Fu and Cullen (2008) credit the central state directly for the increased rights awareness of citizens, which in turn has bolstered the work of public interest lawyers in the "rights protection" movement (维权运动)(Fu and Cullen 2008).[6] They note that "[i]n at least one sense, the central government itself can claim substantial credit for these achievements. China is probably the only country in the world were the government makes it an explicit and specific long-term strategy to imbue its citizens with knowledge of the law" (Fu and Cullen 2008, 125). The "rights-protection" movement that is now viewed with heavy suspicion by the government, with widespread arrests of lawyers and activists since 2014, has its early foundations in the regime's own campaigns to bring law to the people. As this section notes, these campaigns have morphed over time to fit the state's needs, with a rising attention to individual rights and rights-protection over time, particularly in the realm of labor and employment law. In more recent years, these areas of emphasis have waned as rights-protection became associated with instability and disharmony.

Boosting the population's legal knowledge and awareness became an early reform goal of the Chinese state. In 1986 the central CCP Propaganda Department and the Ministry of Justice initiated a series of five-year legal dissemination campaigns "for popularizing common knowledge of the law." Since then there have been six five-year campaigns to disseminate legal knowledge to the population. The third five-year campaign, which began in 1996, was the first to extend to labor and employment law in a significant way, timed with the passage of the 1995 Labor Law. These are state-led attempts to imbue the population with legal consciousness, which includes knowledge and awareness of law as well as an inclination to invoke the law to protect individual rights and collective goals, such as "social order," "social stability," and the control of crime and "bad elements."

However, the role of the legal dissemination campaign in China's larger process of rule of law building has not received much scholarly attention.

---

[6] 维权运动 (weiquan yundong) is translated by Fu and Cullen as "rights protection movement." Others translate it as "rights defense." I use both translations interchangeably.

II. The Institutional Context of China's Rights Consciousness 79

A few early essays describe its main goals and how they evolved over time since 1986 (Troyer, Clark, and Rojek 1989; Exner 1995). Following the turbulent period of the Cultural Revolution, early legal dissemination campaigns emphasized the contribution of citizens to social stability and control. In the official documents, the early proclamations and speeches on popular legal knowledge are couched in terms of using citizens' legal knowledge to protect the state and the socialist system from bad elements and ne'er do well cadres. At the work conference in 1985 where the first five-year plan for legal dissemination and education was announced, the Minister of Justice Zou Yu invoked the words of Deng Xiaoping, "as Comrade Deng has said, we must discuss the legal system, so that every person understands the law, so that more and more people not only do not break the laws, but also that people will protect the laws." Zou argued that the main problem in building a legal system is not that regular people do not know the laws, but that most government officials do not know or respect the law. In a speech at the same conference, Deng Liqun also laid out the dual goals of legal dissemination: control and mobilization: "the goal of disseminating common knowledge of the law to all people, put all together, is to make the majority of cadres self-consciously do things according to law, the great majority of the masses self-consciously obey the law and correctly use the law to protect their legitimate rights, and at the same time to struggle against all kinds of illegal activity" (L. Deng 1985). CCP leaders envisioned law, again pragmatically, as a tool to govern society, but more importantly they aspired to use the power of society to control their own agents – local officials and cadres. Even as early as 1979, the state's decision to revive the legal system led to a concomitant emphasis on the concept of law as something that could be widely used and invoked. As the official People's Daily proclaimed on its front page, "we can use these legal weapons to improve the social order, more closely unite specialized government offices and the broad masses, and more effectively combat criminal elements" (*People's Daily* 1979).

Later work by Benney (2013) and Fu and Cullen (2008) on the "rights defense movement" by activist lawyers and civil society organizations attribute the rise of "rights talk" among Chinese social actors to the state's own promotion of legal education and legal knowledge. O'Brien and Li's work on the notion of rightful resistance is closely connected as well (O'Brien 1996; O'Brien and Li 2006). In their work, protestors often justify their resistance through their awareness of central laws and regulations that protect citizens against predation and injustice at the hands of local officials. Activists exploit the difference between central guarantees and local realities via their knowledge and awareness of their legal rights.

The legal dissemination campaigns around workplace rights reflect the evolution of the legal dissemination campaigns away from social control and toward individual protection of individual rights. While the instrumental nature of rule of law is still evident in the later campaigns, the emphasis has shifted from legal education of individuals so that they can help protect the state to an emphasis on the legal education of individuals so that they can protect themselves. In the later campaigns for legal education, individual citizens are the foot soldiers in rule of law building, becoming knowledgeable about the law and mobilizing it for their own protection (Michelson 2008; Stern 2014). The 2008 White Paper on China's rule of law stated these goals explicitly: "The target of popularizing the knowledge of law is every citizen, and the focus is civil servants. For ordinary citizens, popularizing the knowledge of law not only aims to make them know the laws and abide by them, more importantly, is to enable them to use the laws as a weapon to protect their lawful rights and interests. For civil servants, popularizing the knowledge of law aims to make them develop a clear understanding of the rule of law, and to act according to law more consciously" ("China's Efforts and Achievements in Promoting the Rule of Law" 2008).

In the first five-year campaign for legal dissemination, 1986–1991, citizens were taught to know "ten laws and one rule." This included the marriage law, the criminal law, the criminal procedure law, the civil procedure law, and the punishment rule for the maintenance of public order. Campaigns took place at schools, workplaces, and through the media. Workplaces tied bonuses to whether workers could demonstrate knowledge of important laws. Elementary schools on through elite Party Schools for training of cadres were major locations for legal education and training. Over time, however, the media became the major conduit for legal knowledge as newspapers, magazines, and television and radio programs were developed to expose citizens to "rule of law," legal rights, and using the law as a weapon to protect your rights by using "vivid legal news and literature." By the end of 1993, during the second campaign, there were already forty-four legal newspapers and thirteen legal periodicals.[7] At the beginning of the 3rd fifth year campaign, the Ministry of Justice convened the "national legal literature publicity seminar" to study how to make "legal literature" more available to the public. As early as 1980,

---

[7] For examples of these periodicals, see Liu 2011; Michelson 2008.

II. The Institutional Context of China's Rights Consciousness

stories and novels were written to encourage a popular shift toward law and to signal to the post-Cultural Revolution population that law was no longer a dirty word, but something to be revered and respected. In Kinkley's analysis of the short story, The Trial, he writes:

"The Trial" may be called propaganda for the "rule of law." Descriptive passages emphasize law's majesty and its strict procedures.... Statutes are quoted verbatim with their number, as in many a law story of this era. This renders rule of law more self-conscious, "popularizes (spreads the word about, makes universal) new citizen rights and procedures under the law...." (Kinkley 2000, 120).

In the third campaign (1996–2000), the year after the implementation of the 1995 Labor Law, labor and employment law became a central focus of the campaigns, with workers, enterprise managers, and cadres as the targets of the campaign. While the first major goal of the campaign was to uphold Deng Xiaoping thought about rule of law construction, the second major goal quickly turned to how people should know and use the law. "We should continue to promote legal education related to knowledge of the constitution, knowledge of laws that are closely connected to the work of citizens, and related to the preservation of social stability. Strengthen citizens' concepts of rights and responsibilities, raise the ability of citizens to use the law to protect their legitimate rights and interests, and their self-awareness to use the law as a weapon and to struggle against violations of the law"(Bučar et al. 2014). As Kinkley finds with the popularization of legal literature, the larger campaign of legal education and dissemination had both conservative and liberal adherents. For CCP conservatives, especially in the 1980s, teaching people about law was part of restoring social order after the chaos of the Cultural Revolution. It was a modernizing and civilizing project that targeted both ordinary people and cadres. Liberals and those who advocated for political reform increasingly emphasized the protection of individual rights and the use of law to control the powerful, including abusive cadres, but also as the market economy developed, private and public enterprise managers who abused the rights of their employees. The development of labor and employment law in the 1990s was critical to the shift away from "law as weapon" to protect the socialist system, the constitution, and normal people from crime and toward "law as a weapon" to protect individual rights in arenas like the workplace out of which the state was steadily withdrawing. From the early reform to the beginning of the Hu Jintao administration's "turn away from law" in 2004, the official media triumphed the idea of "law as weapon" for individual protection against malfeasance. (See Chart 3.4.)

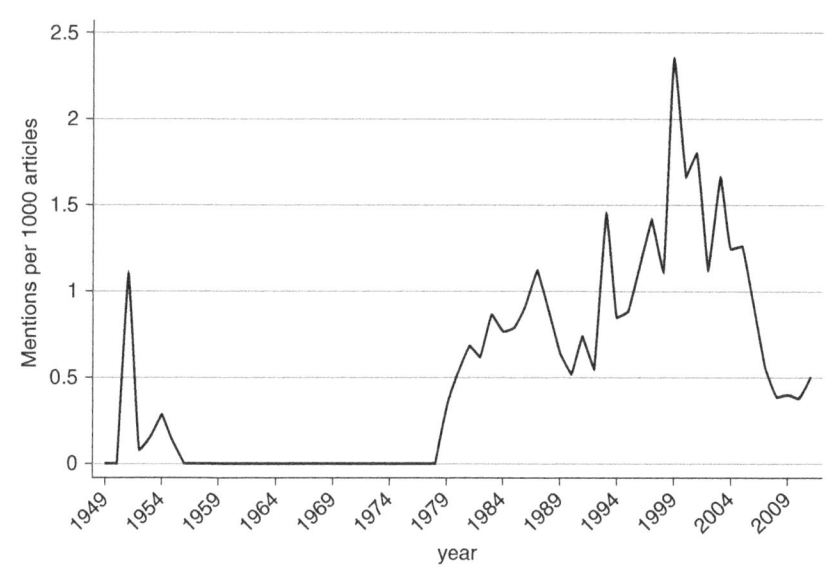

CHART 3.4. "Law as a Weapon" Mentions in People's Daily, 1949–2011.

After Hu's exhortation for Chinese society to become more "harmonious" in 2004, a sharp decline occurred in the government's encouragement of legal weapons.

The Chinese government's dissemination of legal information and its encouragement of legal knowledge contrasts sharply with other indicators used to measure its commitment to rule of law more generally. Its performance in legal dissemination, in making law known, far exceeds other measures used by the World Justice Project's (WJP) rule of law index, which ranks countries across eight governance areas in order to compose a composite measure of rule of law (Bučar et al. 2014). In many other areas, China's performance is abysmal, especially in areas of political and civil rights and the independence of its judicial institutions. In civil justice measures, China ranks 79th out of ninety-nine countries evaluated; in fundamental rights, China ranks 96th; in constraints on government power, 92nd. But China is an outlier in one measure of the subfactor "open government": accessible laws. On this measure, China's factor score is .69, the highest it attains for any measure and outpacing the average score for its region (Asia-Pacific) and its income group (upper middle income). In one of the WJP surveys used to measure accessibility, over 66 percent of the respondents in China agree that the government provides "information in plain language about people's legal rights, so that everybody can

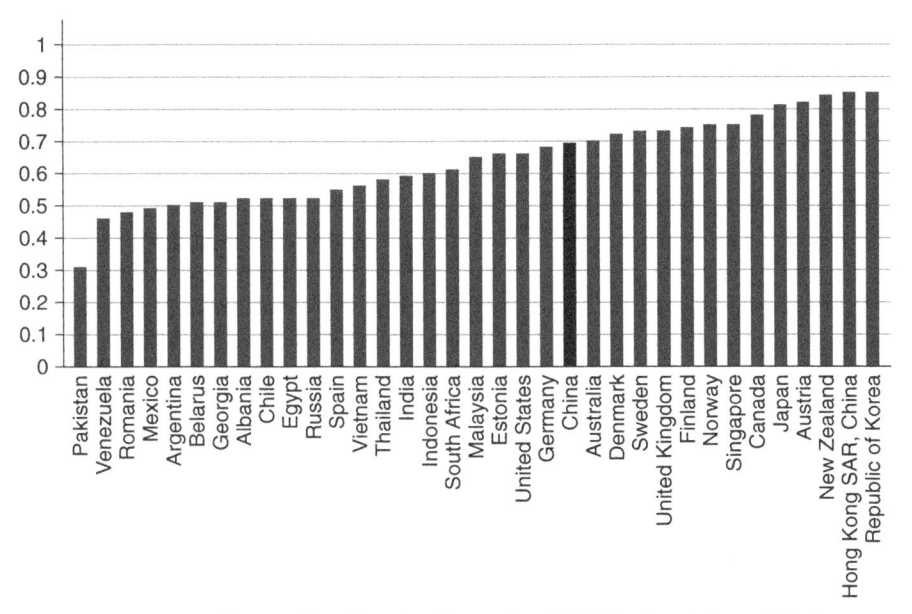

II. *The Institutional Context of China's Rights Consciousness* 83

CHART 3.5. Country Ranking for "Laws Are Publicized and Accessible."
Source: World Justice Project, Rule of Law Index, 2012.

understand them" (Bučar et al. 2014). In this one specific measure of "rule of law" China looks like a developed democracy, while in most others it appears as it is – a single party autocracy (Chart 3.5).

The legal dissemination campaign for labor and employment law included an explosive change in the number of articles, advice columns, books, and periodicals that provided information, gave advice, discussed cases, and criticized firm and government behavior. Bookstores opened sections on law that included popular titles for everyday people, not legal experts. In 2004, a popular series called "Lifestyle Lawsuit" published a volume specifically for employment disputes, adding to its series on travel disputes, medical disputes, consumer disputes, marriage disputes, and real estate disputes among others (朱建新 and 王新阳 2004). Many books use a question and answer format to assist those with little background in legal matters. "100 What to dos: Lectures on Labor Contract Law Cases" provides cartoons of disputes with examples from real cases (许淑红 2008). Each case concludes with analysis and reference to the exact laws and regulations that are relevant. Some volumes are written for specific groups, such as "200 Legal Knowledge Questions about Employment of Migrant Workers" (董保华 and 杨杰 2003). Other volumes target employers and those in human resources, "Navigating Labor Suits Made Easy" and "Ending Labor Contracts Made Easy" are volumes in a series to make life easier for the overworked in-house counsel (黄健, 黄雷, and 章琼怡 2008). "Why do companies always lose labor suits? What are the causes of these defeats? This book provides practical suggestions with applied services via our legal website for both employers and employees."

Similar legal advice and consultation is provided in the print media, especially popular newspapers writing for the ordinary citizen and specialized papers published by official organizations, such as the trade union or local labor bureaus. In Shanghai, the *New People Evening News*, the most popular evening paper in the city for many years, published special columns on labor issues. The Shanghai Municipal Trade Union publishes *Labor Daily*, which runs a weekly insert "Labor Rights." The insert usually features a real case that highlights a problematic issue in the resolution of labor disputes. Smaller columns might offer details on regulations, how to calculate various types of compensation, and related information. The May 25, 2013 edition, for example, featured a case of an injured worker, Mr. Song, who should have received occupational injury compensation from his employer and a period of recovery from his injury. Instead the company fired him before the recovery period had expired. After Song filed and won an arbitration suit for reinstatement, they fired him again as soon as the recovery time had ended, but still with no compensation. The company forced Song to file multiple claims, and then appealed each claim through the civil court system. Powerful companies with access to legal representation use these delay tactics to frustrate and wait out workers, who often give up because the time and costs of a long legal battle are prohibitive. In an article entitled "Don't Constantly Force Workers to Sue," the paper does not mince words criticizing company behavior that uses the legal system to thwart justice, "When a worker and a company have a labor dispute and each side sticks to their own version of events, in the end it can only be resolved through legal channels. This commonly occurs. However, when a company knows that it should pay and doesn't pay, instead intentionally making it hard for the worker, this is a bastard's logic" (*Labor Daily* 2013).

The *Labor Daily*'s use of a real case, vivid language and images (several photos of the worker with various types of evidence are displayed), and sympathetic analysis of the worker's plight repackages the state's propaganda on law. It is slicker, more compelling, and more realistic. It does not avoid discussion of problems, but it teaches the reader how to interpret the problems and what are the correct (state-sanctioned) methods to resolve this problem. As Stockmann and Gallagher (2011) have shown, propaganda that is displayed in a more commercialized manner is more believable. By combining real news (via cases) with propaganda messages about the legitimacy of law and legal mobilization, the Chinese legal dissemination campaign won over hearts and minds that were eager to find new channels to resolve their problems.

Labor Dispute Resolution: Fire Alarms and Firefighters

The 1995 Labor Law made commitments to workplace rights and new state responsibilities at the same time that it codified in law a system of labor dispute resolution. The law drew on earlier practices of the 1950s that outlined a multi-stage process of dispute mediation and arbitration but was abolished in the late 1950s as private enterprises were completely phased out of the economy (Cooney, Biddulph, and Zhu 2014). In 1987 similar regulations were passed to resolve disputes in state-owned enterprises. These were then passed as an ownership-specific law in 1993, before being extended to all types of firms in the 1995 Labor Law. A three-tiered process of voluntary mediation, compulsory arbitration, and litigation moved labor conflict out of the firm and into the administrative units of the bureaucracy and the courts (Ho 2003). (See Figure 3.1) The decision to formalize and codify the dispute system grew out of the growing fear of the state that it was increasingly unable to manage labor conflict, especially in the new non-state sectors. This was equally feared in the public sectors, as reformation through privatization (for small to medium-sized) and corporatization (for larger SOEs) led to intense disputes. A series of wild-cat strikes in development zones in China's north and south were important in pushing for the legal changes in the 1995 Labor Law as the government became more aware of the potential danger of large-scale copy cat strikes in coastal development zones (Davis 1995).

This new system of dispute resolution preserved the older system of voluntary mediation and conciliation at the firm via labor mediation committees, which were bodies directed by the firm-level trade union to manage labor conflict. However, the importance of this internal mediation declined over time as the new external system opened up and workers believed that they would have a better chance of favorable resolution outside of the firm itself. Internal mediation also declined because many new firms, especially foreign and private firms, lacked the internal institutions necessary to do mediation, and the older, state firms with those institutions were restructuring them out of existence privatized, or went

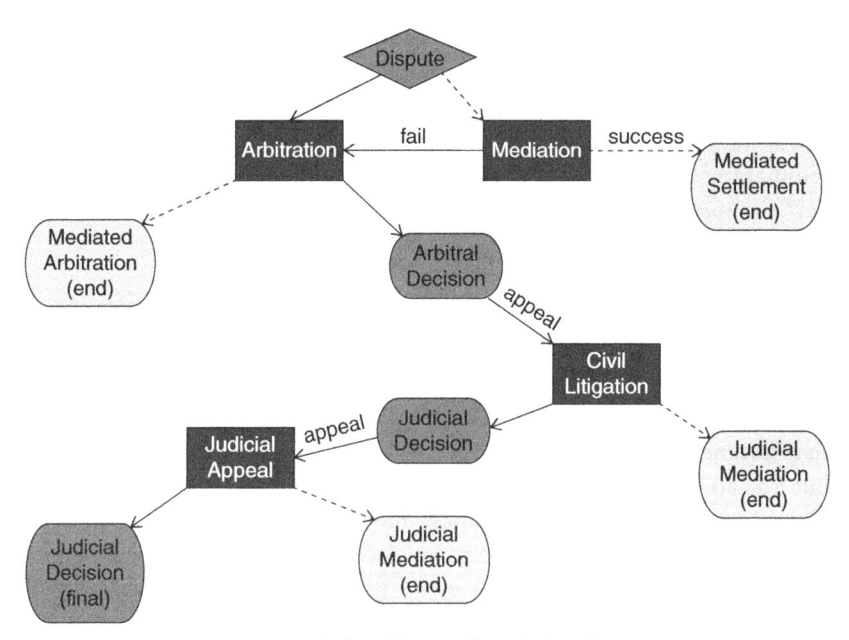

FIGURE 3.1. Labor Dispute Resolution Process.

bankrupt. The decline of internal mediation enhanced the importance of the two external steps – arbitration and litigation – and required local government to quickly build up a new dispute processing organization within local labor bureaus.

The regulations for labor dispute resolution in the 1995 Labor Law required local Labor Bureaus to set up Labor Arbitration Committees (LAC) to adjudicate labor disputes within their jurisdiction. While in theory the LACs were tripartite in nature with representation from the trade union, the employer, and the labor bureau, in reality, single arbitrators within the labor bureau arbitrated most disputes; large or complicated disputes might use the tripartite structure through coordination with the ACFTU and the employers association, the Chinese Enterprise Management Association. This new institution allowed labor conflict to leave the workplace and enter the administrative and legal realms. In doing so, the state signaled its willingness to serve as a third-party arbiter of private disputes. The 1995 Labor Law also provided the right to court appeal in the event of dissatisfaction with the arbitral judgment. Both sides have the right to appeal the arbitration decision in local courts for a de novo hearing of the case. This system allows workers in the non-state sectors to head directly to labor arbitration, bypassing firm mediation, and also

II. The Institutional Context of China's Rights Consciousness 87

the opportunity to appeal the arbitration decision at court. In the years since its inception in the labor law, this system of dispute resolution has drawn workplace disputes out of the firm and into the local political and legal arenas.

Although usage of these institutions increased rapidly after 1995, the labor dispute resolution system was rife with problems. The process was bureaucratic, complicated, long, and costly. The path from mediation, through arbitration, and two court appeals was lengthy and often frustrating. In many localities, the cost of arbitration was prohibitively expensive, costing about 300 RMB (about USD$45). Court fees were lower (50 RMB in Shanghai), but combined with the costs of legal advice and lost time at work, the procedural barriers discouraged workers and benefitted employers who had the resources to pay for professional legal advice and bear the long process. Workers particularly criticized compulsory arbitration, which was far more expensive than civil courts, and furthermore was under the jurisdiction of the local labor bureau and therefore seen as biased toward employers.

These concerns were partially addressed by the 2008 Labor Dispute Mediation and Arbitration Law (LDMAL), one of the major labor laws passed by the Standing Committee of the National People's Congress in 2007. The law further enhanced access to justice for workers and enabled greater bottom-up mobilization at a critical time. It also reiterated the state's commitment to mediation and non-adversarial negotiation of labor disputes. Both of these aspects of the law would become extremely consequential as disputes increased dramatically as these new laws went into effect in 2008, just as the global economy was imploding. The LDMAL improved access to justice for workers in three major ways. First, the LDMAL cancelled fees for arbitration, making it free of charge. Second, the LDMAL extended the statute of limitations for violations from sixty days to one year, giving workers more time to find out about a violation and make a claim for redress. Third, the LDMAL increased the evidentiary burden of firms, noting that when evidence required for adjudication is only in the hands of the employer, it has a duty to provide it. Under previous law, the evidentiary burden was on the side that made the claim, which hurt workers if they needed evidence such as time records, wage and social insurance records, and other documents that are the property of the employer.

The LDMAL also further emphasizes mediation as an important resolution option. It is important to note, however that the law does not require mediation as a preliminary step in the dispute process. Each side may choose to bypass mediation and head directly to the more formal stages of arbitration and litigation. The law outlines three types of labor mediation: enterprise mediation, which already existed but had declined in importance; people's mediation, which is a long-standing traditional dispute resolution system run by basic level governments; and, finally, specialized labor dispute mediation committees created at the neighborhood or township level. In 2012, the MOHRSS further decreed that large companies must establish internal labor mediation committees in order to reduce the number of disputes overwhelming the formal system.

While the LDMAL certainly reiterates a commitment to mediation, the labor dispute resolution system has always privileged mediation in practice. Mediated agreements are reachable at the arbitration and litigation stages with the arbitrators and judges incentivized through salary and bonuses to achieve high mediation rates. In arbitration, mediated agreements are reached in lieu of an arbitral judgment. In courts, judges lead a process of judicial mediation that results in a mediation agreement sanctioned by the court. However, despite the renewed emphasis on mediation in the LDMAL, labor disputes continue to rise up through the multi-tiered system to the courts for a final decision – either through judicial mediation or a civil judgment. Arbitration, while required, has been beset by a number of problems that undermine its authority and legitimacy. These problems include weak institutional capacity, a lack of professionalism and training, political interference from powerful local actors, lack of legitimacy due to the committee's strong dependence on local labor bureaus, and lack of finality given the court appeal option. A large portion of arbitral decisions are appealed in civil courts (BJ201301; Cooney 2007, 679). The opportunity to appeal to court reduces the arbitration process to a stepping-stone on the way to final resolution. This has added to the burden of the civil court system, undermined the authority and legitimacy of labor arbitration, and complicated and lengthened an already difficult process for workers.

Despite the problems and frustrations of the formal resolution system, workers continue to make use of these institutions in increasing number. The LDMAL and the 2008 Labor Contract Law, promulgated and implemented in the same year, were key legislative changes that granted workers new rights and protections and facilitated access to dispute resolution institutions by lowering fees, relaxing time limits, and transferring evidentiary burdens. One key legislative leader at the Standing Committee of the NPC, Xin Chunying, iterated the laws' significance this way, "a harmonious society is not one without disputes, but rather a society

III. Consequences for Mobilization, Compliance, and Enforcement

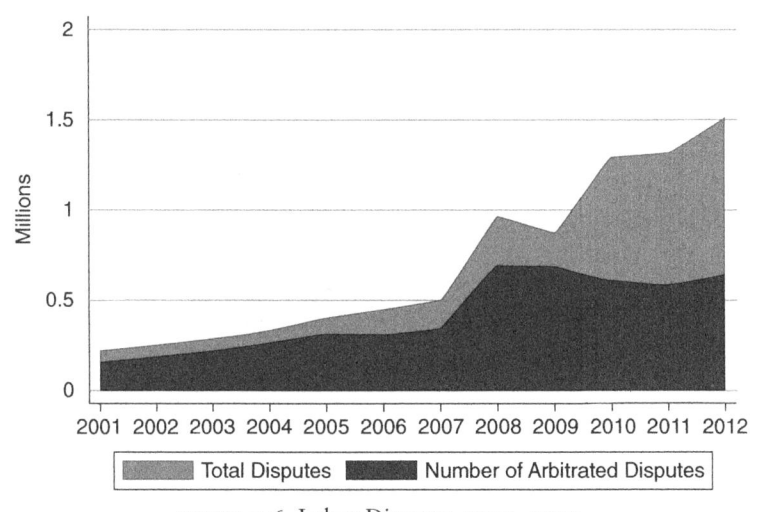

CHART 3.6. Labor Disputes, 2001–2012.
Sources: China Labor Statistical Yearbook (2013: 348–9) and Chinalabour.net.

that has an exemplary mechanism to resolve disputes. If we take labor disputes as water, then the LDMAL is a channel; a channel that flows easily should be able to lawfully, justly and promptly resolve disputes" (Peng 2008, 20).

III. CONSEQUENCES FOR MOBILIZATION, COMPLIANCE, AND ENFORCEMENT

Workers' Legal Mobilization

Xin Chunying's prophecy about the LDMAL was all too correct. The new channel to resolve disputes, both cheaper and easier than before, created a deluge in the year that the LDMAL, the Labor Contract Law, and the Employment Promotion Law went into effect. In 2008, these new laws, in combination with the Global Financial Crisis and its effect on China's export sector, led to a watershed year for labor disputes as workers responded to the new protections and economic instability with waves of legal claims, strikes, and street protests. In that year, arbitrated disputes increased by nearly 100 percent, reaching 693,000 filings. The total number of disputes, which includes disputes that were mediated prior to arbitration climbed to 970,000. (See Chart 3.6.) These high rates continued long after 2008. Internal figures of the MOHRSS indicate that by 2012 total disputes reached over 1.5 million. In 2001, there were less than two

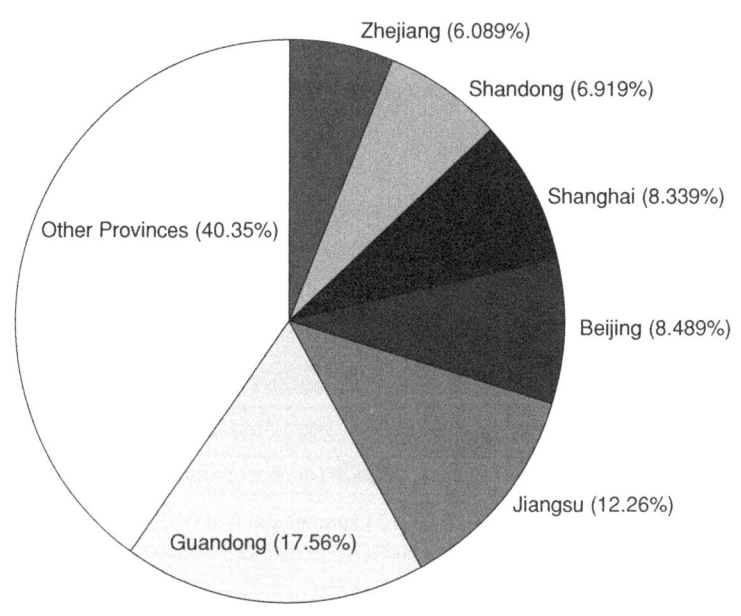

CHART 3.7. Arbitrated Labor Disputes by Province, 2004–2011.
Source: China Labor Statistical Yearbook (various years).

disputes per 1,000 workers employed in urban units in China; by 2008 this had increased to five disputes for every 1,000 workers on average across the country.

While the rise in disputes after 2008 was a nationwide phenomenon, labor disputes continue to be highly concentrated in a few regions: the provincial level cities (Shanghai, Beijing, Tianjin, and Chongqing) and in two provinces, Guangdong and Jiangsu, epicenters of China's manufacturing power. (See Chart 3.7.) As shown by Cai and Wang, labor disputes are highly correlated with provincial GDP and the proportion of export value to overall GDP (Cai and Wang 2012). Cai and Wang hypothesize that the incidence of labor disputes reflects the relative legal awareness of the workforce and local labor markets. The provincial level cities have more workers with higher skills, education, and resources. Guangdong and Jiangsu, with their heavy concentration of export-oriented manufacturing, have been severely affected by labor shortages in production and technical workers. In both cases, these conditions have enhanced the bargaining power and confidence of workers to protect their rights. These provincial level results accord with the disputant data from the 2010 CULS, which indicates that workers with higher levels of education are

III. Consequences for Mobilization, Compliance, and Enforcement 91

far more likely to report labor dispute experience (Cai and Wang 2012; M. Gallagher et al. 2014). According to the CULS, there is no significant difference between male and female workers or urban local workers and migrant workers in the propensity to have a labor dispute. Wage-related grievances are the major reason for labor disputes among both migrant and local workers (48 percent and 43 percent respectively), but urban local workers are far more likely to file disputes related to employment security (17.9 percent and 0.6 percent respectively). A 2014 study of labor disputes in Guangdong courts found similar trends. Out of 13,168 disputes that reached civil court appeal, 34 percent were disputes regarding employment termination while 31 percent were wage and salary disputes (Jiang and Li 2015).

This deluge in rights-claiming was predicated on expanded knowledge of the new laws among workers. Chinese workers know a great deal about what the law provides especially in regards to the most important and general benefits of the new laws. In the 2005 LLMS, respondents were given a list of eighteen questions on the labor law to evaluate their awareness. These questions surveyed knowledge on termination, contracts, dispute resolution, rest time, social insurance, and others. If seen as a "test" of knowledge, over 75 percent of the respondents passed with a score of 67 percent or higher. Nearly 23 percent scored over 80 percent. In the 2010 CULS, we see a similar level of knowledge, and for questions about basic rights, extremely high levels of knowledge. The CULS also finds that the gap between migrant and local resident knowledge is narrow. (See Chart 3.2)

Disputants emphasize the importance of acquiring knowledge as one of the first steps in the mobilization process. In the context of structural reforms and changing legislation, workers are often not sure if their legal rights have been violated or not. Searching out legal codes and administrative regulations takes time and commitment, but as the interviews show, there are many avenues to knowledge: newspapers, books, legal hotlines, Internet sources, and special publications by the trade union. A poorly educated middle-aged female disputant (SH20044) recounted how she and her husband went about the process of claiming a right to protect: "*we bought a book about labor law at the bookstore and read every line to make sure that we hadn't done anything wrong.*" The availability of information helps to sharpen the problem, instructing on the law and the process for dispute resolution. As one older disputant recounted in his dispute over his layoff, "*We all knew from the media that the law was eight hours of work per day, and that one should get paid overtime. I* understood labor law a little bit at the time. We had heard about it from the workplace as well. We didn't bother looking for the trade union; they have no use. Wouldn't be able to protect us. According to the newspapers and the media, the labor law would help us workers." (SH200448)

Feisty disputants enjoyed gaining legal knowledge and using it against powerful employers during and even after the dispute. Some disputants spoke about using their newly gained knowledge to help other people, including former colleagues, to also protect their workplace rights. An older saleswoman (SH200450) who had a drawn-out dispute with her employer over termination was reinstated. She recounted coming back to the workplace in a triumphant manner; singing the opening line of the Chinese national anthem, *"Stand up! Stand up! You no longer are slaves,"* and then adding *"you now have a legal weapon to protect yourself!"* She invoked law and patriotism to show that what she had done was right and just.

Access to legal knowledge via the media helped disputants evaluate their own claims, often by viewing cases that seem similar to their own. One young male disputant (SH200437) described his path to legal mobilization this way, *"I saw in New People Evening News that there would be free legal aid at Meilongzhen in Xujiahui. ... Also the Liberation News featured a case that was very similar to mine. A friend showed it to me. Then I had more confidence. A law office was also mentioned (in the article). I went there as well but they only wanted money. Normal of course but it was all that they would talk about. I had seen the column in the New People Evening News about legal aid every Sunday and it seemed very just. I also listened to the people in line with me at Meilongzhen. Many had already gone to the trade union and then were sent to legal aid by the union. I thought that this was a good sign. The problems that the union can't solve are pushed to this center. Not money but justice."*

Gaining legal knowledge did not always lead to empowerment or satisfaction. Workers with unsuccessful lawsuits often criticized the media after the fact for giving them "false hope." A young kindergarten teacher in a private school (SH200427) who was fired when she became pregnant knew that the firing was illegal. She recounted looking in the newspapers to find laws and even found an article about the same issue. She presented this information to her boss who nonchalantly challenged her to sue. Her case ended in failure when her wealthy boss fled China for Italy. The case attracted a lot of media attention and she found that her fame made her less employable. Few schools wanted to hire a "troublemaker." She dismissed the law as something *"that I could use to protect myself, but in*

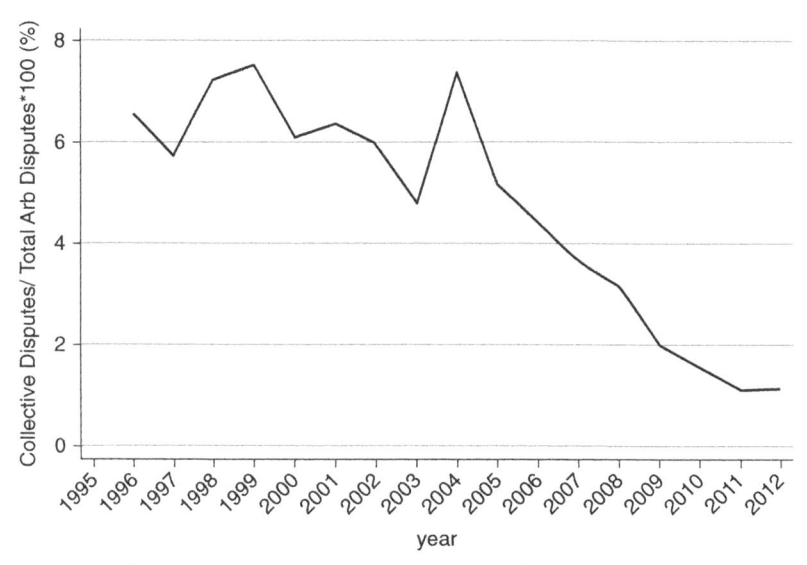

III. Consequences for Mobilization, Compliance, and Enforcement 93

CHART 3.8. Collective Disputes as a Propotion of All Arbitrated Disputes, 1995–2012.
Source: China Labor Statistical Yearbook (various years).

the end not only did it not protect me, it injured me." Legal knowledge became useless; *" We have the law; we all know the law, but do companies give us eight hours a day? Of course not!...The reason people go crazy and do extreme things is because they don't have any way out."*

This immediate impact of the post-2008 surge in disputes, which was combined in Guangdong with much more active collective mobilization, was a state-led push for increased mediation and pre-arbitration settlement led by local state agencies focused on "stability preservation." This response, sometimes construed as a "turn against law" is examined in Chapter 6. This trend of extra-legal settlement is clearly reflected in the growing gap between the total number of disputes each year and arbitrated disputes. Arbitrated disputes have remained relatively static since hitting 693,000 in 2008 while total disputes are now almost double that number.

Collective legal claims were also incessantly individualized. Although China's labor legislation does allow for the resolution of collective disputes via the labor dispute resolution system, collective disputes as a proportion of all disputes has fallen significantly over time. This decline in arbitrated collective disputes has occurred alongside very rapid increases in strikes, demonstration, and worker protests. (Chart 3.8). By 2011, less than 2 percent of all labor disputes were collective disputes, despite consistent increases in other types of collective action. The collapse in the number of collective disputes going through the formal systems of arbitration and litigation indicates that government's unwillingness to process collective grievances via the legal system; it does not indicate the lack of collective mobilization (Yang Su and He 2010; F. Chen and Xu 2012). The decline in collective disputes is the result of active fragmentation of disputes by arbitrators and other government units tasked with social stability maintenance. Individual disputes are easier to resolve; they divide workers up by small differences in contract terms or dispute details; and they contribute to a larger settlement rate for individual arbitrators. A similar dynamic also occurs at the civil litigation stage (F. Chen and Xu 2012).

Firm Compliance

These institutional reforms, especially the laws of 2008 and after, have had major impacts on Chinese firms. Compliance has improved in some important areas, but it is happening unevenly across different types of sectors, firms, and workers. Evasion has also become more sophisticated. The driving motivation for compliance and evasion is fear of worker mobilization through arbitral or judicial claims. Firm managers blame the increased knowledge and awareness of their employees and their relatively easy access to information and dispute resolution.

These changes reflect real and important achievements through the legislative agenda promoted under the Hu-Wen administration. The inclusive and protective goals of the 1995 Labor Law were aspirational and unreachable given the lack of enforcement and the low costs of ignoring the law. Firm compliance was poor as the law did not mandate severe penalties for failure to conclude contracts. Without access to labor contracts, workers were also then denied entryway into the law's other protections and access to social insurance benefits. One of the major concerns of the Hu-Wen administration in the legislative changes of 2008 was the lack of employment security for workers without contracts or extremely short and insecure contracts. Deputy Director of the Legislative Affairs Office of the Standing Committee of the National People's Congress (SCNPC), Xin Chunying, noted in an interview that before 2008 not only was the proportion of contracted workers low, 60 percent of those workers had only short-term contracts, usually one-year

III. Consequences for Mobilization, Compliance, and Enforcement

TABLE 3.2. *Awareness of Labor Law (Percent Answering Correctly)*

	Local Residents	Migrants
Q1. Do you think that when you are hired your employer should set a labor contract with you? (yes)	95.34	89.48
Q2. Do you think employers must pay you double wages for each month you worked beyond the allotted time for completing a labor contract? (yes)	80.87	77.00
Q3. If a worker violates the rules set by an employer can the employer terminate the worker's labor contract? (yes)	70.19	73.60
Q4. If you meet the required conditions and suggest an open-ended contract, must your employer comply? (yes)	70.17	67.76
Q5. Within how long do you think the labor contract should be signed after being hired? (one month)	39.58	45.83
Q6. For a one-year labor contract, what is the maximum probationary period? (two months)	22.04	23.75
Mean score	63.03	62.90

Source: CULS 2010.

contracts or even shorter (Peng 2008, 19). The 2005 Labor Law Mobilization Survey (LLMS) shows similarly low rates of contracted workers across the cities surveyed, averaging about 51 percent. The three waves of the China Urban Labor Survey (CULS) show that the proportion of workers with contracts even declined from 2000 to 2005. (See Table 3.2.) In 2005 only 12 percent of migrant workers worked with a contract. Without written contracts most workers were unable to claim the basic standards and rights of the 1995 Law.

Despite the continued controversies over the Labor Contract Law since its passage in 2008, the progression from the 1995 Labor Law to the laws of 2008 has yielded some improvements in key workplace conditions, especially in two areas – formalization of labor relationships and social insurance participation. In the 2010 CULS, the percentage of migrant workers employed via the labor contract system increased by over 20 percent from the low of 12 percent in 2005 (Table 3.2). As Table 3.2 shows, by 2010, the percentage of the workforce working with formal labor contracts had increased significantly, especially for migrant workers. These improvements were even more pronounced among wage workers. For migrant wage workers, by 2010, 60 percent had formal labor contracts, compared to 31 percent in 2001 and 37 percent in 2005.

Among local workers, the increase was smaller but from a much higher base, from 74 percent in 2001 to 80 percent in 2010.

Formal worker status also increased the likelihood of participation in social insurance, especially for migrant workers. Workers with formal labor contracts, both migrant and local, are far more likely to participate in social insurance. The 2010 CULS data show, for example, among migrants without labor contracts, 15 percent had pension insurance and 13 percent had health insurance in 2010. For those with labor contracts, however, these numbers are 44 percent and 39 percent. (See Table 3.2) Migrants with formal contracts had more than double the rate of participation in pension programs, rising from 13 percent without contracts to 33 percent between 2005 and 2010. Local residents' participation also increased, from 77 percent without contracts to 95 percent with contracts for pension participation; in healthcare insurance, the increase was from 75 percent to 91 percent (M. Gallagher et al. 2014).

Access to social insurance among migrants in the 2010 CULS is still relatively low compared to local residents, but given that the 2010 survey captures trends before the 2011 Social Insurance Law was in effect, these achievements are still impressive. The 2011 Social Insurance Law and the regulatory changes since then have improved the portability of social insurance accounts, which is and was one of the main barriers to migrant worker participation in long-term insurance programs. Not only do employers resist paying social insurance for their non-resident workers, these workers are often hesitant to pay into social insurance accounts when they doubt their long-term ability to make use of these funds. Although it is difficult to compare informality and social insurance coverage between countries given the different regulatory rules and statistical categories for measuring informal employment and the informal sector, China's performance in reducing informality and expanding access to social insurance is not poor. According to the ILO, China outperforms many other large developing countries, including Brazil, India, Philippines, and Vietnam among others.[8] (See Table 3.3). Driving these improvements is the sustained mobilization of workers, both legal and on the streets, in demanding better firm compliance with the new labor

---

[8] The ILO data for China also come from the 2010 CULS, which is a city-level study not a national sample. For this reason, China's nationwide formality rates are probably lower than reported. Even with this caveat, however, China and other transitional (post-socialist) economies tend to have higher rates of formality than other developing countries.

TABLE 3.3. *Workers with Social Insurance, 2005 and 2010*

	Pension 2005	Pension 2010	Health 2005	Health 2010
No contract local	59.8%	74.5%	44.8%	72.1%
With contract local	85.4%	92.3%	77.5%	88.3%
No contract migrant	15.8%	14.9%	13.6%	13.2%
With contract migrant	33.7%	43.8%	34.2%	38.5%

Source: CULS.

and social insurance laws. In recent years, social insurance disputes have increased rapidly in number, from about 30,000 disputes in 2001 to over 165,000 disputes in 2013. Disputes over social insurance consistently account for about a quarter of all disputes on an annual basis. These official statistics on social insurance disputes mask other important trends, however. Strikes and demonstrations by migrant workers demanding social insurance coverage have also been on the rise. In 2014, factory owners in Guangdong Province faced massive demonstrations by migrant workers demanding social insurance back payments and more equitable treatment of migrants in social insurance coverage (Mitchell 2015). Strikes over social insurance have increased measurably over this time period, especially among aging migrant workers ("Strikes Continue Unabated in China during First Half of the Year" 2016).

However, as predicted by some labor law specialists in China, the restrictiveness of the 2008 labor Law also led to a marked expansion of labor subcontracting, as firms sought to evade the new restrictions on short-term fixed contracts. Firms hired workers via subcontracting agreements with labor service companies. Workers established contractual relations with these third-party companies, but were not formal workers of their place of work. This arrangement enhanced flexibility and reduced social insurance and wage obligations for firms. Workers employed indirectly through labor service companies generally have lower standards of compensation and are hired to work for short-term periods. Some firms transferred substantial parts of their operations to subcontracted workers; other firms sought out student workers (实习工) who are not protected by the law to the same degree as formal workers, but employed via relationships with technical schools that provide students as part of their education and training (Su 2010). While estimates of the extent of subcontracting varied widely from a low of twenty-seven million (state-owned

Assets Supervision and Administration Commission) to a high of sixty million (All China Federation of Trade Unions) it was widely acknowledged that the 2008 Labor Contract Law had opened another loophole to evade the burdens of formal employment (B. Wang 2012).[9] As subcontracted workers tended to be at the lower levels of the labor market, it adversely impacted migrant workers and workers with less education and fewer skills. As discussed above, 2012 revisions to the LCL attempted to close loopholes for widespread use of labor subcontracting, but anecdotal reports continue to find widespread use of temporary and short-term labor. These problems also tend to affect the less skilled and educated segments of the labor market (Fan 2011; Lan, Pickles, and Zhu 2015; Harney 2016).

In terms of minimal standards for overtime and wages, compliance has also been extremely poor. Despite China's strict overtime restrictions, many manufacturing firms are in constant violation of the thirty-six-hour limit (S.H. Lee, McCann, and Messenger 2007). Chronic and systemic overtime and long working hours have plagued Chinese manufacturing since at least the 1990s. Compliance with minimum wage requirements is also very uneven. In a study of low-paid workers in China, Deng and Li find that many workers, but especially migrant workers are paid well below the legal minimum of their localities (Q. Deng and Li 2012). Improvements in working conditions are happening, though gradually, but the benefits are accruing at the higher end of the labor force, among those with higher levels of education and in more developed regions. In the 2010 CULS, high school graduates were 28 percent more likely to have a labor contract compared to someone with a middle school education. College graduates were 55 percent more likely. Workers in Shanghai were also far more likely to have a contract than workers surveyed in the other cities (M. Gallagher et al. 2014).

Firms have responded both with better compliance and more sophisticated techniques of evasion as the laws have tightened. In 2010, managers at a small number of Shanghai firms were interviewed about the effects of the 2008 Labor Contract Law on internal firm practices. These managers profess some new attention to employment law and regulations, but they also detail new ways in which they try to evade the law or reduce the

---

[9] SASAC is the State Asset Supervision and Administration Commission, which is the government agency tasked with oversight over all state-owned enterprises at that level. The ACFTU is the All-China Federation of Trade Unions, which is the central umbrella organization of all legal trade unions.

III. Consequences for Mobilization, Compliance, and Enforcement 99

costs of compliance. These interviews highlight the reactive adjustment of firms to workers' mobilization. "Angela" (SH201001) is the office manager for Swiss company that serves as a middleman for a Swiss department store. With over eighty workers in Shanghai, she says that the company mostly employs college graduates for low-level office work. She targets non-Shanghai hukou college graduates who are "less demanding" and "more innocent." Since the LCL was passed in 2008, Angela describes a more contentious and confrontational workplace with constant vigilance needed against litigious employees.

Overall, the labor (contract) law has really increased our labor costs, risk, and workload in dealing with workers. Even by rewriting company policy, we cannot write such detailed policy to guard ourselves against all circumstances. It's impossible. Hence, we live with increased risk that our workers will misinterpret our company policy or find loopholes in it to file labor disputes against us.

In terms of the workers' behavior, Angela blames changes on the laws and on the media for promoting it too actively. She notes:

The legal consciousness of workers is substantially higher. The former labor law was just about legal principles and was quite flexible. Now the law has changed to become rigid (死板). And it's very detailed.... Workers will use the labor law everyday to threaten the firm ... The labor law has created more grumbling among our workers, creating more conflict between employer and employees. The media has been too active in promoting the law. Plus it is unreasonable that arbitration is free. Arbitration should be at least 1000 RMB! Given the local wage level, workers can definitely afford it.

As a manager involved in human resources, Angela describes strategies of becoming more compliant with the law, hiring legal professionals to rewrite company policy, but she also details strategies to avoid litigious workers. *"If we can, we really want to create an employee black list. That way, we can look up which employees have labor disputes with their previous employers. Right now, we can run background checks on employees, but nothing shows up on their records about past workplace conflicts."* She also complains bitterly about the long maternity leave for pregnant workers, the extended protection from termination for sick employees, and the high costs of termination. Angela recounts an instance when her boss caught an employee playing cards on the job. *When the boss threatened to fire him, the employee replied, "you have no right to fire me because company policies do not state that we cannot play cards during working hours. To fire us, you will have to give me severance pay. If you fire us, we can go to court about this."*

In a Korean clothing company with over 2000 workers in Shanghai, Ms. Hong (SH201002) from the legal department also finds that the combination of intense media attention and workers' legal conscious has created new burdens for the company:

The firm has to be more careful about labor relations. Media and propaganda on the labor (contract) law have been intense. Workers know that they can call 12333 anytime of the day... Our company is more lawful now, it is taking labor more seriously. The firm is afraid of inspection and penalties. Workers can sue us and the government can inspect us. As a result, our risk of being sued is much higher than before. Previously workers only have 60 days to file a complaint, but now they have one year to file. So even after they leave their current position, they can still file a case against us. Previously the laws were more about principles without any enforceable quality. The 2008 law has clearer responsibilities and penalties. Thus we feel that the government is more serious about implementing the law. Secondly, workers' rights consciousness is clear. For instance, our workers will ask us for overtime during training programs. Unless there's overtime, none of our workers would be willing to stay one minute after business hours. They will often threaten to file a complaint at the arbitration office.

Mr. Liu is the CEO of a HR consulting firm that he started just as the 2008 laws went into effect. He offers consulting and advice to firms that struggled to comply with the new law. His company also offers subcontracting opportunities to firms that want to reduce labor costs by employing staff through a third party. The practice of labor subcontracting boomed after the 2008 LCL went into effect as companies tried to evade the new restrictions on short-term contracts and the higher severance costs of the law. Mr. Liu describes the post-2008 environment this way:

The biggest difference between before 2008 and after is that before 2008 the conflict is between employers and labor enforcement agencies. After 2008 the conflict is between employers and workers. Through media promotion of the Labor Contract Law, workers are more conscious about their rights. Moreover, the 2008 law is more specific than previous laws on the penalties for violations.

Mr. Liu notes that workers' escalating legal mobilization puts new pressure on firms and increases their risks and labor costs. But he also recognizes that even in Shanghai, workers with low education and skills are much less likely to be able to avail themselves of these legal weapons.

Workers are more likely to file labor dispute cases against their employers. Since the hotline 12333 is available, they can call anytime to ask about their labor contracts. Also previously they only had 60 days to file a labor dispute, now they have one year. But at the same time, workers in some sectors still do not file labor disputes. For instance, restaurants and beauty salons are least likely to follow the

III. Consequences for Mobilization, Compliance, and Enforcement 101

labor contract laws. Most workers [there] do not have labor contracts, earn less than the minimum wage, and may have to pay a deposit. But the government does not inspect them and the workers do not file suits against them. I don't think it's because these workers do not know their rights, but because they are stuck in this sector. There is less mobility in this sector. There are a few key salon chains. ...the owners of these chains all know each other and will run background checks on their employees. So if a worker files a labor dispute case against his workplace, he will be blacklisted from employment at other salons.

Mr. Han (SH201006) works in HR in a German-invested glass manufacturing company with factories in the Shanghai suburbs and Zhejiang. As with the other managers, he describes a workplace environment more fraught with conflict and distrust.

Previously our hiring was much more casual. A worker will come and he'll try his hand at the job. If he's good, he can stay. Neither party has to sign a contract. As long as he gets his wage, labor relations are good. The atmosphere at the firm was more like a family. Right now, we are rushing to sign contracts with all our employees. Depending on the worker, we have one-year, two-year, three-year and non-fixed term contracts. Previously if we forgot to sign a contract with an employee, it wasn't a big deal. Now it is a big deal because employer-employee relations have become tense. Both parties feel that they have to protect their rights and guard against each other.

Mr. Han regrets the loss of the family atmosphere, finding workers to be "callous" and only interested in money and their rights. He also criticizes the media and propaganda activity as excessive, making workers too uppity and no longer "humble."

Also, workers are learning about the labor law themselves. They know they can call 12333 for legal advice. They can also go to the labor bureau for information. If anything happens at the workplace, they would go directly to the labor bureau and ask for a form. If not, they would call 12333 to ask questions about their situation. The workers feel empowered by this, especially in 2008 when the government was very pro-labor. Now the government is more neutral. Previously, workers were very humble about their skills and rights, but now they are vocal about their rights and demand benefits from the firm. Right now, the workers know more about the labor law than their immediate supervisor. Many times, we receive calls from the production supervisor to ask about the labor law because a worker mentioned a certain procedure in the law.

The deluge of disputes that followed the 2008 laws affected firms and managers in a visceral way, as empowered workers upended longstanding beliefs about the docility of workers, especially migrant workers who had entered the cities years before with few rights and low expectations. Harsher penalties for noncompliance and the fear of worker-initiated disputes drove changes in behavior including both better compliance with key aspects of the laws, such as formal contracts, and strategic evasion of the same. Labor subcontracting, outsourcing, and other forms of casualization became more common, particularly at the lower end of the labor market.

Government Enforcement: Reactive and Constrained

The importance of the labor dispute resolution system in improving firm compliance with the new labor laws stands out against the consistent weakness of other modes of compliance and enforcement, especially the government's own system of labor inspection. In this regard, enforcement of labor laws through labor inspection in China reflects common problems with weak local government enforcement of regulatory standards.[10] For example, experts in environmental protection have noted that China's environmental standards are quite well developed and sophisticated as written, but they fall far short in actual implementation and enforcement (Rooij 2006; Lorentzen, Landry, and Yasuda 2014; Stern 2014). Two major barriers are responsible for this gap between law and its enforcement: the *constraints* of labor inspection within the decentralized system of governance and the *reactive* nature of the vast majority of inspections.

First, in China's decentralized system of governance, local governments have conflicting incentives; first, to grow the local economy, but also to mitigate the negative externalities of rapid growth, such as environmental pollution, rampant violations of labor codes, and industrial violations of health and safety standards. With almost all of the local bureaucracy tied to the territorial government, which controls promotions and budgets, most local officials are not encouraged to enforce the law vigorously if doing so will impact the local economy. Although labor inspection and

---

[10] This section is based on interviews with labor inspectors, secondary literature, official statistics and reporting on labor inspection. I also participated in two training programs for labor inspection. The first was held in Shanghai in 2004. The other was a US-China labor cooperation program that began in 2004 with a joint training session between Chinese and American labor inspectors in Qingdao. Perhaps reflecting its relatively weak role in labor law enforcement, in-depth studies of labor inspection are few. Exceptions include Christina Chen, "The Politics of Labor Protection in Authoritarian Systems: Evidence from Labor Law and Enforcement in Post-Reform China" (2011); Sean Cooney, Sarah Biddulph and Ying Zhu (2013); and Zhuang and Ngok (2014).

III. Consequences for Mobilization, Compliance, and Enforcement 103

the labor dispute resolution system exist side-by-side as mechanisms to resolve grievances and to correct firm behavior, labor inspection is even more hampered by its bureaucratic position and general lack of adequate financing and capacity. As Zhuang and Ngok (2014) have argued, under this decentralized governance model, labor inspection is fragmented and weak. Since the passage of the 1995 National Labor, labor inspection and arbitration have been the responsibility of the local labor bureaucracy, which is a unit within the local government. These functional units in charge of labor policies are directly supervised by the territorial government of which they are a part. While they take professional advice and instructions from the upper level labor bureaucracies at the provincial or national level, their "professional relations" with the central labor bureaucracy are superseded in practice by their "leadership relations" with the local Party-State (Lieberthal 2004). Appointments, budgets, and promotions are also controlled at the local level, which further ties the functional bureaucracies to the fate of the locality. Local cadres in charge of labor affairs are first and foremost local officials, rather than trained labor functionaries embedded in a national civil service. Wang (2014) also recounts how local firms can seek out protection from inspection from local government agents who value their investment in the area over enforcement of labor and environmental standards.

Although labor inspection and labor dispute resolution are both hampered by the growth orientation of local governments, labor inspection is more affected for several reasons. First, pro-active labor inspection is at the discretion of the local government while labor arbitration is responsive to workers' filing claims against specific employers. Under the new rules of the LDMAL, labor disputes that are not accepted by labor arbitration committees can be heard in civil courts directly. This new opening to the courts restricts the ability of local labor bureaucracies to deny workers access to dispute resolution. Second, the legal framework for labor inspection does not encourage more active and authoritative enforcement. While the 1995 Labor Law gave the power of inspection to local labor bureaucracies it did not grant them adequate punitive measures to require compliance (Zhuang and Ngok 2014). There have been some recent improvements, however, at least in the area of wage arrears. The problem of wage arrears led to a nation-wide campaign in 2004 to target sectors such as construction that routinely experienced widespread protests, strikes, and violence related to protracted non-payment of wages (Halegua 2008; Ngai and Lu 2010; Biddulph, Cooney, and Zhu 2012). In 2011, illegally withholding wages became a criminal offense (Zhuang and Ngok

2014, 569). Finally, labor inspectorates are woefully understaffed and lack capacity. A labor official from Tianjin recounted these problems of both government interference and capacity. *"In a Tianjin district, our labor supervision team went to enforce the law, as soon as they arrived, the district head immediately called us. He did not permit (the labor inspection). Said it would adversely affect economic development … Tianjin has 6 million workers, at the municipal and district levels, we have 67 labor inspectors officially on staff (在编的), I brought in 100 more, but in total this is still less than 200 people"* (BJ201503). A report on Ma'anshan City found that labor inspection was critically understaffed with only four inspectors in a single county. Each inspector was responsible for more than 1,000 enterprise and 27,500 workers, far beyond the 1:8,000 goal set by the central government (Party School Research Group 2009).

In addition to the constraints of the decentralized system, China's dominant mode of state-led enforcement is heavily reliant on reactive responses to worker-complaints from below or campaign-like surges in targeted enforcement mandated from above. These campaign surges often follow incidences of social unrest and are centrally-mandated episodic reactions to compliance failures (Biddulph, Cooney, and Zhu 2012). Top-down campaigns from the central government to address particularly pressing problems, such as wage arrears, failure to conclude written labor contracts, or pay social insurance supplement these two local modes of inspection. In addition to those campaigns from higher levels, labor inspection occurs in two major ways: 1) active inspection by local labor bureaucracies (what might be called "police patrols") 2) reactive inspection by local labor bureaucracies as a result of worker complaints or anonymous reports (a "fire alarm" system similar to labor dispute initiation).

Since the 1990s, labor inspection has been mostly reliant on bottom-up complaints from workers below or top-down mandates for targeted campaigns. Labor inspection via external complaints expanded from 2002 with 233,747 settlements before peaking in 2008 with 482,659 cases. In 2011, there were 379,865 cases. 53 percent of the cases were wage disputes; 19 percent were related to social insurance; and 16.3 percent were contract disputes related to signing or termination. Zhuang and Ngok show that since 2006 over 90 percent of all cases settled by labor inspection have been through reactive inspections following complaints (Zhuang and Ngok 2014, 575). Unfortunately, budgetary allocations to labor inspection have not kept pace with the rapid increase in labor conflict. In analyzing the budgetary expenditures allocated to labor

III. Consequences for Mobilization, Compliance, and Enforcement

inspectorates during this time period, they find that expenditures on labor inspections have fallen dramatically since 1998 as a proportion of all spending on labor affairs. During the surge of complaints and unrest following the passage of the Labor Contract Law, expenditures on labor inspection made up less than 5 percent of all labor affairs spending. While overall spending on labor inspection increased during this period, it does not seem to track the surge in labor conflict and worker complaints (Zhuang and Ngok 2014, 572).

Official statistics on labor inspection results also indicate the weakness and impotence of labor inspection penalties. While labor inspectors have the right to issue administrative penalties, warnings, and fines, inspections overwhelmingly result in orders to make corrections, a minor charge that can have little effect on company behavior. From 2002 to 2011, labor inspectors responding to workers' anonymous complaints settled more than three million complaints via firm inspections, but in every year the majority (from 73 percent to 78 percent) of cases were settled "by orders to make corrections." Fines were exceedingly rare, from 5 to 8 percent of all cases; moreover, the proportion of fines has declined over time, from a high of 8 percent in 2002 to 5–5.8 percent in the last three years for which data are available (2009–2011). In most cases, labor inspection results in "slaps on the wrist" (Zhuang and Ngok 2014).

Official statistics of labor inspection also display the worrying trend of a decline in inspections during a time of increased labor conflict and unrest. The aggregate number of labor inspections over the last decade increased on an annual basis before declining after 2008. These numbers underscore how reliant the state is on "fire alarm" systems: labor inspections via complaints and labor disputes filed by workers outpace "active inspections" by a large margin. There were 1.3 million labor disputes in 2011 and about 726,000 reactive labor inspections. The MHRSS also reports 1.8 million active labor inspections, which is a large number of inspections. However, the reported results by the Ministry itself are hard to interpret. Some researchers report that these active inspections are often simply "desk-based" inspections based on employers' self-reported labor compliance. In interviews with labor inspectors in 2004, desk-based inspections were by far the most common kind of inspection (QD200401; Cooney 2014, 123). Even in an area that has been targeted by the central government for campaign-style enforcement, wage arrears, the results seem anemic. While the MHRSS reports that wage arrear cases did produce repayment to over 5.3 million workers, only .002 percent of all inspections resulted in a serious violation (National Bureau of

Statistics)! As has been detailed by many Chinese scholars, labor inspection is an underfunded and understaffed bureaucracy embedded within a local political economy built on generating growth, investment, and employment (J. Deng 2007; Party School Research Group 2009). Moreover, even when a labor inspector finds a violation, the labor bureaucracy has limited tools with which they can require compliance, usually just issuing a notice for correction.

Disputants who attempted to use labor inspection mechanisms to censure firm behavior were also overwhelmingly negative about their experiences. Many report that when they complained, the labor inspection bureau simply redirected them to labor arbitration instead, absolving the bureau of any need to investigate the grievance. One middle-aged male worker decried the unfairness of the system while underlining the common suspicion that labor inspection is weak because of the close relationship between firms and local officials. *"Implementation of labor law is difficult. It's all too weak. Look at how weak labor inspection is! They pay you 3 RMB an hour; it's not even enough to live on! But if you report the violation, it's no use. In our district, this factory is a big customer. They do something wrong and it is just forgotten about."* (SH200448)

A young worker in a Shanghai supermarket (SH200414) first reported his workplace's failure to pay overtime via the labor inspection office of the local government. However, his anonymity was not protected, as afterward it was widely known at the company that he had reported the infractions. He believes that his termination was in retribution for the complaint. The teacher fired for getting pregnant (SH200427) also reported, "Labor inspection!? It's not worth it. Nobody answers or they just tell you "it's just like that." You have to go to the next level to get anything done."

The "next level" is to work the system on your own by filing a labor arbitration claim against the company. With labor inspection weak and anemic, rights-protecting workers fill in the gap. This system is overwhelmingly reactive to worker initiative and mobilization. As many of the case narratives demonstrate, workers often exploit all means available to resolve a labor grievance, from calling the labor bureau's hotline, to reporting the firm anonymously to labor inspection, to filing a claim at arbitration and proceeding to court. State-led enforcement through the labor inspection system is both notoriously weak as local officials prioritize economic growth over compliance and exceedingly fleeting as top-down campaigns ebb and flow.

III. Consequences for Mobilization, Compliance, and Enforcement 107

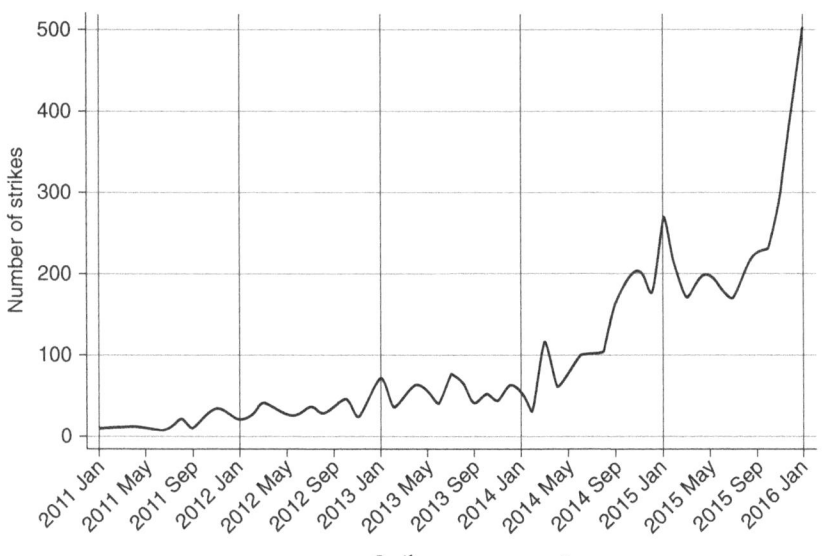

CHART 3.9. Strikes, 2011–2016.
Source: China Labor Bulletin.

Fire alarm mechanisms are preferable to costly and inefficient police patrols, particularly if the police patrols are not only weakly armed but also incentivized to look the other way as much as possible. Perhaps because of the weak authority of the labor inspection system, the number of reactive inspection cases filed has actually fallen since 2008 even while labor disputes and grievances lodged at arbitration and at the courts have skyrocketed. The numbers of workers filing these suits have risen drastically over time, even as the bureaucracy has been overwhelmed and delays and frustration are the norm. Since 2001, labor disputes have increased by 277 percent. While accurate data on strikes are difficult to attain, nongovernmental organizations that track strike activity also report steady annual increases in the number of industrial work actions. (See Chart 3.9). In 2011, fifteen strikes occurred on average per month. In 2012 this number jumped to thirty-two and in 2013 to fifty-nine. With the deceleration in growth and large numbers of factory closures after 2014, strikes skyrocketed. In the first half of 2016 there were 1,454 strikes, an average of 242 strikes per month ("Strikes Continue Unabated in China during First Half of the Year" 2016). In this context of increasing legal and extralegal mobilization on the part of workers, the decline in labor inspections and the lack of effective financing and staffing are only comprehensible in the context of the political logic of regulation in China's decentralized system of governance.

CONCLUSION: LEGAL MOBILIZATION AND CHINA'S REACTIVE GOVERNANCE

In the vocabulary developed by McCubbins and Schwartz to describe Congressional oversight over the executive branch, China relies much more heavily on "fire alarms" mechanisms of regulation and enforcement than "police patrols" (McCubbins and Schwartz 1984; C. Chen 2011). While the state developed both "police patrols" and "fire alarms" as part of its labor law reforms, bottom-up, worker-initiated, fire-alarm mechanisms for labor law compliance are far more important in practice than top-down, active, police patrols by state actors. As discussed in Chapter 2, the allure of fire alarms goes back to China's decentralized system of governance, which grants local governments ample room to pursue key economic goals while leaving the central government less able to ensure compliance with laws that impede economic growth or that are against the interests of key local actors, especially powerful officials and enterprises. In other words, if the central state does not trust locally-run "police patrols" to function effectively, it must rely on fire-alarm mechanisms from below. Fire-alarm mechanisms encourage individualized mass mobilization around centrally mandated high standards. The central government can take credit for the high standards, while the local government takes the blame for the lack of enforcement. The central state cultivates lower level actors, such as workers, to earn political support and legitimacy while also using actors at the bottom as "fire alarms" to put pressure on its agents in the middle – local officials and the firms that they should regulate but with which they often collude.

In the original application of the terms, fire alarm mechanisms involve the creation of channels and mechanisms to mobilize individual and group actors in society to alert the legislative branch of violations or overreach by executive branch bureaucracies, which are not elected. Other research extended the concept to signify more general action by individual citizens or groups to notify governments when private or public actors violate laws or regulatory standards. Public policy goals (of enforcement and compliance) are realized through private action. Regulatory oversight is delegated to citizens who must mobilize, either individually or in groups, to check the power of bureaucratic actors. McCubbins and

Conclusion: Legal Mobilization and China's Reactive Governance

Schwartz argue that Congressional oversight of the bureaucracy occurs mainly through this mechanism, which is both politically rational and economically efficient. Politicians in democratic systems should prefer fire-alarm mechanisms that allow them to be responsive to citizen initiative. A politician prefers to "take as much credit as possible for the net benefits enjoyed by his potential supporters – by citizens and interest groups, within his constituency and elsewhere, whose support can help him win reelection" (McCubbins and Schwartz 1984, 167). Fire alarm mechanisms are also superior to police patrols because they allow politicians to react to grievances once they have occurred, but not to spend much time, resources, or effort on looking for potential grievances via police patrols. Moreover, fire alarm mechanisms through delegation to citizens also pass on the costs of enforcement to the individuals and, eventually, to administrative agencies or courts that must deal with the complaints.

While efficient and rational, a government's overdependence on fire alarms raises important issues of equality and fairness. "Fire alarm oversight tends to be particularistic…it arguably emphasizes the interests of individuals and interest groups more than those of the public at large." In the democratic context of the United States, McCubbins and Schwartz mostly discount these concerns because "nowadays even disadvantaged groups often have public spokesmen" (McCubbins and Schwartz 1984, 172). Congress can help groups organize; and individual Congressional offices can provide constituent services that can also provide assistance. They also note that the federal government can establish institutions to facilitate fire alarms, such as the Legal-Services Corporation, which was set up to provide legal assistance to disadvantaged citizens. In democratic systems with responsive politicians, strong civic associations, and an activist federal government, they argue, fire-alarm mechanisms can overcome the inequalities that might bar some citizens from active participation and mobilization.

While Congressional oversight is a world away from labor law enforcement in China, China's reliance on fire-alarm mechanisms for labor law enforcement raises similar issues. Why does China overwhelmingly rely on an individualized fire-alarm mechanism, the labor dispute resolution system, for enforcement of labor standards? What are the implications of this reliance – for the larger goal of general compliance and enforcement and the more specific goals of the individual worker who plays the important role of "firefighter" via their own mobilization? As Weil analyzes at the micro level in the United States workplace, which also privileges individual mobilization (especially when unions are absent), the threshold for claiming rights is higher for the individual worker than if the entire workforce was mobilized, as individuals do not take into account the collective benefits that would arise from better compliance. Compliance based on individual fire alarms will be suboptimal if collective mobilization is blocked or intermediaries such as unions and NGOs are weak (Weil 2004, 22–23). The concerns about equal access to fire alarms and whether fire alarms can satisfy public goals via individualized grievances (raised then dismissed by McCubbins and Schwartz) are especially prominent in the Chinese labor context, in which collective mobilization is restricted, intermediary associations are weak and/or repressed, and vast differences of skills, resources, and education exist in the workforce. Within the Chinese political system, reliance on fire alarms has a strong political and economic logic, but it is also reinforces existing and new patterns of inequality and leads to suboptimal enforcement of labor standards.

The allure of rights-protection has brought many aggrieved workers to the state's door – first in arbitration and then in the courts. Imbued with a new sense of empowerment and unrealized codified rights, feisty litigants have challenged powerful employers to abide by the rules. Workers have consulted newspapers, books, the Internet, and their friends as they investigate their options and their chances in the courtroom. Since 2008, their options have expanded as barriers to litigation were relaxed and prohibitively high administrative fees were cancelled. The mobilization wave that followed the 2008 legislative drive continues unabated, though the state has tried to champion mediation and non-adversarial settlement more aggressively as a way to dampen conflict and reduce pressure on these new formal institutions.

These institutional reforms have engendered a workforce that is increasingly aware of their workplace rights and inclined to make use of third-party dispute resolution to force changes in firms' behavior. China's turn to law in the 1990s to structure labor relations granted workers new rights under the labor contract system. The legal dissemination campaigns widely proclaimed these new rights. The dispute resolution system offered space for grievances to be heard and adjudicated in the civil justice system. As the following chapters demonstrate, at the individual level, legal mobilization yields varied outcomes. For former SOE workers attempting to challenge the loss of job security and employment benefits that they enjoyed under the old system, legal solutions offered meager

Conclusion: Legal Mobilization and China's Reactive Governance 111

compensation. Workers with higher levels of education and access to legal representation tend to do better and also feel better about their legal experiences. But the dispute resolution system remains highly individualized and unable to manage the rising collective demands of workers emboldened by labor shortages and the rhetoric of inclusive protection.

4

By the Book

Learning and the Law

"When I graduated, you entered into a company that you were never going to leave. Then you might not care about the law, but now you're switching from company to company every year, signing contracts all the time. Of course you're going to start to pay attention to the law. Now all the newspapers have information about the law, about how to negotiate, how to sign labor contracts...."

(SH200426)

These next two chapters examine legal mobilization from the perspectives of aggrieved workers, that is, from the bottom and often in their own words. This chapter focuses on a topic that is critically important to the legal mobilization process: education. Remarks about the importance of learning, becoming knowledgeable about the law, and having or not having formal education were raised again and again by workers themselves as they made sense of their legal experiences. Formal education and specific knowledge about labor law also stand out in the quantitative analysis as major factors in leading people to the law and shaping their attitudes toward it. Using case narratives of legal-aid litigants and surveys, I explore this role of learning, of being or becoming educated, in bringing people to the law and legal institutions as a mode of conflict resolution and rights protection.

Three main points emerge in the analysis. First, and unsurprisingly, people with higher levels of formal education are more likely to know about their legal workplace rights, use formal institutions to protect them, and to find these institutions more effective. The elite bias in law, especially in individualized litigation, confirms long-held expectations that the legal system and the "judicialization of social rights" are not ideal mechanisms if the goals are greater inclusion and protection of marginalized groups (Galanter 1974; Black 2010; Brinks and Gauri 2014).

Second, in some contrast to the importance of formal education, I also find that litigants with high levels of specific knowledge about labor and employment, however attained, share more positive attitudes about the legal system and are more likely to make use of these institutions for rights protection. In other words, with China's populist promotion of "legal weapons," there are alternative pathways to legal mobilization for those who do not have high levels of formal education. The state's own propaganda work in legal dissemination and access to various modes of self-education and legal aid, as well as engagement with explicitly law-based transactions (such as signing labor contracts), can *substitute* for formal education in bringing less-educated workers to the system and imbuing them with confidence. As detailed in the previous chapter, access to legal information and knowledge is possible and often facilitated by state agencies and the media. Aggrieved workers often begin their road to the courts with an intense period of self-education, using the media, books, the Internet, and social networks to discover their rights "by the book." Both in the case narratives of legal aid plaintiffs and in the general population surveyed, higher levels of legal knowledge are correlated with greater propensity to use the law and to find the legal system effective.

Third, while more educated and knowledgeable citizens are more likely to use these new institutions to foster their own political participation and advance their interests in the increasingly law-bounded market economy, prior dispute experience, or "experiential knowledge," complicates a person's propensity to seek out legal institutions for rights protection and may contribute to a general lack of faith in the formal channels. This point emerges in case narratives of legal aid plaintiffs and in general surveys among respondents with dispute experience but who are almost always lacking legal representation. This lack of representation probably explains the deep disappointment that emerges in the surveys among workers with real legal experience, and is discussed more fully in the following chapter. Focusing here on the role of experience, I show in this chapter that even among those with adequate legal representation through legal aid, experiencing the law first hand can diminish expectations.

In earlier work (Gallagher 2006), I introduced the concept of "informed disenchantment" to explain the contradictory effects of legal mobilization. Legal mobilization as a process has an important educative component, which can lead to strongly negative evaluations of legal and administrative institutions such as labor bureau arbitration committees and courts. However, this same process can have positive effects on an individual's own sense of internal efficacy. Many disputants leave the process with strong opinions that the law doesn't work well, but that they have learned to work the law more effectively. This contradictory effect of legal mobilization warns against any linear or simplistic notion of "rising" rights consciousness in China. This interpretation also explains the contradictory bundle of beliefs that many legal aid recipients exhibited during in-depth interviews, including very negative evaluations of the law and the political system within which it is embedded, coupled with affirmative evaluations of their own future chances using the law to protect their rights. Thus, the educative components of legal mobilization include not only the prior period accumulating legal knowledge and information via the media, books, and the state, and law-based transactions (like contracting), but also the process itself, which tends to lead to more measured, sometimes cynical, evaluations of the institutions along with a stronger sense of internal efficacy.

This chapter concludes with a discussion of the role of education and political participation in theories of political change and modernization. In taking legal mobilization as a form of political participation under authoritarian rule, I do not necessarily interpret such participation as a signal of support for *or* defiance against the regime. Educated, knowledgeable citizens may simply be more demanding of their political system, whether democratic or authoritarian, and more inclined to engage it. In the aftermath of participation, these citizens are more critical and discriminating, focusing on structural and procedural issues that impede the formal legal process. While disenchantment with legal institutions is not a problem unique to China (see, e.g., Benesh 2006), it is possible that these problems are more endemic to authoritarian regimes, where the gap between expectations for formal institutions and how they actually operate is large. In China, this gap is even more consequential as the state's protective legislation and its large-scale legal education campaigns have heightened the expectations of the population. To understand the effect of legal mobilization on regime support, we must understand not only how and what kinds of citizens use formal channels, but their evaluation of the experience. This chapter presents evidence that the CCP's embrace of institutions tied to democratic rule, such as "rule of law" to sustain authoritarian rule may be backfiring. While the state encourages citizens to use these institutions to advance their interests and protect their rights, such use exposes the flaws of these institutions and the local state's ambivalent role in ensuring rights.

LEGAL MOBILIZATION AS POLITICAL PARTICIPATION

Education is a critical variable in the decision to embrace legal institutions and in shaping one's responses to the legal system. As with other types of political participation, using the law to advance one's interests requires skills and resources. Research on political participation has paid significant attention to the role of education, but much less attention has been directed at legal mobilization as a political act (Zemans 1983). In democratic societies, such as the United States, the study of political participation centers around the act of selecting public officials and includes standard behavior such as voting, campaigning, and lobbying. Legal mobilization has been much less emphasized, unless it is part of a broader social movement around public policy issues, such as civil rights, pay equity, or gay marriage.

Zemans' early call for the inclusion of legal mobilization into debates about political participation was based on the notion that invocation of the law to solve problems is political. It is "a form of political activity by which the citizenry uses public authority on its own behalf" (Zemans 1983, 690). Legal mobilization is a process that invokes politics by transforming a social or economic problem into a legal one. It may begin as a dispute between two private parties, but it often ends as a triadic public issue when the state steps in to resolve the conflict. The disputing parties might also invoke other types of conflict resolution, such as protests, petitioning, or seeking out the media, which also enlarges the public and political impact of the dispute.

Legal mobilization can also be linked to important public policy goals, such as enhanced implementation and enforcement of law. Much of law enforcement and rights empowerment only occurs when people invoke laws and rights around their own personal interests. As Zemans notes, rights are "contingent," when they are given by the state in legislation but often not realized until citizens mobilize to press for enforcement. "Whatever rights are conferred are thus contingent upon the factors that promote or inhibit decisions to mobilize the law" (Zemans 1983, 695). As discussed in other chapters, the state's encouragement of legal mobilization is partly motivated by its weak capacity to monitor local level actors in their enforcement of central laws and policies. Bottom-up legal mobilization serves as a "fire-alarm" monitoring and regulatory system (McCubbins and Schwartz 1984) that compensates for a fragmented local state tasked both with economic growth and control of the negative externalities of growth, such as pollution and labor violations. Legal mobilization of citizens as "private attorney generals" is part of a policy environment that relies on non-state action at the local level to achieve the center's goals. In his study of "private attorney general" behavior in China, Clarke notes, "in order to achieve the public-policy goal of effective monitoring and enforcement, the state enacts a structure of incentives designed to mobilize citizens ... " (Clarke 2009). He finds that while many aspects of Chinese civil procedure norms are not welcoming to citizens' bottom-up enforcement of law through legal mobilization, there are areas where private litigation is increasingly important. Legal mobilization around workplace grievances is one of them. This public role of legal mobilization further bolsters the argument to take individual legal action as inherently political. Its consequences not only affect individual outcomes, but also have consequential ramifications on policymaking and the quality of law enforcement, compliance with the law and rights protection, and other similarly-situated claimants. While the state might be self-serving in its promotion of legal mobilization, there are also important consequences of state-led citizen activism beyond those intended by the state.

In an authoritarian political context in which most political institutions are formalistic and highly constrained, the importance of legal mobilization as a mode of political participation is heightened. In China, electoral and legislative institutions do not offer many opportunities for individual citizens to participate in meaningful ways. As Shi notes in his study of Beijing, many people participate in politics via informal or administrative channels where policy preferences, complaints, and suggestions might receive more attention (Shi 1997). When formal political participation is restricted, the few channels that exist become more significant as space for state-society interaction, for individuals to have a sense of voice.

As political participation then, legal mobilization requires that individuals use their own resources and skills to participate effectively. In studies of political participation in developed democracies, the "resource model" – one's ability to marshal "time, money, and skills" toward political participation – finds that education is the "single best predictor of political activity"(Burns, Schlozman, and Verba 2009, 94). In the Chinese context, many have found that political participation can also be interpreted using these general models (Shi 1997; W. Tang 2005). The decreasing importance of work-unit type and occupational group in predicting political participation reflects the growing individualization of Chinese society with increasing importance placed on individual skill, education, and achievement.

In a study of rural China, Jennings reiterates this importance of individual resources, not only in the light of the decline of administrative power, but also in the context of weak civil society and associational life. He finds that China's participation patterns are "quite compatible with participation models developed for more open societies" and that individual traits may be even more consequential in China because of its weak "secondary associations" (Jennings 1997). In a more focused study of Chinese workers, Tang finds that young, urban workers with higher levels of education are more likely to use institutional channels to press for their rights, even more so when they are also CCP members (Tang 2009). These studies confirm the expectation that political participation in China, as elsewhere, requires resources, skills, education, and income. In the context of legal mobilization around workplace issues, inequality in resources affects outcomes, while the paucity of civil society organizations affects the legal experience, which is alienating, bureaucratic, and frustrating for many aggrieved workers who try to access the system on their own.

Structural inequalities that are built into the legal process make it difficult for those without the requisite skills, tools, or resources to use the law effectively. The law and society literature on legal mobilization also finds that structural inequalities are built into the legal process (Galanter 1974). In her study of individual contact with the courts, Benesh (2006) finds that in the American context, education and knowledge tend to produce more confidence in judicial institutions. Relis (2002) also finds that individual-level attributes can have critical effects on how one experiences and evaluates the legal system. Those who approach the legal system with low levels of education and little knowledge of the system find that they need to constantly redefine and scale down their moralistic claims to something legally acceptable. This process can be frustrating and disempowering, especially when the plaintiff lacks adequate legal representation. Legal representation is critical to managing expectations and helping a plaintiff scale down requests. A competent lawyer makes sense out of the law for the uninitiated, dramatically improving a disputant's experience in the courts. Not only does having a lawyer improve perceptions of fairness among litigants (Relis 2002, 160), many disputants profess satisfaction with their own lawyer even when unhappy with the entire system. However, for the vast number of unrepresented litigants the legal mobilization process is unsatisfactory, confusing, and frustrating (Relis

2002, 178). I examine the issue of representation further in the following chapter.

Epp's (1990) study of legal mobilization for employment discrimination also emphasizes the role of education in increasing the likelihood of litigation. Education may increase awareness of codified rights and confidence in one's skill in claiming those rights through formal legal institutions. Education provides disputants with greater capacity for legal mobilization and also may raise awareness or "rights consciousness" about unfair treatment. Many studies have noted that more disadvantaged workers will be less likely to file formal claims. Lower levels of educational attainment are commonly collinear with other factors that suppress mobilization, including race, gender, and class (Bumiller 1988; Ewick and Silbey 1998). Other work has noted the importance of civil society organizations in assisting marginalized workers in making formal claims and moving through difficult administrative processes to resolve disputes (Gleeson 2009).

While there are many examples of activist lawyers, NGOs, and academics involved in the advancement of workers' rights in China, the political environment hampers the ability of these disparate actors and organizations to organize and act collectively in a sustained and strategic manner. At the local level, NGOs and activist lawyers are co-opted and/or repressed (Cheng, Ngok, and Zhuang 2010; Spires 2011). When they push the boundaries of current practices, they do so on the margins and in quiet ways; they often seek out official patrons and protectors rather than social support or initiating formal litigation. At the central level, the strictures on independent trade unions allow the official trade union to monopolize representation, even when the union does not fulfill that role adequately. In McCann's study of the pay equity movement in the United States, legal mobilization over discrimination was the beginning of a social movement for public policy change (McCann 1994). Change happens via social organizations, activist lawyers, and movement leaders who take advantage of shifts in the political opportunity structure. In the Chinese case, a nascent social movement has begun but under much more challenging political conditions. These issues are discussed in depth in the Chapter six.

GETTING SCHOOLED IN THE LAW

Education plays an integral part of a person's decision to seek justice. Because resolution of labor disputes in China is so dependent on an individual's own motivation and tenacity, the process of getting information and becoming aware of rights can be transformative. Education is important to every step in the legal mobilization process from gaining specific knowledge of labor rights, to naming a workplace problem as a legal violation, to claiming protection by going to court, and, finally, to evaluating the process and outcome.

Knowing and Naming Rights

One precondition of legal mobilization is knowledge and awareness of codified rights (Albiston 2005). If one is unaware of rights on the books, then the process of legal mobilization, moving from "naming, blaming, claiming" (Felstiner, Abel, and Sarat 1980) cannot even begin; discovery of a grievance requires awareness that another person's behavior contravenes a rule. It is widely accepted in China today that people's awareness and consciousness about their legal rights has increased (Pei 1997; O'Brien and Li 2006; Yang and Calhoun 2007). As discussed in Chapter 3, much of the legal dissemination and knowledge dispersion about rights in China has been done either by the state or with the state's encouragement. While it is hard to judge in comparative terms if Chinese people know a lot or a little about their legal rights at the workplace, evidence from the LLMS and the CULS show several interesting and important trends. First, people seem to know a good deal about their basic workplace rights in statute and regulation, though many do not know the specific details. Second, the gap between urban residents and migrant workers in knowledge may be narrowing, especially among younger workers and more educated workers. Third, formal education is associated with higher levels of knowledge, but there is no relationship between dispute experience and higher levels of legal knowledge.

In the 2005 LLMS, respondents answered a battery of eighteen questions related to labor and employment law. The questions ranged from relatively general to very specific. Given the level of specificity, range of topics, and number of questions, it is surprising that a large number of respondents did relatively well on this test of their labor law knowledge. As displayed in Table 4.1, over 75 percent of the 4,000 respondents exhibited medium to high levels of specific labor law knowledge. In the 2010 CULS, using a truncated battery of similar questions, both urban residents and migrants displayed high levels of knowledge on major issues (M. Gallagher et al. 2014). For example, 95 percent of local residents and 89.5 percent of migrants knew that they were entitled to a written labor contract. 80 percent of local residents and 77 percent of migrants knew that

TABLE 4.1. *Legal Knowledge*

	Freq.	Percent
Legal knowledge low (knowledge score<0.67)	1,016	25
Legal knowledge medium (0.67–0.8)	2,156	52
Legal knowledge high (0.8–1.0)	940	23
Total	4,112	100

* Out of 36 questions, the percentage of respondents who answered the knowledge questions. Less than 67% correct is coded as low knowledge. 67%–80% is medium knowledge. 80%–100% is high knowledge.
Source: LLMS 2005.

the penalty for failing to conclude a contract is double wages for every month worked without a formal contract. Migrant workers with high school education and above trail their urban counterparts only slightly in awareness of the labor law and in detailed knowledge of the law's content. (See Chart 4.1). The smaller gaps in the 2010 survey may indicate that migrants are catching up quickly in what they know about workplace rights.

In both the 2005 and 2010 surveys, formal education is associated with higher levels of knowledge. In the 2005 LLMS, being educated, male, and

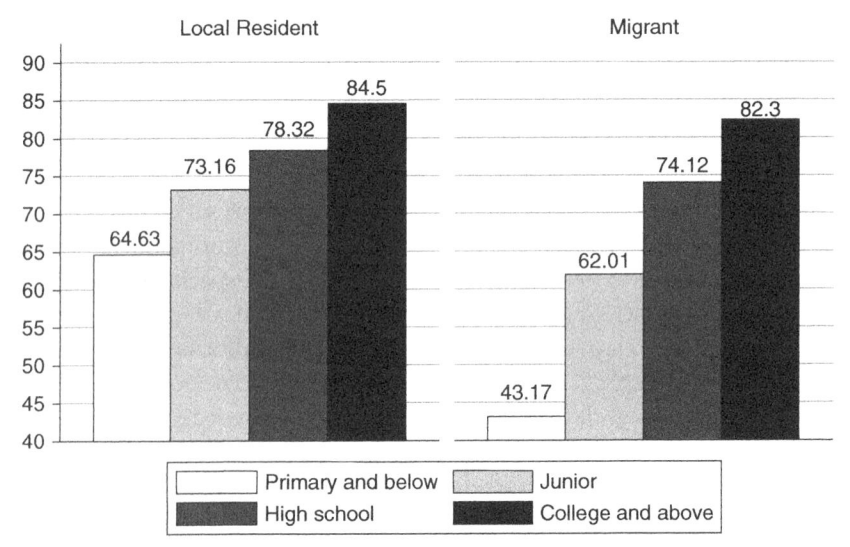

CHART 4.1. Med-High Labor Law Knowledge by Education Level.
Source: LLMS 2005.

TABLE 4.2. *Determinants of Legal Knowledge*

	DV: Legal Knowledge Score		
Variables	(1)	(2)	(3)
Education year	0.277***	0.257***	0.241***
	(0.028)	(0.029)	(0.029)
Log (income)	0.105	0.056	−0.001
	(0.114)	(0.114)	(0.118)
AGE	−0.008	−0.007	−0.004
	(0.008)	(0.008)	(0.008)
Female	−0.475***	−0.499***	−0.472***
	(0.154)	(0.154)	(0.157)
Migrant workers	−0.823***	−0.799**	−0.761**
	(0.317)	(0.317)	(0.321)
Dispute experience	0.613	0.545	0.424
	(0.521)	(0.521)	(0.525)
SOE	0.622***	0.625***	0.441**
	(0.182)	(0.182)	(0.190)
FIE	1.460***	1.484***	1.230***
	(0.416)	(0.416)	(0.423)
Government/party unit	0.068	0.043	−0.086
	(0.236)	(0.236)	(0.239)
High media exposure		0.671***	0.723***
		(0.199)	(0.202)
Labor contract			0.578***
			(0.167)
Constant	21.195***	21.563***	21.745***
	(0.906)	(0.911)	(0.930)
Observations	2,720	2,720	2,631
R-squared	0.079	0.083	0.085

Notes: Ordinary Least Squares analysis of the labor law knowledge scores.
Standard errors in parentheses.
***$p < 0.01$, **$p < 0.05$, *$p < 0.1$.
Source: LLMS 2005.

younger are associated with relatively high levels of legal knowledge.[1] (See Table 4.2.) Rural migrants are less likely to have high levels of knowledge. Those working for foreign-invested enterprises (FIE), those with a labor contract, and those with high rates of media attention are also more likely to be knowledgeable about labor rights. These results may indicate that

---

[1] Scoring above .67 on the Labor Law Knowledge scale was grouped as "medium-high levels" of knowledge. The scale was made from a series of questions about the 1995 Labor Law. This scale was significantly more complicated than the scale used in the 2010 survey.

respondents employed in more 'legalistic' settings absorb legal knowledge at the workplace as part of the socialization process. Many FIEs emphasize law as a way to limit employment security, avoid litigation, and please domestic audiences back home. The 2010 CULS also found that education was significantly associated with awareness of the law but in contrast to the 2005 survey, women and older workers knew more about the Labor Contract Law than men and younger workers (M. Gallagher et al. 2014). These changes may indicate that workers who are particularly vulnerable to discrimination, either due to sex or age, have intentionally sought out information on their workplace rights. The 2010 CULS also shows an impressive decrease in informal employment of migrant workers. The proportion of migrant workers with a written labor contract increased from 12 percent to 34 percent between 2005 and 2010. Formal employment via exposure to contracts also provides more opportunities to learn about workplace rights and is associated with higher levels of knowledge in both surveys.

Claiming Rights

After gaining knowledge about legal rights, legal mobilization begins with the process of pursing redress for violation of legal rights. As much of the China literature has shown, pathways of rights-protection are multipronged and not mutually exclusive (Michelson 2007; Peerenboom and He 2009). Aggrieved workers can seek protection through a variety of mechanisms, simultaneously or in sequence. Litigation, as the most formal mechanism, may often be delayed as the claimant pursues less costly, more expedient and private ways to resolve conflicts. There is a strong relationship between formal education and propensity to pursue a grievance, particularly to pursue resolution through litigation (Jiang and Wu 2015). However, informally gained specialized legal knowledge can compensate for lower levels of education and is also correlated with claim-making in general and with litigation in particular.

The two surveys used different strategies to examine patterns of labor conflict resolution. In the 2005 LLMS, 8.6 percent (391) of the respondents reported having a labor problem in the last ten years. Of those 391 respondents with a problem, 82 (or about 21 percent) pursued their claims. Using a hypothetical vignette of a common labor dispute, patterns of resolution across the entire sample are examined, using dispute experience as an independent variable. The 2010 CULS examined the dispute patterns only of those with actual dispute experience. Despite the differences in the surveys' design, we find an association between education and propensity to pursue claims, both extralegally and via the law, across both. As can be seen in column 1 of Table 4.3, in the 2005 LLMS, a unit increase of education year increases the odds of pursuing resolution of the grievance by 8.6 percent. The significance of education year is not interrupted even when the media exposure level and the legal knowledge level are controlled, as shown in columns 3 and 4. Analysis of the 2010 CULS respondents who had actually participated in a dispute also found that the only significant determinant of experiencing a labor dispute is education, and the effect of education is particularly strong for migrant workers. Migrant workers with a junior high school education have a 27 percent higher likelihood of initiating a claim than those without; those with a high school education are 59 percent more likely. For migrants with a college education, they are more than 78 percent more likely to initiate disputes than those with a primary school education or less (M. Gallagher et al. 2014, 21).

Formal education generally has a positive effect on increasing workers' awareness of substantive law and labor rights as well as legal procedure. This makes educated workers more knowledgeable about the legal system and imbues disputants with a sense of personal efficacy. This internal efficacy facilitates workers' engagement with legal institutions and helps them pursue resolutions for their grievances more proactively. For educated migrants in particular, educational resources and skills may substitute for social connections and networks in their adopted cities. Migrants with high levels of education may also be more aware of and angered by unequal treatment and discrimination, seeking out restitution when they are treated differently because of their social background.

What are the factors that encourage or discourage Chinese citizens from choosing the courts as a method of rights protection? In the 2005 LLMS, when asked which method they would use first, 86.9 percent said mediation, 3.1 percent administrative methods, 5 percent arbitration, and 2.7 percent litigation.[2] However, choice of first method does not indicate which method is seen as most *effective*. In a second question on effectiveness, 44 percent said litigation was the most effective, 18 percent said arbitration, 17.9 percent said mediation, and 8.1 percent said administrative methods. 2.7 percent responded that no method is effective. A large proportion of people see the courts as most effective in resolving a work

---

[2] "Administrative methods" indicates the use of direct petitioning of government offices for redress.

TABLE 4.3. *Propensity to Pursue Grievance*

DV: coded 1 if the respondents pursue a resolution of a work-related grievance; 0 otherwise

	(1)	(2)	(3)	(4)
Education year	1.086***	1.076***	1.056***	1.045**
	(0.020)	(0.021)	(0.020)	(0.021)
AGE	0.994	0.991	0.991	0.992
	(0.006)	(0.006)	(0.006)	(0.006)
Female	0.938	0.997	1.030	1.027
	(0.102)	(0.112)	(0.117)	(0.116)
Labor contract	1.537***	1.598***	1.549***	1.538***
	(0.183)	(0.196)	(0.192)	(0.191)
SOE	1.232	1.221	1.201	1.200
	(0.162)	(0.163)	(0.162)	(0.162)
FIE	1.423	1.305	1.229	1.230
	(0.541)	(0.499)	(0.472)	(0.473)
Government/party unit	1.478**	1.267	1.242	1.212
	(0.256)	(0.234)	(0.231)	(0.226)
Manufacturing & construction	0.918	0.965	0.941	0.954
	(0.109)	(0.117)	(0.115)	(0.116)
Migrant worker	1.318	1.291	1.369	1.380
	(0.302)	(0.297)	(0.318)	(0.320)
Dispute experience		0.969	0.934	0.894
		(0.354)	(0.343)	(0.329)
Med-high knowledge			2.160***	2.116***
			(0.254)	(0.249)
High media exposure				1.561**
				(0.277)
Wuxi	1.667***	1.677***	1.574***	1.543***
	(0.271)	(0.278)	(0.263)	(0.259)
Chongqing	1.159	1.239	1.135	1.134
	(0.171)	(0.189)	(0.175)	(0.175)
Foshan	0.955	0.930	0.923	0.902
	(0.142)	(0.142)	(0.142)	(0.139)
Constant	2.957***	3.400***	2.448**	2.526**
	(1.114)	(1.335)	(0.968)	(0.999)
Observations	3,759	3,381	3,381	3,381

Notes: Logit analysis. Reported are odds ratios.
***$p < 0.01$, **$p < 0.05$, *$p < 0.1$.
Source: LLMS 2005.

dispute, which suggests that the courts seem authoritative. On the other hand, less than 3 percent of the 2005 survey respondents would choose the court first, as it is costly, time-consuming, and public. Litigation was also the least preferred method. In each separate question that queried whether the respondent would use the method, 82 percent said they would mediate, 72 percent arbitrate, 70 would use administrative methods, and 67 percent would litigate. While people may value litigation's effectiveness, they take seriously the higher costs of this approach.

In statistical analysis of the propensity to litigate, the respondent's decision to use litigation as one possible method to resolve an employment dispute is examined. Formal education and specific knowledge of labor law are again both consistently associated with the propensity to choose litigation. (See Table 4.4). In column 1, a unit increase of education year increases the odds of choosing litigation by 4.1 percent. The positive and significant relationship between years of schooling and the propensity to litigate remains even when the income level and the legal knowledge level are controlled, as can be seen in column 2 and column 3. A unit increase of education increases the odds of choosing litigation by 4.9 percent and 4.1 percent, respectively.

The important roles of education and knowledge accord with the case narratives below: litigation is more acceptable when a person's internal efficacy, skills, and knowledge are more developed. Respondents employed in government or party units are also more likely to pursue litigation compared to other workplaces. This corroborates other findings that demonstrate the importance of political connections and status in legal mobilization (Su and He 2010; Ang and Jia 2014).

Evaluating the Experience: In Theory and in Practice

Formal education and even informal learning about the law are protective in that they increase disputants' knowledge about the law and legal procedure, their own efficacy, and their confidence in using legal institutions effectively. In the LLMS, educated respondents are more likely to choose litigation as a strategy to solve a workplace grievance; they are also more likely to evaluate litigation as an effective strategy. As can be seen in column 1 and column 2 in Table 4.5, education is positively and significantly associated with the evaluation of litigation as an effective strategy. A unit increase of education year increases the odds of evaluation of litigation as an effective strategy by 4.3 percent when income level is not controlled (column 1), and by 2.9 percent when income level is

TABLE 4.4. *Propensity to Choose Litigation*

DV: Coded 1 if the respondents choose litigation as a way to respond to the vignette; 0 otherwise

Variables	(1)	(2)	(3)
Edu year	1.041**	1.049**	1.041**
	(0.017)	(0.020)	(0.020)
Female	1.043	0.954	0.981
	(0.094)	(0.100)	(0.104)
AGE	1.001	0.999	1.000
	(0.005)	(0.005)	(0.005)
Labor contract	0.943	0.891	0.867
	(0.094)	(0.102)	(0.101)
SOE	0.975	1.128	1.122
	(0.106)	(0.142)	(0.142)
FIE	0.833	0.995	0.949
	(0.194)	(0.265)	(0.254)
Gov/party unit	1.336*	1.424**	1.421**
	(0.201)	(0.240)	(0.241)
Manu.&construct	1.044	1.101	1.090
	(0.103)	(0.126)	(0.125)
Migrant worker	0.793	0.880	0.949
	(0.144)	(0.183)	(0.199)
Dispute	0.535**	0.525**	0.527**
	(0.141)	(0.160)	(0.161)
Log (income)		1.019	1.007
		(0.085)	(0.084)
Med-high knowledge			1.804***
			(0.216)
Wuxi	0.994	0.949	0.907
	(0.122)	(0.136)	(0.131)
Chongqing	2.229***	1.824***	1.710***
	(0.315)	(0.292)	(0.276)
Foshan	0.806*	0.771*	0.764*
	(0.101)	(0.116)	(0.116)
Constant	1.980**	1.805	1.348
	(0.651)	(1.160)	(0.873)
Observations	2,999	2,291	2,291

Notes: Logit analysis. Reported are odds ratios.
***$p < 0.01$, **$p < 0.05$, *$p < 0.1$.
Source: LLMS 2005.

TABLE 4.5. *Determinants of Effectiveness of Litigation*

DV: coded 1 if the respondents evaluate litigation as effective; 0 otherwise			
	(1)	(2)	(3)
Education year	1.043***	1.029*	1.021
	(0.013)	(0.016)	(0.016)
Female	0.925	0.883	0.892
	(0.067)	(0.074)	(0.075)
AGE	0.995	0.993	0.994
	(0.004)	(0.004)	(0.004)
Labor contract	1.037	1.080	1.054
	(0.082)	(0.099)	(0.097)
Manufacturing & construction	0.937	0.942	0.938
	(0.074)	(0.087)	(0.087)
Migrant worker	0.977	0.982	1.023
	(0.148)	(0.171)	(0.179)
Dispute	0.505**	0.574*	0.584*
	(0.139)	(0.177)	(0.181)
Log(income)		1.004	0.999
		(0.065)	(0.065)
Med-high knowledge			1.669***
			(0.175)
SOE	1.083	1.174	1.157
	(0.095)	(0.121)	(0.119)
FIE	0.861	0.758	0.721
	(0.177)	(0.178)	(0.169)
Government or party unit	1.146	1.250*	1.235
	(0.131)	(0.162)	(0.161)
Wuxi	0.952	0.987	0.955
	(0.095)	(0.114)	(0.111)
Chongqing	1.532***	1.549***	1.484***
	(0.151)	(0.177)	(0.171)
Foshan	0.561***	0.528***	0.525***
	(0.060)	(0.068)	(0.068)
Constant	0.511***	0.597	0.460
	(0.133)	(0.300)	(0.233)
Observations	3,483	2,631	2,631

Notes: Logit analysis of determinants of effectiveness.
Reported are odds ratios.
***p < 0.01, **p < 0.05, *p < 0.1.
Source: LLMS 2005.

controlled (column 2). However, as with earlier discussions above, high levels of specific knowledge of labor law are also associated with more positive evaluations of litigation's effectiveness. Education loses its significance in predicting the effectiveness of litigation when legal knowledge is added to the model, though the sign is still positive (column 3). If a respondent has medium-high level of legal knowledge, the odds of expecting litigation to be effective increase by 66.9 percent. If a person uses the various available channels to self-educate about workplace rights, they are also likely to view litigation as an effective method of resolution.

The positive relationship between education and legal knowledge and the propensity to use and believe in the law is an important sign of the potential value of law in China as a "durable" social institution that can reinforce existing inequalities of resources and power structures (Kagan, Garth, and Sarat 2002; Silbey 2005), but also push forward new ideas of workplace rights and employer responsibility – ideas that the state itself promotes because they are beneficial to the regime's developmentalist goals. Given the survey's reliance on a hypothetical workplace problem, the responses capture popular belief and confidence in the law as an institution that promises justice. Do these beliefs and confidence carry forward to those with actual experience? Does law live up to the hopes and expectations of the uninitiated?

Dispute experience does not dissuade respondents from rights' mobilization; survey respondents with labor dispute experience (hereafter, *disputants*) are no less likely to pursue resolution of the hypothetical grievance. They are, however, significantly less likely to choose litigation as a resolution method. As seen in Tables 4.4 and 4.5, dispute experience has a consistently negative association with choosing the litigation option. Dispute experience also has a significant and consistent role in diminishing expectations about the law's effectiveness. In response to the question on which method is the most effective, among disputants only 28.6 percent say it is most effective (compared to 49.3 percent of non-disputants). Disputants are also much more likely to say that none of the resolution methods is effective (15.9 percent of disputants vs. 2.8 percent of non-disputants).

The findings of the 2005 LLMS find additional corroboration in the evaluation of dispute processing in the 2010 CULS. In the 2010 CULS, disputants also showed relatively high rates of dissatisfaction with the dispute process. 63 percent of local residents and 29 percent of migrants reported that they were "not at all satisfied" or "not satisfied" with the results of the dispute process. The higher rates of dissatisfaction among local residents may be the result of two factors. First, as local residents with legal "hukou" in their place of work, local residents may have higher expectations for their judicial institutions. Second, migrant cases are often much simpler to solve as they tend to involve wage and overtime disputes that can be settled through monetary compensation. As discussed in more detail in the next chapter, local residents, especially older residents, often have disputes over employment security and enterprise restructuring, which are much harder to solve, as some of the case narratives below demonstrate. The CULS disputants' experiences bear this out. 68.9 percent of local residents report that their dispute was either not resolved (56.5 percent) or resolved but not enforced (12.4 percent). 67 percent of migrant disputants, on the other hand, report that their dispute was completely resolved and only 1 percent reported unenforced resolutions.

NARRATIVES OF LEARNING

The survey results can tell us that formal education and specific legal knowledge matter consistently in encouraging people to use the law and enhancing their experience of the law. They also indicate that actual experience with the legal system tends to lead to diminished expectations and much less enthusiasm for legal solutions. Using the case narratives of legal aid plaintiffs, I explore why these patterns exist. The role of formal education is most straightforward and reflects the basic relationships posited in the literature on education and political participation. Formal education can imbue litigants with greater confidence and skill in using these institutions, which require mastery of difficult procedures and unfamiliar vocabulary. This accords with findings in Chapter 3 where I argued that these institutions are market-conforming because their benefits tend to accrue to those with the skills and resources necessary to use them effectively. Second, workers with higher levels of formal education can find themselves in leadership positions among similarly aggrieved colleagues in collective disputes. These workers are encouraged by colleagues to serve as representatives in the hope that a well-educated spokesperson will maximize the chances of a good outcome.

While formal education is consistently important to legal mobilization, we should not discount other pathways to knowledge and awareness. It is extremely important that gaining specific knowledge about workplace rights can also be protective, imbuing workers with greater confidence and trust that these institutions are effective and authoritative. This avenue of education is open to anyone with a grievance and the legal dissemination campaigns make information about rights widely available. Legal aid litigants overwhelmingly reported that the legal mobilization process starts, first and foremost, with self-education – buying books, reading newspapers, studying cases, searching on the Internet, calling the government hotlines. If the dispute resolution process is a long, punishing battle for justice, then becoming educated about the law is a form of battle armor.

The importance of gaining specific knowledge also casts doubt on the singular role of formal education in shaping patterns of political participation. It is entirely possible that other unobserved variables related to earlier socialization, social networks, or family environment are more important in imbuing some people with the desire to become savvy engagers with the political system. Among the legal aid plaintiffs discussed below, many were shut out of educational opportunities because of bad timing as their schooling years coincided with the upheaval of the Cultural Revolution and nearly a decade of closed schools. When presented with opportunities to become knowledgeable about the law, they reacted with alacrity and made full use of the resources available notwithstanding their low levels of formal education. In other words, there may be other reasons for why certain types of people pursue education, either formal or informal, and these unknown variables may also be linked to their higher rates of political participation. As keenly displayed below, the narratives of these aggrieved workers with their stories of long-drawn-out legal battles, arguments with bosses and officials, and petitioning crusades to every available government office and media outlet certainly suggest personal characteristics that are not evenly distributed throughout the population. Once the political system opened up enough to allow workplace disputes to emerge out of the firm and into the courts, these people, even with low levels of formal education, took on the challenge and embarked on an education in the law.

Finally, there are complicating effects of experiential knowledge, the "learning by doing" that occurs through the process itself. This allows workers to synthesize what they have learned "by the book" with what they have learned "on the ground." At the end of the legal mobilization process, workers come to terms with their experience and pass judgment on themselves and on the legal system. Workers who believe that justice has been thwarted because of corruption or bias judge the system very harshly. Others come in with high expectations that are dampened down by the complicated realities of legal procedure and evidentiary burdens.

Law and Formal Education

Peng (SH200437) worked in the personnel department of a local SOE. In his thirties, he entered the workforce at the cusp of the transformation from socialist administration to market regulation. The state allocated his first job, sending him to the well-known Shanghai Watch Company, but then he decided to "jump" to a higher earning position, moving to an SOE in the financial sector where he was employed for nine years, but each year on a one-year contract. When he was fired, Peng decided to fight for severance compensation because after his last contract expired, he had continued to work for two months. He worked in personnel so thought that he was *"pretty familiar with labor law. (I) thought it was a comprehensive law that was intended to protect the rights of workers."* When his company refused to negotiate a settlement, Peng sought out specialized legal advice from newspapers and from free legal aid given in a Shanghai park by lawyers and students from a university legal aid center. He also visited a law firm, but didn't want to commit to paying in advance. As Peng researched his options, he realized that effective use of the law is difficult. The open consultation legal aid at the local park was crowded with so many people asking questions and seeking out representation, he noted that *"there are not enough people to receive all the complaints – so many people waiting in line. The lawyer can't explain everything completely, this is even worse for people who aren't well-educated."* Peng went to arbitration by himself with help and advice from the litigator who realized that he would lose the case there but could then appeal. *"I wanted Lawyer Xu to go to arbitration with me, but she said it was no use. She said "Just go to arbitration by yourself. If you win, you win. If you lose, we will go to court together."* Peng lost in arbitration and was severely disappointed by the quality of the arbitrator who he considered too young and inexperienced. Peng reported the low quality of the arbitrator to the petitioning office of the Labor Bureau and then prepared himself for the court case.

Peng won RMB 40,000 (USD 4,878) in severance and compensation at court and although the company appealed and delayed payment until Peng asked for enforcement through the courts, he eventually succeeded. Peng's formal education and background in law helped him navigate the long process and his experience served as a catalyst for other colleagues. He noted, *"I've become an expert in labor law and the legal process. I've learned a lot. I've also given consultation to many people, including many old co-workers. It's led to many more labor disputes at that company.*

I've also recommended legal aid to them. Many people have already gone there, plus I also tell them about the TV shows." He also found himself using his specialized knowledge at his new workplace, a large state-owned insurance company. *"I've given many suggestions on how to improve our labor contracts ... I helped standardize our labor relations ... we are also paying more in social insurance. One dispute has already happened while I've been with this company. A temporary worker was paying his own social insurance, but he was leaving and was going to sue us. I told my manager that what we are doing is obviously illegal. So we negotiated instead. We gave him the money (social insurance payments) back."* But Peng was not enthusiastic about the prospect of using the legal system again, noting how long, complicated, and risky the process was. *"I would try to make sure that things have improved. Better laws, more complete. A better guarantee of winning before suing again. Protect myself from retribution. If these things happened, then I would do it again. If not, then I would look for legal aid and also calculate my opportunity costs."*

Yao Li (SH200413) belonged to the "floating population" or "people from the outside" – designations used by city people to describe the millions of rural people who work in the city but are rarely able to become legal residents. Yao, from rural Jiangxi Province, had a college education, which at the time allowed her to relocate to Shanghai as her Japanese employer agreed to sponsor her hukou transfer. On a typical one-year contract, she also had a five-year service term with the company that required her to stay at the company for five years in exchange for training and the hukou transfer.

Yao's dispute began when she took a leave of absence from work to return to her home village following an industrial accident that injured some of her family members. Although she states that she had permission for the leave, when she returned to work she was demoted out of an office position to the factory. When she resigned in protest, the company demanded 20,000 RMB ($2439USD) for early abrogation of the service period. She refused and filed an arbitration claim against the company for the right to resign and receive severance compensation. Yao's experience was transformative, as she emphasized how she used the law to overcome her outsider status in Shanghai and how she learned to defend herself using her formal education and skills to do the work required in a lawsuit.

While Yao lost in arbitration and only received part of her demands in her first court appeal, she won overwhelmingly during the second appeal, receiving compensation for her termination and the right to leave the company freely. After one year of unemployment and the lawsuit, she found new employment in a Sino-French company. She attributed her success to her own hard work and the help she received from legal aid. She reported more confidence in herself now. She did a lot of research to find out what her rights were – she went to the library, found newspapers and magazines, read about legal aid in the *New People Evening News*. "*[The lawsuit] strengthened my personality, nobody can take away what is mine. I used to give up.*" She professed faith in using the law and legal institutions and would do so again, but also believed that it's always better to negotiate first. "*You should negotiate with good people, but with people who don't talk reason, you need the law.*" She was also critical of the law's inability to protect employees who are the weaker side in the employment relationship. Yao never petitioned, because as an outsider in Shanghai, she believed that no one "would even pay attention" to her. She continued to pay more attention to labor law after her dispute. She cried during the interview when discussing some of the hard parts of the lawsuit, but as she discussed her strategy and her determination in persevering to the end, including to applying to the court for enforcement of the final judgment, she sat up straight and spoke forcefully.

Yao's written documents attested to her abilities to rely on her own formal education. Unlike Zhao's petitioning letters, discussed below, that were scribbled in longhand and combined detailed citation of laws and regulations with conversational language, her letters to the company were typed and sent by registered mail. She listed by number the violations and the relevant laws and regulations. Yao was not devoid of emotion or nationalist outrage, however. She assailed the Japanese-invested company for treating its Chinese employees unfairly. In one letter, she accused her Japanese managers of "using Fascist methods to deprive me of the freedom to take leave so that I can search out legal support." She employed "rights talk," claiming that they have violated her "right to know" and her "right to work" – a basic right of the Chinese Constitution. Finally, she hoped that the company would proactively change its decision and its attitude, if not she was quite willing "to use law as a weapon to defend my due rights." In a second registered letter, after relations had grown worse, she invoked both rule of law and nationalism. "*China is a rule of law society. The Chinese people have long ago already stood up! As a 100% Japanese company, you cannot just have your way, forcing your Chinese employees to resign through terror and coercion! You cannot just evade your duties, allowing your base conduct to run amok in China! As for your disregard and violation of the People's Republic of China*

Labor Law and Labor Contract Law, I solemnly express my strongest protest!"

Yao utilized her own skills and capacity to write up her own initial arbitration claim made prior to her legal claim, checking it with legal aid experts for accuracy. She also brought the company back to court twice after the final judgment on her own with no legal assistance, first to seek enforcement of the compensation award and second, to require the company to issue her a notice of termination, without which one cannot be legally employed elsewhere. Yao credited her experience for strengthening her resolve and her awareness about her rights at the workplace. She noted that she checked her new labor contract thoroughly and now pays attention to labor cases in the media. Although she identified as an "outsider" in Shanghai, her formal education set her apart from true "peasant workers," rural migrants who work in Shanghai but can rarely get access to legal urban status (Tang and Yang 2009).

Law and Formal Education: Becoming a Leader

Hong (SH200438) was a middle manager in a large Sino-Australian joint venture that was nearing the end of its twenty-year term.[3] As the company prepared for its dissolution, a large number of employees worried about their employment security and their chances for severance pay in the event of termination. When the headquarters in Beijing announced that only workers with over ten years tenure would receive severance pay, employees in the Shanghai branch decided to mobilize. Hong was voted in as their representative because he was better educated, more confident, and skillful than many other workers. While he had a vague notion of his rights at the workplace, he began to actively research labor laws and regulations on the Internet in preparation for the case. He became known as the resident expert in labor law and was asked by co-workers and friends for assistance. He found a chart in a popular local paper on how to calculate compensation for early termination and used it to prepare for negotiation. He visited the office of the general manager and tried to negotiate a solution. The company, fearful of the precedent it would set across all of its operations across the country, declined to reach a

---

[3] The dissolution of the joint venture was largely due to changes in the restrictions on foreign investment following China's accession to the WTO. The Australian company wanted to form a wholly foreign-owned subsidiary going forward, so the joint venture was dissolved when its term expired.

compromise. Hong filed a collective claim in arbitration for himself and over 100 other workers.

Hong did not receive legal aid during the early and middle stages of the dispute, doing everything on his own and trying to keep the large group of employees together, despite their different statuses and contract specifics. The company issued a document specifying lack of severance for all but ten workers and invited workers who disagreed to seek resolution through the legal system. Hong followed these instructions to the letter, filing an arbitration claim against the company. His complaint was successful, resulting in a combined award of RMB 1.6 million (USD 195,121) for all the workers whose contracts had not expired when the joint venture was liquidated. However, nearly half of the plaintiffs did not receive any severance as their contracts had expired prior to this date, depriving them of compensation for early termination.

Hong turned to legal aid when the company contested the arbitration ruling in civil court.[4] Hong worried that he did not understand complex legal procedures. While he had been successful on his own, it was a lot of work and time and required much coordination to keep the group together. Legal aid was a tool to improve his chances and balance against the company, which had hired an experienced lawyer. At the court proceedings, the employee group agreed to judicial mediation at the judge's encouragement. In the end, the company agreed to pay 80 percent of the 1.6 million RMB arbitral award plus an additional 50 percent compensation to the employees whose legal claims had been rejected. The plaintiffs' legal aid litigator praised the mediation as a just solution – granting the employees immediate compensation, curtailing further litigation, and providing "moral compensation" to those plaintiffs who were not legally entitled. Hong's confidence is apparent in his desire to continue to rely on legal institutions. While he clearly acknowledges problems with the legal system, he believes that more utilization will pressure the courts to improve. "*I would definitely sue again. And I tell all my friends; I tell them the same thing. I give them help, support, and advice. If other people did the same to protect their rights, if more people use the legal system, it will improve, become more responsible, with higher costs for people who violate the law.*"

---

[4] As noted in chapter 3, labor arbitration is a compulsory step in the dispute resolution process, but it is not binding. Either side can contest the arbitral decision in civil court litigation. While often colloquially referred to as "two appeals," the first court hearing is a de novo hearing of the case. In general, the disputants may also appeal that first judicial decision to the next level, usually the intermediate level court of the locality.

Hong's sense of confidence in himself and in the legal system comes, of course, at least partially from a very successful outcome. But similar dynamics exist even when the end result is less ideal. Chen and Jin (SH200447) were interviewed together as the two leaders of a collective dispute involving twelve workers against a restructuring SOE. Both had higher levels of education and had worked in low-level management at the company. They had experience with labor law through the workplace and were chosen by their fellow workers to lead them in a fight for employment security. As with many SOE restructurings, this enterprise had already gone through many changes. These employees were part of a merger between two SOEs in 1992. In 1998, when this company began to fail, many of the original workers were sent back to the original SOE. In 2000, these twelve workers were simply laid off and given a small monthly stipend of 290 RMB (about USD$35). In 2003, the money stopped completely. Jin, with forty-two years of tenure, was in danger of losing his pension and retirement security if he lost his connection to the work unit less than a year from retirement. Chen, with twenty-six years of tenure, did not believe that he would survive in the new economy. Along with their colleagues, they pursued the case in order to have some security and some attachment to a work unit as they approached old age. They note, *"we had the highest education and the best knowledge of law, it's natural that we would do it together. We held many meetings about how to do the lawsuit. After this, I have learned a lot. I myself have become a little expert."* They also describe a long process of diversion and channeling as state officials redirect them away from petitioning toward the law. As SOE workers they tried hard to leverage connections to the state, visiting the city government, the trade union, the labor bureau, and the labor inspection bureau, all to no avail. The state pushed them to arbitration and litigation and to the educative process of legal mobilization. *"We had to hurry up because of the 60 day expiration [to file an arbitration claim]. We had already studied the labor law so we knew about this regulation. He (Jin) had taken classes in law, learned a few things about labor law. It used to be that labor regulations were all internal. We didn't know. We couldn't know. It's not like that now with so much media dissemination, newspapers and the Internet. Everyone can find out ... We knew that we could use the law to protect our rights."*

In the aftermath of their lawsuit, Chen and Jin were pessimistic about the law's ability to protect their rights. They noted the long, difficult process of a collective dispute. It was hard to keep the twelve workers together; each separate legal claim had to be pursued individually so that they filed three claims for salary, for social insurance, and for their housing fund payments. *"After two years, we are really tired. Both the labor arbitrators and the judges sympathized with us because we are the victims."* In their evaluations of the law, they were gloomy about its prospects. *"Implementation is too weak, the law has too many holes, legal consciousness is not high enough. There is no punishment when enterprises withhold wages."* Although they conceded that the procedures and the officials were *"relatively just,"* they had gained enough knowledge to judge the system's failures and problems. They also spread the word, noting *"we now consult with a lot of other family and friends, we tell them how they should sue."*

Law and Informal Learning: From Petitioner to Citizen Representative

Zhao (SH200449), born in 1957, was sent down during the Cultural Revolution to a farm in Subei, a poor rural part of Jiangsu Province. He stayed there until 1977, losing out on educational opportunities and facing a period of unemployment upon his return to the Shanghai. Finally, in 1984, he inherited his mother's SOE position. The practice of passing on one's position to a child was common in the SOE sector and was especially important in the early 1980s to relieve the unemployment of rusticated youth as they returned to the cities to restart their interrupted lives. Zhao's company formed a Chinese–foreign joint venture with a Korean firm in the early 1990s and Zhao signed an open-ended contract with the joint venture in 1997. Two years later, due to restructuring and the buy-out of the foreign partner, Zhao was laid off and put in a precarious legal and economic position, as the central state signaled its support for massive restructuring of the public sector. Zhao's employer shut down and sold the worksite to a local hospital. Control of the former employer was transferred to a large state-owned group in charge of restructuring many defunct municipal SOEs. While Zhao was allocated a small living stipend, the succeeding enterprise's management offered him new employment at a new firm under new conditions with a short-term contract and low pay. As a middle-aged, poorly educated, former rusticated worker, Zhao was fearful that this move would sever his relationship with his former employer and leave him to the vagaries of the market. He refused and began to petition, seeking out the government and the media at various levels to resolve his case.

The petitioning system (*xinfang*) has its roots in the Imperial Period, but was also encouraged by the CCP as a way to link the masses to the party via direct contact and supplication (Minzner 2006). Chinese citizens can write letters, visit petitioning offices, and now also petition online. Petitioning can be used to expose corruption, plea for intervention in a private dispute, and alert higher levels of government to malfeasance at lower levels of government. Zhao became a petitioning expert. In a two year time period, he petitioned over twenty-five times, including all major government and trade union offices in Shanghai. After exhausting recourse to the offices in Shanghai, he turned to Beijing, petitioning twice to the State Council, the All China Federation of Trade Unions (ACFTU) and the Ministry of Labor. During his first petitioning sojourn to Beijing he was apprehended by Shanghai police who sent staff to Beijing to look for Shanghai petitioners. Once returned to Shanghai, Old Zhao put a sign around his neck and walked around outside the gate of his former employer, demanding that the enterprise continue to pay him a basic salary based on the minimum wage until he reached retirement age at fifty-five. (He was then in his mid-forties.) Zhao feared that his low level of education and his age would prevent him from finding new employment in the non-state sectors. He was also angry that he had missed out on his own opportunities because of political campaigns during his youth, but could be just tossed out by his state employer when circumstances (and reform policies) changed. In his petitioning, he emphasized this moral reasoning as well as the corrupt and shady behavior of enterprise management during the restructuring.

In addition to petitioning to over twenty-five offices, in Shanghai and in the capital, Zhao also attempted to use traditional socialist institutions at the workplace to stop the restructuring of the factory where he had been employed. He called on management to hold a Workers Representative Committee meeting to vote on the restructuring plan. The enterprise's trade union (part of the CCP-dominated ACFTU) was, he alleged, "bought out" by management and did not help other workers. Zhao was initially joined by over thirty workers in this mobilization to reverse the restructuring plan. However, they were bought off one by one and given individual severance packages until only he was left. Zhao's strategies, while traditional, increasingly utilized his growing legal knowledge as he researched laws and regulations on SOE restructuring, labor law, bankruptcy proceedings, and policies designed for low-income residents. His petitioning letter to the Beijing government cited laws and regulations on foreign investment, employment, early retirement policies, and payment of social insurance. Even before he engaged with legal aid two years into his dispute, he had used considerable time and resources to educate himself about the various laws and regulations that might help his case. He reported spending over 3,000 RMB ($365 USD) on books about the labor law and contract law.

Zhao's petitioning proved to be a dead end. For each letter he sent, regardless of where he sent it, responses came from the enterprise group in charge of his factory's restructuring, the defendant in his lawsuit! His letters to Premier Wen Jiabao, the ACFTU, the Central Disciplinary and Inspection Committee (CDIC), the *Xinmin* Evening News were all passed back directly to his former employer for a response. Each letter repeated the same message – Zhao should accept his fate; he should accept the new positions that he has been offered; he should "change his way of thinking" and "solve his subsistence problems with labor from his own two hands." As he accounted in another petitioning letter to Beijing, when he meets with the enterprise manager, Comrade Shen, Zhao was ridiculed and taunted. Zhao quoted Shen in the petition as saying, "you can sue, and you can write letters, and you can petition, but in the end it is me who answers these letters and my future response will be the same as my past responses." In a final petitioning letter to the central government, Zhao used Shen's words to justify his long petitioning battle: "*He (Shen) closes the door like that to any resolution! With no alternative, I feel I must come to Beijing to report, I hope that the Mayor and responsible leaders will quickly and properly resolve[this dispute], allowing me to return home as early as possible to take care of my aged mother.*"

As petitioning proved fruitless, Zhao turned to the legal system wholeheartedly. He tried two district government legal aid offices but both refused to take his case, one for jurisdictional reasons and the other because he failed the means test. Finally, he received legal aid from the labor law legal aid center at ECUPL. As Zhao's dispute progressed through arbitration and then litigation, he became more interested in new legal protections for workers. He began to study laws and legal cases in the newspapers despite that prior to his dispute he "never even read newspapers or books." He began to sit in on court cases to observe how other cases are decided. Finally, as his dispute began to wind down, he began to assist other workers and former colleagues in their own disputes. As a "citizen representative" entitled under PRC civil procedure norms to represent private parties in civil litigation, Zhao won three labor cases in court for friends. He proudly boasted that his win of RMB 18,000 (USD 2,195) for a colleague attracted the attention of the opposing lawyer who had never been able to win such a large settlement in a labor dispute.

The resolution of Zhao's own dispute was underwhelming from a monetary compensation standpoint, but it guaranteed his long-term connection to the enterprise succeeding to his former employer. He received a paltry amount of compensation, the gap between what the company was paying him as a stipend and what they would have paid as minimum wage. The arbitration committee rejected his claim for compensatory damages for the withholding of the correct wages for "lack of evidence." The decision also split the RMB 300 (USD 36) fee between Zhao and the employer, a clear sign of the committee's intent to show favor to both sides. In the negotiation stage, he rejected a negotiated offer of RMB 50,000 (USD 6,097) to buy out his work tenure, instead choosing to remain as a formal employee of a defunct company. For Zhao, this was preferable to complete abrogation of the labor relationship. He received the minimum wage salary as a basic guarantee of livelihood but he does not have to go to work at the factory, because it no longer exists. Most importantly, he would still have his retirement pension when he turns fifty-five years old. Although the enterprise contested the arbitration award in civil court, the courts continued to support Zhao's case.

Zhao was not overly sanguine about the formal resolution system or the political system after his dispute ended. He was bitter that China's labor laws have become too protective of employers, especially in Shanghai. He complained that too many laws and regulations were still not public, unknown to the regular person who appears at the courthouse. He traced these problems back to the political structure, that there is *"only one party without supervision."* He had lost faith in the Labor Bureau's hotline for legal advice and consultation, believing that it is only there to *"trick the regular people."* He preferred instead to read documents and new laws on his own, to cultivate relationships with people in the courts so that they would tell him about new internal regulations. He planned new letters and petitions to the media to expose problems of corruption and ineptitude in the bureaucracies. But Zhao was energized by his experience, reporting that he doesn't regret the experience at all, it was *"an exercise"* – a learning experience that helped fuel his new work as a citizen representative.

Zhao's torturous road through petitioning and litigation was an educative experience. He actively pursued learning about the law and availed himself of all the possible tools to do so – the media (including case reports in newspapers), books, sitting in on the courts, reading documents, calling the government hotline, consulting with knowledgeable friends, and gaining specialized knowledge from legal aid. While the financial compensation gained from the proceedings was small, he was overwhelmingly successful in his goal of employment security and the assurance of a pension. Even when there was no real employment to be had, he preserved his right to a state pension, which then gave him the basic income guarantee that allowed him to continue his work as an informal labor law expert. In 2013, he was still helping other workers with their labor grievances in formal legal proceedings. As the discussion in Chapter 5 details, Zhao's metamorphosis from a socialist worker to a litigious "citizen representative" is unusual. Many aggrieved workers of his generation were also pushed to the law via an unsuccessful petitioning sojourn, but rarely were they able to appropriate the law effectively as a tool for protection for themselves, much less others.

Experiential Knowledge: Law on the Ground not by the Book

Higher levels of education and legal knowledge improve the dispute experience, with legal knowledge, in particular, contributing to beliefs about the effectiveness of litigation even for those with negative dispute experiences. The educative process of legal mobilization contributed to a greater sense of internal efficacy and confidence, even when these litigants were more cynical and skeptical of the legal institutions themselves (Gallagher 2006). However, even in this group, unusual in their access to legal representation, some litigants were utterly disaffected, condemning the legal system wholesale for its inability to provide what they consider "just" results. The dominant factor among this group of disaffected disputants is the suspicion that the law cannot function properly because of bias and corruption. These disputants believe that powerful state firms and influential foreign investors can pull connections and use the allure of gifts and bribery to swing the results in their favor. In the cases highlighted below, plaintiffs recount the pathway of disenchantment, which begins with confidence and knowledge that they know the law and are in the right to feelings of despair and anger that the facts of the case matter less than the identities of those involved.

Qian (SH200436) was confident in his abilities and in the law to protect his rights. He was a former SOE worker in his mid-fifties with a technical degree in mechanical engineering who had "jumped into the sea" of the market economy at the end of the 1990s. In 2001 he was unemployed and visited a local job fair looking for new opportunities. He was hired on the spot by a Chinese-foreign (Hong Kong) joint venture in real estate development and golf course construction. The Taiwanese boss of the joint venture was out of the country and his manager resisted his requests for a formal labor contract, telling Qian that the labor contract would be settled when the boss returned. After five months of no pay, Qian quarreled with his manager over the continuing failure to conclude an employment contract and the lack of pay. The next day the joint venture office locks were changed and Qian found himself again unemployed and without several months of pay. He filed a claim against the company at labor arbitration. Qian considered the case "simple" and "clear": he had worked for the company and had not been properly compensated. Qian considered himself well-educated and familiar with the law. He had even received special legal training at his previous employer. He did not seek out a lawyer or legal aid but pursued the case himself.

Qian lost in arbitration on the grounds that he did not have a formal labor contract. Without a formal labor contract, the arbitration committee ruled that it was unable to determine the existence of a labor relationship and thus there was nothing to support his claims for compensation. Qian filed a separate arbitration request for social insurance benefits; this was also rejected. Upon losing arbitration, Qian realized that the case was not simple because the labor law's emphasis on a written labor contract provided a loophole for companies that wanted to evade their legal responsibilities to employees. He continued to mobilize the law for his protection, but he looked to legal experts, reading up on newspaper articles on the issue and seeking out legal aid at several places. He then contested the arbitration claim in civil court.

Qian's lawyers instructed him to collect evidence that attested to his employment at the company. In all, he compiled over twenty pieces of evidence that confirmed an employment relationship, including a registered letter from the district electric bureau to the company that included Qian's name as the company's contact person and internal company documents that listed Qian as an employee. The Shanghai Municipal Trade Union also supported the case and made this known to the court. But all of this was to no avail. Qian and his seasoned legal team lost both the first and second instance civil litigation. In his lawyers' six-page written appeal to the Intermediate Court, they charged the courts with fraud, bribery, and perversion of justice.

In discussion with Qian after the case, his dejection was clear. "*I used to think law was just. Now this case has made me lose my confidence in the law. The people who used these tricks to avoid the law are the* ones who determine how the law works. Many people sue because they have confidence in the law; (but) many people don't believe in the law so (they) use non-legal measures." Qian's new lack of confidence in the legal system comes directly from his impression that those with power and connections easily manipulate the law. "*At the center law is just, but as it goes down to the lower levels it gets twisted.*" In explaining his disenchantment, Qian disentangled "law," which is made at the center, and its enforcement, which is done locally. "*Both court appeals – there was no difference with arbitration. The same logic applied from the arbitration claim. (They) knew that there was this loophole. Those who won understand law, (and) used this loophole. Not a problem with the law, but a problem with the system.*" Qian's deep distrust in the ability of the courts to act fairly was heavily influenced by the opinions of his litigators, who believed that the preponderance of evidence demonstrating a labor relationship would close the loophole in the law. In a written evaluation of the case after the fact, the legal aid lawyers questioned why the courts did not apply Supreme Court explanations that they believed applied to the case, further insinuating that government intervention into the case had occurred to protect the Hong Kong investor.

Qian interpreted his disenchantment as a problem with the "system" not the law itself. "*I've lost confidence in law, but this is not my personal tragedy, it's the law's tragedy. Law is our last choice, if that choice is also useless, then we really don't have anywhere to go.*" Among the disenchanted, Qian's articulation of desperation is common. Pei (SH20042), an older worker who was transferred from his SOE to a Chinese-foreign (Hong Kong) joint venture, was fired after he sued the joint venture for an occupational injury suffered during a fight with a person trying to enter the factory compound. (Pei was then working as a guard at the joint venture.) He recounted in an interview a long process of multiple lawsuits, confusing procedures, and ultimate failure. When asked if he would resort to the law again, he vehemently exclaimed, "*No way. I couldn't stand it. It's been enough. On my new job, I'm also on a one-year contract, it's not stable; actually, I can be let go at any time. I no longer believe in labor law. The rule of law has nothing advantageous for the common person. I know the law; (but) the case (decision) is wrong. The work-unit knows people in the court and at the labor bureau. (I have) no proof but suspect it. There is a conspiracy. They have money, while I have none.*"

Ding (SH201301) was a middle-aged migrant worker from Anhui Province who worked in the Shanghai suburbs for nearly twenty years. He had long-term, stable employment at a corporatized SOE that produced commercial water heaters, but the hard work and the unsafe conditions ruined his health. He suffered from black lung disease and hearing loss. In 2010, his enterprise struggled and finally laid many middle-aged migrants off. One by one as these workers looked for new employment, they discovered their health predicament. Not only were they unemployable – as they failed any medical exam they were given to qualify for new employment – they faced heavy medical expenses and long-term chronic disease. Ding and a fellow migrant worker from Chongqing, Lu (SH201302), found assistance at legal aid and began a collective lawsuit against the employer for proper diagnosis and insurance for occupational disease and injury. Ding, as the more outspoken and confident person, educated himself about the law, looking at books while sitting in bookstore aisles, reading the newspaper, and researching on the Internet. He first looked to the government for redress – petitioning and inquiring at various government offices including the local district government, the Health Bureau, and the municipal trade union. But he was constantly directed to more formalized channels – first arbitration and then litigation. His employer refused to negotiate or engage in mediation, which also left him little choice but to pursue more formal and ultimately legal channels.

While his case started as a group of workers suing together, they were fragmented and separated into individual cases during the arbitration process. Ding's evidence and his employment contract worked to his advantage. He received occupational injury compensation from the employer and now has a safety net to help him pay his long-term medical expenses. His other coworkers were not so lucky, and none of them is now employable given their health conditions. Lu, who was also represented by legal aid, was denied compensation because of the timing of his termination. After a year of waiting, he finally lost the case in court, which upheld the original arbitration decision. Ding's attitude about his own legal experience is that it was successful due to the help, advice, and strategy from legal aid, but also because the government expressed support for his claims. The government felt pressure after a famous case in 2009 when Zhang Haichao, a migrant worker with black lung disease, underwent open chest surgery to prove his disease (Dongfang Jinbao 2009; China Labour Bulletin 2010). Ding believed that this case helped him a lot. It put social pressure on the government to intervene in cases like his. Ding's interpretation was that the courts work when the government allows them to work well. Individual claimants must bring attention to their claims to elicit the government's attention and support

Even before their claims, Ding and Lu had some sense of their rights under China's new labor laws. Once they began to suspect their illnesses, they requested a non-fixed term contract as a hedge against termination and lack of social insurance. When this request led the company to lower their salaries and force them out, they began to look for legal assistance on-line. They knew that they could not possibly manage the complicated processes of proving an occupational disease and obtaining government-approved evidence. After discovering that private lawyers were too expensive, they found legal aid on the Internet. "*We just searched on Baidu, looking for something that helps peasant workers protect their rights, and [the legal aid center] just appeared. I called ahead to make an appointment and then came with all my materials. They helped us defend our rights for the past three years. During all of it, Lawyer Zheng has done everything.*" Ding and Lu's path to the law corroborates the argument offered by Becker (2012) about the importance of urban ties to foster legal mobilization. These migrant workers rely on factory co-workers and legal aid lawyers, not native-place ties and informal associations. According to Ding, their early action on black lung sparked new waves of lawsuits that continue to inundate their former workplace.

Ding's case materials are as impressive in their complexity as Yao's – even more so given the difficult nature of occupational disease cases and the need to gain government certification of the disease before the suit can be processed. However, Ding and his fellow workers were much more dependent on their legal aid lawyer than either Yao or Zhao. They relied on him to do "everything." Just as the government showing support was important, these plaintiffs required knowledgeable and competent legal assistance to pursue their claims. In the end, Ding was mostly successful as he received compensation, though it's unlikely that he will be formally employed again. His colleague, Lu, who sued alongside of him was denied compensation because his employment contract had expired before he was diagnosed with black lung. Yet even Lu, still unsuccessful in gaining compensation and unemployable in his early forties, was relatively optimistic about formal legal processes and institutions. He noted that he still believes in the law because "if you just go out and create a disturbance, there are some things that still cannot be resolved." Ding and Lu had more faith in the law despite various obstacles to gaining complete redress, including the time required to resolve the case, which for Ding was three years and for Lu lasted another year and ended in failure. While both workers had been involved in strikes before, they did not believe "creating a disturbance" would work for their cases. Engagement with formal legal processes had tamed their expectations and their behavior.[5]

CONCLUSION

The cases described here involve workers of different generations, of different hukou, with varying types of disputes and individual situations. One common thread in their dispute narratives is the role of *being or becoming educated*. Given the different backgrounds and situations of these disputants, learning emerges in disparate ways but the role of education is a constant throughout and was a theme raised again and again by legal aid plaintiffs. Yao is educated, a university graduate, but an outsider in Shanghai. Her educational credentials imbue her with internal confidence to learn about the law to fight against her employer. As with Zhao, self-education and confidence building (as well as consciousness-raising) are important parts of her story. Her confidence in her own efficacy leads to subsequent use of the courts as well as attempts to avoid recourse to ex post adjudication by legal institutions through more law and regulation-based practices at the workplace. She will check her next contract; she will pay attention to these issues as a means to avoid having a bad experience at the next workplace.

In Zhao's case, he is uneducated, a classic example of the "lost generation" of the Cultural Revolution who returned to the city too late for educational opportunities. For him the process of legal mobilization involves self-education and via knowledge, a kind of empowerment. Law is a tool that is given to him by the state. He then wields it in his individual battle against an SOE. He deftly appropriates the law and has fun with it. While he is critical of the political system, he interacts with it constantly and brings his friends and colleagues to it as well. Chapter 5 turns to a more in-depth examination of the generational differences exhibited in the different mobilization stories of Yao and Zhao, but among the older generation he is somewhat unusual in his enthusiastic embrace and mastery of legality.

Ding and Lu, with low education and migrant status, learn law vicariously through the assistance they receive in legal aid. Although they pay attention to the law and seek out legal information, they see the courts as a way to involve the state in the delineation and enforcement of their

---

[5] See Becker (2012) for general patterns of migrant mobilization.

legal rights after they are rebuffed by local labor officials. As migrant workers with low education they believe that they need others for rights-protection, both legal aid and the government. But they also express belief in the law because getting to a trial showed the government's concern for their case. They do not have a personal sense of empowerment like Zhao, but rather a sense of fulfillment that others, including the state, are paying attention and coming to their help. However, they are not passive; they use their recognized political status as a "weak group" to entreat support from the government and the media. Ding also reports that he has helped others with similar disputes, providing evidence for a co-worker in another case. He also notes that the company now "hates" them for drawing attention to the problem of occupational disease. Many more cases have been filed at the firm since their case began three years ago.

China's Legal Dissemination Campaign began in the mid-1980s. Since that time, the government has invested a significant amount of time and resources in teaching the population about law at schools, the workplaces, and in the media. In the case narratives above, disputants make use of these resources to become informed consumers of legal institutions. In some cases, they make up for a lack in formal education and become seasoned experts, helping friends and colleagues with similar problems. While we see the important effects of education and specific knowledge among the general population as well, the role of experience looms large in leading people away from the law. This may not be unique to China, as Relis and others have found evidence that citizens with close interactions with the legal system tend to evaluate it more negatively (Relis 2002).

Since the 1950s modernization theory has put great emphasis on the role of education in fostering political change (Lipset 1959). Models of political participation also show the importance of education as part of the standard resource explanation for variation in political participation across the citizenry (Brady, Verba, and Schlozman 1995). However, the causal role of education in political change is not well understood (Acemoglu et al. 2005). Rather broad processes of increased education, urbanization, and more sophisticated communication are associated with equally broad phenomenon such as increased political participation, social mobilization, and democratization. This chapter went beneath those broad trends to show in a specific context how citizens use education and knowledge (often provided by the state itself) to engage with their political institutions. While political participation in authoritarian regimes is, by definition, circumscribed and restricted, the Chinese state's promotion of rule of law and its encouragement of rights-protection by aggrieved workers has expanded the space for political participation. But the effects are contradictory. The citizenry is more active, engaged, and discriminating. In gaining knowledge about rights on the book, they feel empowered to engage in rights-protection. Disputants, however, are more critical in their evaluation of legal institutions and less enthusiastic about future iterations of legal mobilization.

5

Great Expectations

The Disparate Effects of Legal Mobilization

> I used to think that the law was just. Now this case has made me lose confidence in the law. The people who used these tricks to avoid the law are the ones who determine how the law works. Many people sue because they have confidence in the law. Many people don't believe in the law, so they use extra legal measures. I've lost confidence in law. Not my personal tragedy, it's the law's tragedy. Law is our last choice. If that choice is not worth it, then we really don't have anywhere to go.
>
> (SH200436)

Legal mobilization is the act of engaging with the legal system to solve a problem. It necessarily involves being exposed to legal instruments (like contracts), gaining legal experience, and interacting with judicial actors, legal professionals, and the institutions in which they work. Through this process an individual's attitudes and evaluations of these institutions change as they become more familiar with the legal realm, its vocabularies, and its landscape. Law, which once seemed distant and grand, becomes close and in focus. Positive attitudes toward and confidence in the legal system are important to generate citizen trust and legitimacy of the government. Trust in the legal system can also inculcate citizens with the values to resolve disputes legally and peacefully, to accept defeat, and to distinguish between procedural and substantive justice. In democracies, these values are important to sustain democratic rule. In authoritarian China, the construction of a modern legal system is also inextricably linked to many Party objectives: the attempt to build more effective and efficient governance and in turn provide the necessary infrastructure for a market economy; to enable the center to monitor and control local power; to persuade citizens to accept legal adjudication of disputes and grievances; and to rule in a less repressive manner while still maintaining power and control. Legal reform, then, is a substitute for democratization, not a precursor to it. Creating positive citizen attitudes toward the legal system is part of a strategy to avoid democracy by supplying some functions of a legal system without the complementary institutions that accompany it in a liberal democracy such as a representative government, an independent judiciary, a vibrant civil society, or a free press.

In this chapter, I examine legal mobilization patterns that followed the Chinese state's rhetorical switch to rule of law, its promulgation of protective workplace rights, and the expansion of legal propaganda and education to increase legal rights awareness among the population. Unlike Chapter 4, which focused on the common role that education and knowledge has in bringing people to the legal system and encouraging aggrieved workers to make use of the law and legal institutions, this chapter examines legal mobilization's *disparate* effects on citizens through three focused comparisons. First, I examine what kinds of people use the legal system to protect their workplace rights. By examining differences between users and non-users, we can see who selects legal mobilization as a pathway to justice and compare differences in attitude and behaviors between users and non-users. Chapter 4 established that legal experience does not inculcate users with enhanced trust and confidence in legal institutions. Here I use in-depth follow-up interviews with survey respondents that reported experiencing a labor grievance to explore how actual contact with the law can bring about disenchantment. For disputants who missed the opportunity to engage with the law, the law is still majestic and inspiring, but far away. For those who tackled their problems with the law, they are almost uniformly disappointed and dejected.

In the second comparison, I examine these dejected disputants by contrasting them with the Shanghai group that had access to high-quality legal aid and representation. Representation is a critical problem in labor disputes as the trade union system does not function well as a representative or advocating institution and many legal professionals are loath to take on labor cases that are both hard to win and offer little chance of large fees and billing (Michelson 2006). This comparison reinforces the importance of legal aid/representation to outcomes and subjective understandings of legal outcomes.

Finally, in the third comparison, I examine differences within this group of legal aid recipients, focusing on two "political generations": those workers who came of age during the stage of mature state socialism and those who entered the labor force in the reform era, after the initial construction of the labor contract system. These comparisons move in concentric circles from the largest differences to the smallest: users vs. non-users, users with legal aid vs. users without any legal representation, and a within-group comparison among users with legal aid.

The law's disparate effects are not unexpected. China's construction of legality is an instrumental, state-led project employed as a means to reform social and economic institutions, not an end in itself. It was put into place *not* to manage or govern existing social institutions or norms, but to utterly transform them: to smash iron rice bowls, to reduce dependency on the state, and to build commodity, services, property, and labor markets, all of which were non-existent in the Maoist era. The aforementioned three comparisons get at these intentional "functions" of law; however, they also reveal unintended consequences of authoritarian legality. At the most general level, the widespread dissemination of legal knowledge and awareness contributes to people's willingness to invoke legal rights. This first comparison shows that until people have personal experience with the law, they are prone to see it as a potential resource, an authoritative institution that offers protection. Engagement with the law and gaining legal experience can have a transformative effect, shifting people from vague enchantment to informed disenchantment, from casual believer to cynical utilizer (Gallagher 2006). The second comparison, focusing on legal representation, exposes the problems of legality without institutional complementarity. As a 'fire-alarm' mechanism for labor law enforcement, workers' legal mobilization is an extremely individualized process in the context of weak civil society support, limited access to legal aid, and repression of labor activists and their organizations. Most claimants go through the process without legal representation due to the high cost of legal counsel and limited availability of legal aid. The ability of such claimants to learn is limited and bad experiences are more likely to lead to complete rejection of the legal system. Legal experience mediated by legal aid contributes to better processes and substantive outcomes. More importantly, disputants with access to legal aid tend to have more positive interpretations of their outcomes (whether good or bad) and of the legal process that delivered those outcomes. They highlight their own mistakes due to unfamiliarity alongside their decreased faith in the institutions. But they believe in the possibility of better outcomes in the future via enhanced internal efficacy and the availability of quality legal assistance.

Finally, turning to differences within the privileged group of claimants who went through the process with professional and gratis legal assistance, I show that the state's use of the law as a mechanism to disrupt existing social cleavages has been largely successful. Socialist workers experienced the adoption of workplace legality as a diminution of their previous social and political status. When forced into the legal arena by a state that was actively cutting the ties of the socialist contract, they found the law to be inadequate. It did not protect them from what they feared most – the loss of employment security. It did not honor their particular history as a generation of citizens who, despite being born during the promise of the founding of the PRC, met with misfortune throughout their lives; in their early years the Cultural Revolution blocked educational attainment and their later years were rocked by reforms and restructuring. As this generation moves on into retirement, the generation taking its place has lower expectations about workplace security and understands the state has diminished obligations. As this generation ages and as migrant workers become more thoroughly integrated into urban institutions, expectations for social inclusion and security will grow, but the starting point of their expectations is already lower.

This last comparison between generations underlines one of the key functions of authoritarian legality: the law acts as a device to empower some and to disenfranchise others. Even among marginalized groups, whether older socialist era workers or young rural migrants, the law has had disparate effects. In their desire to keep employment ties with declining state firms, older socialist workers found that law was impotent. At best, the law might vindicate their broader demands for employment security with a monetary settlement. Rural migrants, on the other hand, with lower expectations and smaller claims, had better outcomes and more positive experiences. Even more importantly, they experienced the process of legal mobilization differently, as a process of inclusion into a system that had long ignored the basic plight of migrants and *any* rights they might have.

LEGAL EXPERIENCE AND INFORMED DISENCHANTMENT

Michaelson (2007) points out that in understanding Chinese patterns of legal mobilization, we should understand first who is more likely to identify a grievance and then ask who among those with grievances is more likely to mobilize the law for resolution. In the 2005 LLMS, 319 respondents (8.6 percent) reported that they had experienced labor problems over the last ten years. Common problems involved contract termination or change, working hours, compensation, social insurance, and occupational injury. But what kinds of people are more likely to identify a workplace problem? Identification of a problem obviously means that the person perceived something was wrong, which may indicate that their workplaces are more likely to be problematic. However, this is not necessarily the case. Perception of a problem also requires knowledge and consciousness about what legally compliant workplace practices should be. Perception of a workplace problem may also be an indication of the individual's ability to correctly identify and name legal violations.

In statistical analysis of those 2005 respondents who reported having a labor problem, respondents with higher levels of education, formal labor contracts, employment at foreign-invested enterprises (FIEs), and in the manufacturing and construction sectors are statistically more likely to report labor problems. (See Table 5.1). In the 2010 CULS, a similar analysis using dispute experience as the dependent variable also finds that survey respondents with higher levels of education are more likely to have experienced labor disputes, as discussed in Chapter 4.

Working in the foreign-invested sector is also positively associated with the initiation of a dispute but the effect is small (Cai and Wang 2012, 22). Legal residency status (*hukou*) and gender are not significant, but older respondents are less likely to experience a dispute. However, the 2010 CULS finds that workers with labor contracts are slightly less likely to initiate disputes compared to those without labor contracts. This difference between the 2005 and 2010 surveys is explained by the enhanced formal protections provided in recent Chinese labor legislation. Both the 2008 Labor Contract Law and Labor Dispute Mediation and Arbitration Law increased the opportunities for informal workers to make legal claims against employers, including longer statute of limitations and explicitly-directed strict penalties for failure to sign formal labor contracts. Therefore, the later survey shows evidence of increased legal mobilization of workers in the informal sector, which was one of the key goals of the 2008 laws.

These individual determinants of dispute experience indicate that people with higher levels of education and some degree of engagement with law and assumed legal protection already (i.e. the existence of a labor contract) have the knowledge and the awareness to identify workplace legal violations. Workplace determinants, including foreign investment and presence in the manufacturing/construction sector, provide greater opportunity for disputes to occur. Foreign-invested workplaces are more

TABLE 5.1. *Likelihood of Experiencing a Workplace Problem*

Variables	Problem (1)	(2)	(3)
Age group	0.960	0.940	0.931
	(0.057)	(0.057)	(0.058)
Edu. group	1.173*	1.195**	1.194**
	(0.097)	(0.101)	(0.101)
Contract	1.443***	1.499***	1.455***
	(0.189)	(0.201)	(0.200)
SOE	1.054	1.008	0.953
	(0.153)	(0.151)	(0.152)
FIE	1.760**	1.759**	1.735**
	(0.465)	(0.465)	(0.460)
Gov/party	1.046	1.040	0.980
	(0.197)	(0.196)	(0.195)
Manu. & construct.	1.272*	1.259*	1.248*
	(0.162)	(0.161)	(0.160)
Migrant worker	1.575**	1.611**	1.618**
	(0.365)	(0.375)	(0.377)
Unemployed		1.206	1.192
		(0.176)	(0.175)
Trade union			1.158
			(0.187)
Wuxi	0.821	0.827	0.827
	(0.135)	(0.136)	(0.137)
Chongqing	0.883	0.894	0.897
	(0.144)	(0.146)	(0.146)
Foshan	0.722*	0.730*	0.740*
	(0.123)	(0.125)	(0.127)
Constant	0.066***	0.063***	0.062***
	(0.020)	(0.020)	(0.019)
Observations	3,657	3,655	3,649

Logit model is used. >1 = positive effect; <1 = negative effect.
Reported are odds ratios.
***$p < 0.01$, **$p < 0.05$, *$p < 0.1$.
Source: LLMS 2005.

likely to respond to and use formal law and regulation to structure human resources (as well as many other transactions) (Gallagher et al. 2014). The conformity of workplace with formal legality, often implemented to protect the workplace rather than the worker, can, as a side effect, inculcate employees with higher levels of legal awareness and consciousness. These sectors also tend to be highly labor intensive, with strict work rules and

Dispute Pyramid

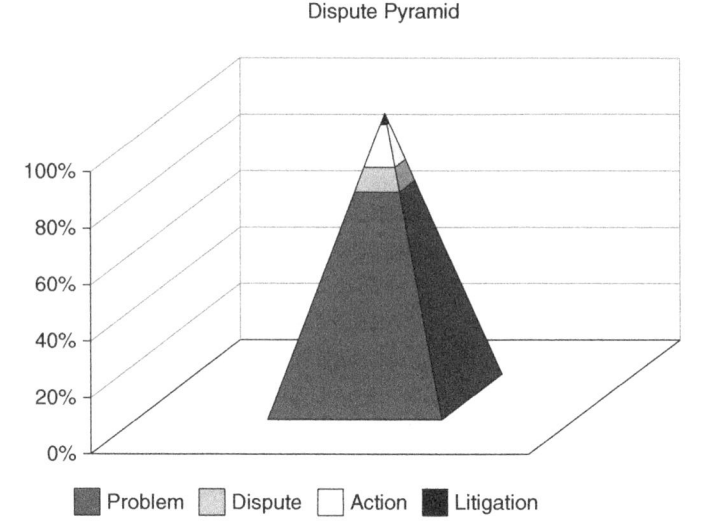

FIGURE 5.1. Labor Dispute "Pyramid" (From Gallagher and Wang 2011, 209). *Source:* LLMS 2005.

stringent demands on workers' productivity. Because of this, the probability of "naming and claiming" labor problems may also be more likely in these workplaces. These patterns also accord with the regional trends of labor disputes nationally. A higher incidence of labor disputes is correlated with higher GDP, a larger export sector, and higher levels of foreign direct investment (Cai and Wang 2012). It is the interaction between the individual's potential awareness of legal workplace rights, on the one hand, and specific workplace characteristics that make a legal problem more likely to occur, on the other, that explains what kinds of workers access these formal legal institutions. Hence, disputes are far more likely to occur in regions with high levels of economic development, a well-educated workforce, and high levels of manufacturing and foreign investment.

By constructing a dispute "pyramid" following the idea of Miller and Sarat (Miller and Sarat 1980) and Michelson (Michelson 2007), we can see that a large proportion of the respondents with work-related problems did not escalate the problem into a dispute (Figure 5.1). Only about one quarter of those with a problem reported that this problem became a formal dispute. Follow-up in-depth interviews were done with this group of eighty-two disputants. Among the eighty-two disputants, fifty-six (68.3 percent) took various measures to resolve their claims including negotiation and mediation, arbitration, administrative methods, and litigation. The vast majority of these disputants used multiple methods: about 39.6 percent used mediation; 26.4 percent used administrative methods; 23.1 percent used arbitration; and 11 percent filed formal claims in court. As in many legal systems, the proportion of claimants who actually went to trial is low. Out of the 319 respondents with labor problems only 3.1 percent actually litigated the dispute. The use of multiple methods is in part a result of the institutional framework set out by the 1995 Labor Law, which requires a multi-step process and encourages mediated resolutions. It also reflects the strategies of many aggrieved persons to use as many options as possible to increase their chance of success.

As discussed above, people who opt into the legal system tend to have higher levels of education, enjoy employment in the formal sector, and work in foreign-invested enterprises (FIEs). Given their education and related skills, they are likely to have greater workplace and market bargaining power (Wright 2000; Silver 2003), making it easier for them to have success in the labor market, which increasingly rewards these attributes (Meng 2012). Their higher degree of efficacy and their increased awareness and consciousness of their legal workplace rights lead them to participate in the legal system. Their efficacy begets participation. However, compared to respondents who have never experienced a labor dispute, post-dispute, these efficacious users have higher levels of disillusionment, more negative perceptions of the legal system's effectiveness, and profess less intention to use the legal system again. While non-users have positive but often vague and uninformed views of the legal system, respondents with legal experience are more realistic and pessimistic about the system's ability to deliver justice.

In the 2005 survey, respondents were asked to evaluate a hypothetical workplace dispute, whether the employer's behavior was illegal, and what their resolution strategy would be if they were the victims of the same illegal behavior. As a hypothetical problem, respondents overestimated their willingness to take action to correct the injustice and there is no significant difference between those with dispute experience and those without: 88.2 percent of non-users said that they would take action, while 87.7 percent of the disputants did so. This is about 20 percent higher than the actual escalation rates among the survey respondents who reported having a dispute, in which 68 percent of those with a dispute took action to resolve it. However, in specific questions about different resolution methods, disputants were always more reluctant to take action and this gap between disputants and non-disputants widens most with litigation. (Chart 5.1).

Chart 5.1. Which Resolution Methods Are You Willing to Use?

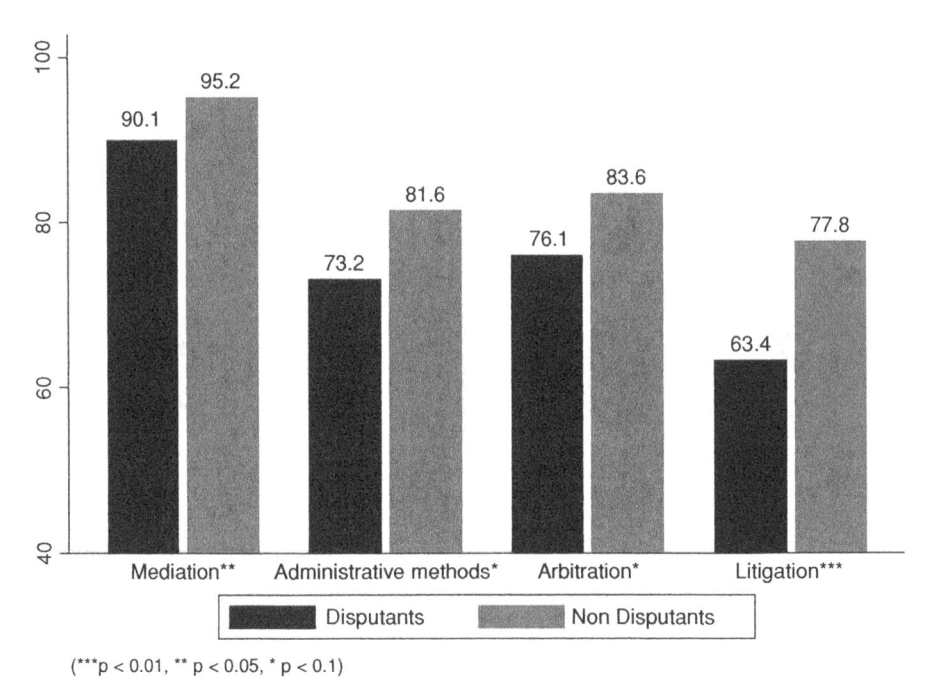

Method	Disputants	Non Disputants
Mediation**	90.1	95.2
Administrative methods*	73.2	81.6
Arbitration*	76.1	83.6
Litigation***	63.4	77.8

(***p < 0.01, ** p < 0.05, * p < 0.1)

CHART 5.1. Which Resolution Methods Are You Willing to Use?
Source: LLMS 2005.

Nearly 78 percent of the non-disputants report that they would have used litigation to solve the hypothetical problem, but only 63 percent of the disputants select litigation as a method. Non-disputants have vague confidence in these mechanisms, even though they have never used them, but those with previous experience are far more likely to feel that none of the options (administrative petitioning, mediation, arbitration, and litigation) is effective or useful. While only 2.8 percent of non-disputants believed that no method was effective, nearly 16 percent of disputants had lost confidence in the entire process. (Chart 5.2).

Dispute experience negatively impacts both propensity to use formal institutions and evaluations of their effectiveness. The differences between users and non-users in terms of vague belief and hope versus concrete suspicion and disappointment can also be seen at the individual level in the follow-up interviews with survey respondents who reported a dispute in the last ten years. For example, not all of the interviewed disputants embraced legal methods; some used protest and demonstrations while others tried more conciliatory bargaining and pleading with bosses for fairness. Some disputants who did not avail themselves of legal

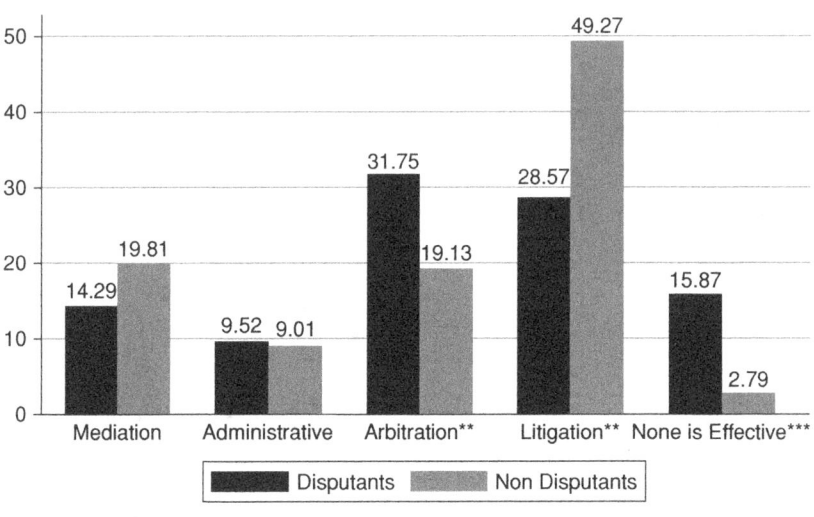

CHART 5.2. Which Method Is Most Effective?
Source: LLMS 2005.

Mediation: Disputants 14.29, Non Disputants 19.81
Administrative: Disputants 9.52, Non Disputants 9.01
Arbitration**: Disputants 31.75, Non Disputants 19.13
Litigation**: Disputants 28.57, Non Disputants 49.27
None is Effective***: Disputants 15.87, Non Disputants 2.79

(***p < 0.01, **p < 0.05)

methods then regretted their decision after the fact. They continued to hold high expectations about the legal system and wished that their ability to access the law had been greater. Zhang (WX538), a migrant worker born in 1969, worked for a Taiwanese-invested enterprise in the city of Wuxi, near Shanghai. After suspecting the management of breaching the law by not paying migrant workers enough overtime or paying into social insurance for local workers, he went to a local bookstore and spent RMB 160 (USD 25) on a labor law manual. He consulted with the city trade union, where he found a sympathetic cadre who took his side and encouraged his mobilization. "*The union cadre really supported me, said I had the power to organize, that I knew how to use the law as a weapon to protect myself.*" Although he consulted with a lawyer, he could not find one willing to accept his case. He then organized his co-workers by showing them that the management was engaging in the above-described illegal practices. He adeptly unified a diverse group of workers with different grievances, but all unhappy with the company. Zhang then turned to protest, leading a strike of over 100 workers. However, the Taiwanese management of the FIE quickly mobilized to divide and conquer the workers, reaching side agreements with many workshop leaders and other mid-level employees. Zhang was forced to negotiate, accepting a payment of RMB 5,000 (USD 609) along with other workers during a meal with the managers. He eventually left the joint venture after being offered the chance to serve as its trade union chairmen. Zhang believes that his strategy was wrong. He should have turned to the law earlier rather than protest. *"Now I think that at the time I should have found a good lawyer to resolve it through legal methods, even if it meant shutting down the enterprise. I wouldn't feel any sympathy for them."* His appraisal of China's labor laws and regulations is positive, with strategic faith in the central government but distrust in local officials' enforcement. *"The country's protection of migrant workers is actually relatively good, but it's local enforcement that has problems."* Zhang uses his experience to encourage friends and colleagues to use the law. *"I tell people to look for a few lawyers, then compare a few of them ... After all they understand these things, I'm just a laymen."*

Liu (WX558), a textile factory worker born in 1963, also regrets her failure to use the legal system and feels that her lack of knowledge prevented her from knowing her options. She was laid off after twenty-three years of employment in a collective-owned company, receiving one-time termination compensation but was deprived of preferential treatment offered to other workers who had been employed by only one month more. *"We didn't know there was an arbitration committee in the city, otherwise, we should have gone there and asked for help. We could have gotten more. We didn't have the awareness at the time."* Liu now looks back regretfully on the experience as a missed opportunity. *"Only after did I know about the labor arbitration committees in the city, we could have gone there for advice. I've already been working outside now for 5–6 years and have seen a lot. Now if the company violates your contract you can go to labor arbitration, you can file a lawsuit. We missed that opportunity."* Liu's belief in the law connects to what she knows about the government and its policies. *"Right now law is good, right? It's being promoted, it's always being talked about. We citizens can now go receive advice. Now I understand a little bit better."*

Despite their lack of real legal experience, both Zhang and Liu become "little experts," telling their friends and colleagues to engage with the law and giving advice about strategy (Gallagher 2006). Liu told her friends with labor problems to go to the arbitration committee for consultancy. *"We have already missed the chance, I wouldn't let my friends make the same mistake."* One of her friends went to court after listening to her advice. *"She will win,"* said Liu very confidently.

Unlike Zhang's confidence in the legal system from afar, Tian (WX536), also a long-term migrant worker born in 1968, experienced the failure of the legal system up close. She and other female migrant workers sued their collective enterprise and the local government after receiving much lower severance compensation than local workers when the company shut down and sold off its land. Tian and her co-workers had all married local men and believed they should be entitled to the same compensation as the local workers. One of her local friends received a RMB 20,000 (2,439 USD) severance while Tian and other outsiders received only RMB 5,000 (USD 609). Tian reports that they bought a lot of books about labor law and consulted a lawyer who initially agreed to represent them pro-bono, but later disappeared. *"At first all of the workers in the factory went to the township offices and sat quietly, but then (the government) said that they would cast us from the urban group (of workers), that's when we decided to file a lawsuit. All along they had been saying that the treatment for us would be the same, then suddenly it changed."* Looking back on her experience, Tian now believes that the lawsuit was a waste of time and may have hurt their chances at receiving better compensation. *"Now I think that the township government used a lot of money to win this case, giving it all to the court. If we hadn't filed a lawsuit, maybe we would have received some of that money. That's how most of us see it....Now I think that the law is unfair and that it is useless."* Her disappointment is similar to that of Old Zhou (SY209), a female worker born in 1945 who had served as her enterprise trade union chairwoman for many years. She resisted the privatization policies of her SOE, even rallying other workers to the cause and fighting for their pensions. After petitioning heavily to no avail, Zhou claims to have filed twenty lawsuits against her company, but with no success. She tried to hire a lawyer, but says that he was paid off by someone and then refused to speak to her. She was accused of corrupt activities and jailed for a period as well. Zhou holds out no hope for legal options. *"The courts are no good! They're never on our side! We have no money, you know. If we had won our case then many officials within the industry and commerce bureau, the city, and the province would have fallen from power, so of course we didn't win. At the time the provincial Governor said that he 'would act after fully considering the case.' Hah! No one settled the case for us...Am I satisfied? Of course I'm not satisfied! It's just like the industry and commerce bureau said, if you file a lawsuit against the Communist Party, how can you win? An arm is no match against a thigh!"* Zhou now advises her friends and former co-workers to give up on lawsuits.

 The legal system attracts citizens who believe that they have the background skills and resources to be successful. But as discussed in Chapter 4, there are other pathways to legal knowledge and awareness. Those without formal education, like Tian and Zhang, go out of their way to gain knowledge, buying law books, watching legal programs on TV, and collecting newspaper articles and case histories on relevant subjects. Their exposure to legal information teaches them about the law on the books, heightening their expectations for state support and intervention in their private dispute. China's rule of law project in labor, at least, is failing those who not only believe in the law, but also believe in themselves. In sharp contrast to the legal aid plaintiffs below, these interviews with disputants drawn from the general population in five cities, there is little sign of enhanced internal or external efficacy. Disputants with legal experience come away from the law with bitter memories and regrets. Only a few of those (who did not use the law) hold out hope about its effectiveness. Out of the twenty-eight follow-up interviews, only four were satisfied with their dispute outcomes and none of these respondents were typical employees. One was an entrepreneur who experienced these issues as an employer and labor contract agent; others were CCP members in higher employment positions who received better treatment in state sector restructuring and were relatively satisfied with the end result.

These negative impressions and attitudes can be partially attributed to the weak position of these individuals, either migrant workers at the margin of urban society or public sector workers under the assault of a national mission to restructure, partially-privatize, and downsize state and collectively-owned firms. However, through a focused comparison between this group and a group of equally disadvantaged legal aid plaintiffs in Shanghai, I argue in the next section that what truly alienates workers from the law is the lack of effective, affordable, and professional legal representation. Atomized by the system of individual labor contracts and the government's tactics of divide and conquer, workers are denied assistance of collective representation via trade unions, while individual representation by legal professionals is too expensive, too unreliable, and too difficult to find. Workers who receive adequate help, assistance, and support from competent lawyers or legal representatives, even when disadvantaged and even when they lose, are more likely to interpret their legal experiences differently and come away with a different set of expectations and judgments about their legal system. Representation is critical to law's durability not only because it improves the legal process for disadvantaged plaintiffs, but also because it manages the expectations of claimants who are initially unrealistic about their chances.

DISPUTANTS: THE IMPORTANCE OF REPRESENTATION

Chinese workers who choose a path of legal mobilization to resolve workplace grievances are often at a disadvantage when facing more seasoned, knowledgeable, and resource-rich employers in the formal dispute resolution system. As Galanter (1974) argues in his work on repeat players, the legal process is often not fair because some players have advantages (of time, money, knowledge, connections) that make a just and fair resolution difficult. Access to justice is inextricably linked to access to legal representation because representation by a competent legal professional can help overcome some of the social, political, and economic disadvantages that individual workers as plaintiffs face when confronting employers as defendants.

Legal representation can facilitate more than just outcomes, balancing against the power that strong defendants possess against weaker plaintiffs. They can affect how the system works. Their know-how can prevent an inexperienced or uneducated plaintiff from making critical mistakes. They can keep the process honest by holding judges, arbitrators, and defendants to the procedural standards set out in formal law. They also, however, reshape and recast the demands and motivations of plaintiffs in light of formal law and legal procedure. By comparing disputants with representation and those without, I hope to shed light on two consequences of representation: first, effective representation can objectively improve the process and outcome for disadvantaged claimants; second, representation can tame and temper demands in ways that insulate the legal system from blame. Effective legal representation can both empower and demobilize.

In this section, I compare the satisfaction and dispute experience of disputants who received legal aid with the experience of disputants who were captured in the 2005 four-city survey and then took part in the 2007 follow-up interviews. The variable animating the comparison is the absence or presence of representation. Obtaining access to legal representation during a labor dispute is often difficult. Plaintiffs are often unable to afford even the flat fee that lawyers charge up front to take on these cases. Moreover, many lawyers are reluctant to take on cases that offer little chance of large compensation (Michelson 2006). Many plaintiffs report that finding lawyers who specialize in labor and employment is difficult. Access to legal aid and free or less expensive legal advice is also fraught with difficulty. While many trade union branches offer legal consultation, the union rarely affirmatively takes on cases and the quality of the consultative advice is not always reliable. While there are some NGOs, like the one featured here, that provide legal aid to workers they are small in number and reach (Perry and Goldman 2007). At the time of the 2004 interviews, the ECUPL Legal Aid Center was the only specialized legal aid clinic on labor law in Shanghai and it received far more requests for legal representation than it could possibly satisfy. In 2004, for example, the center received over 10,000 visits or phone calls for consultation, but took on less than 100 cases for representation in the dispute process. The responses regarding legal representation of the eighty-two LLMS respondents who experienced a labor dispute regarding representation confirm the difficulty of finding adequate and affordable representation. Out of the eighty-two disputants, fourteen (17 percent) consulted a lawyer while six consulted a legal aid organization. Only six disputants (7 percent) actually hired a lawyer. The most common reason given for not hiring a lawyer was the expense. Seven (9 percent) of the disputants consulted the trade union for help and received it, while twelve disputants (15 percent) sought help from the trade union but did not receive any help. These experiences are indicative of the difficulty that Chinese workers face in finding affordable and competent legal assistance. Access to affordable legal representation is difficult and rare, making the Shanghai legal aid plaintiffs interviewed in 2004–2005 and in 2012–2013 very unusual. However, access to legal representation has improved somewhat over time as more trade union branches have opened up legal aid consultation centers, the number of labor NGOs has expanded, particularly in areas with high concentrations of low-skilled manufacturing, and the media has disseminated information about laws, regulations, and legal aid organizations (Spires, Tao, and Chan 2014; Cheng, Ngok, and Zhuang 2010). Despite these improvements, representation and access to justice remain key problems in China's legal system, especially in economically less developed areas.

In transitional or developing countries like China that are relative latecomers to the construction of formal law and legal institutions, there is a tendency to cast legal consciousness as a characteristic that increases or decreases linearly and tracks other phenomena associated with modernization, such as economic development and urbanization. However, experienced disputants who gained legal aid representation displayed sophisticated knowledge and awareness of law and legal procedure. They had a high degree of legal knowledge and awareness. But they also tended to evaluate China's legal institutions very negatively, arguing that the processes were corrupt, confusing, took too long, and tended to benefit those with money or connections. They tended to have a "low" evaluation of legal institutions. After the educative effects of legal mobilization with legal aid, they were also quite positive about their own internal efficacy to use the law more effectively after their lawsuit. Many plaintiffs, despite difficulties in their own lawsuit, professed to have enough confidence *in themselves* to not only use the law again, but also to do it better next time because of their newfound knowledge (Gallagher 2006). These contradictory expressions of resignation and efficacy are an indication of the complex and multi-faceted nature of legal consciousness development in China today. Citizens are emboldened by the power of law and the state's promotion of legal institutions to grasp it as a tool to help themselves, but their actual experiences with the law temper this enthusiasm and dampen hopes. However, many disputants also frame their experience, even when extremely negative, as educative: "a training" (SH20046), "an exercise," (SH200449), "like taking a class" (SH200427). Legal experience enhances their sense of internal efficacy and confidence, reinforcing the perception of the legal system as an effective mode of resolution of social conflict. The disenchantment that is nonetheless coupled with education and information can still reinforce the legitimacy of the legal system. People may come back to the formal legal system not because they believe that the system works well, but because they believe that they know how to work the system. A key component that differentiates the reinforcing experiences of the legal aid plaintiffs from the alienating experiences of the other individuals surveyed is the presence or absence of effective representation.

Workers who go through this individualized, bureaucratic experience alone are unlikely to learn, but are more likely to be mystified and frustrated by the twists and turns of the administrative and legal processes central to dispute resolution. As the earlier comparison between users and non-users demonstrated, legal experience does not typically have this effect of positive reinforcement. In fact, for most respondents legal experience leads them away from the law. In these cases, disillusionment is not tempered by the enhanced internal efficacy or confidence that comes from learning about the law works and can be worked by those with the proper skills. Instead, disillusionment without learning leads to the rejection of law. Representation not only improves the outcomes of the cases, it also transforms the disputant's interpretation of that outcome, even outcomes that are negative.

Zhou (SH200448) was born in 1949 and worked in an SOE until a Korean investor acquired its assets as part of the restructuring process. In order to stay employed, he agreed to work at the newly-formed FIE after being laid off by the SOE; he had worked long hours at little pay for two years when he was suddenly laid off again. He suspected that the boss wanted to hire cheaper migrant labor. Zhou's suit eventually led to a court-mediated settlement for RMB 9000 (USD 1428) in severance pay. Zhou was angry about the entire process, including the buy-out of his old firm, the abusive working conditions under the new boss, and the coercive mediation by a judge who he suspected did not want to offend a foreign company. Zhou remarked, *"I feel cold. Sometimes I think about killing my boss."* He credits legal aid with getting him anything at all. *"Legal aid is needed because we have no money and we need to work. But we are treated badly. [Legal aid] was good because we knew that it had no pressure or interference. It was independent. It is also good because they give you expert advice and just tell you the truth."* Zhou credits legal aid with an educative effect and a taming effect on his more base instincts. He ended the interview with criticism of both firms and the government. *"They pollute the environment! They abuse workers! Who cares? They [the government] just protect the capitalists. We wanted to go to the factory directly and get the money right from Korean boss himself. We wanted him to lose face. But then the lawyer called and said we couldn't do it."*

Among the legal aid plaintiffs, there was an overwhelming disposition toward using the legal system in the future, often embracing the challenge not because they knew the system to be easy or particularly fair, but as an exercise in which they had become more adept. Out of fifty-five legal-aid plaintiffs who answered the question, nearly 82 percent (45 plaintiffs) said that they would use the law again for a labor problem. (See also Gallagher 2006, 804.) Xian (SH201303), a forty-year-old migrant worker from Jiangxi Province in south central China, worked in a large Taiwanese-invested FIE making aluminum alloy wheels for trucks and construction equipment. After less than a year on the job, he was injured when a wheel fell from a shelf in the warehouse, hitting him on the head, leading to a concussion and severe bleeding. Although he was given two weeks to recover, the employer refused to issue him the proper documentation for occupational injury designation, the first step toward claiming compensation and reimbursement for medical expenses. When Xian returned to work, he immediately became dizzy with severe headaches and asked for more time off to recuperate. While he was off work, the employer terminated his labor contract on the grounds that Xian was absent from work without approval. The employer also refused to pay any compensation for the workplace injury.

Xian began the legal mobilization process on his own by first inquiring about his legal workplace rights at the local labor bureau in the development zone, but he was initially unsuccessful. The development zone labor bureau refused to assist him in a mediated settlement, sending him to the district level labor bureau, which then redirected him to the Shanghai Municipal Labor Bureau in the central part of Shanghai. Despite the drawn out process, Xian received advice at the Municipal Labor Bureau and a recommendation to visit the Legal Aid Center at ECUPL. He then began the process of filing a labor arbitration claim against the company with the assistance of a legal aid lawyer. Xian lost in arbitration, as the arbitration committee supported the employer's reasoning that Xian had been absent from work without permission. Xian appealed in court and won. The employer then appealed the court's decision, but it was upheld at the Intermediate Court, which awarded Xian RMB 13,000 (USD 2063) in back pay. He subsequently brought a separate legal claim to the courts for additional compensation on his own, winning a second lawsuit against the company. After three years of a long-drawn-out battle, Xian is satisfied with the substantive outcomes. Given his head injury, however, he decided to no longer work in manufacturing and found a job as a waiter. He enjoys talking about his legal experience, portraying himself as an uneducated itinerant worker who overcame the odds to win against a large and powerful employer.

Xian's final legal outcomes were relatively positive, though the lengthy time (2–3 years) it took to gain them was difficult as it required that he devote considerable time to the bureaucratic requirements of the case as it moved through litigation. He notes that during the Intermediate Court appeal of his first case, he and his lawyer were approached by the judge who asked them to give up the claim and negotiate a private settlement of RMB 4–5,000 RMB. Xian notes, *"The judge called and asked me to settle, just to take 4–5000 and let it go. I thought to myself that to have sued to this point, with 2–3 years already passed, and to only get 4–5000, it's too little, I'd rather not have the money at all ... But the judge knew that our case was representative and a decision would have a big impact on labor law precedence in Shanghai ... Yes, that's what the judge said. I said, I don't care. I'm going to sue to the end. Now that I've gotten to this point, I don't believe that this judge wouldn't have a conscience. In the end, the decision still supported me."*

Xian realizes that he was not at an advantage. Noting that he was *"uneducated,"* he takes his learning experience as something to spread to others. *"I would certainly use the law again, and not only for me, when I see my friends around me, when I see and hear the things going on around me, I can also battle injustice. For example, just recently I saw a group of people on the roadside, I went over to take a look and they said that they were trying to get their wages paid. I said, 'well this is no big deal. You should go to the labor bureau to resolve it. I know a bit about the process, I've had to deal with similar problems.' Now, I can help my relatives, my friends and the people that I meet fight against injustice. I can speak. This case had a huge influence on me.*" Xian is not naïve about the problems that might exist, noting that the labor arbitration committees are likely to be biased in favor of the companies, especially big employers like his. He also experienced how a company can delay a decision by constant appeals and pressure on the courts. When he went to court on his own the second time to get severance compensation, he even had to return a third time to ask for implementation of the decision by the court. "*At this point, many workers don't understand much about labor law, just some superficial knowledge. They might know that when their rights are violated they should go find the labor department. But often if they go once and are unsuccessful, they won't have the nerve to continue, they'll just settle the matter by leaving it unsettled ... That's why we still need a lot more dissemination about this, so that more workers will have a better understanding.*"

Shao (SH200423) was a professional woman in her mid-forties at the time of her dispute. She worked as an accountant in a local SOE, but was shunted from her relatively high-paying position to a low-level one after a management change. With two other employees who suffered similar treatment, Shao began to educate herself about her workplace rights, visiting a district legal aid center, downloading laws and regulations from the Internet, and photocopying evidence from her employer as she braced herself for a lawsuit. "*We knew that we had enough proof, we would definitely win, the law would give us an answer. We had a certain cultural level. The boy from the computer department had even qualified as a basic level legal worker.*" Shao was successful at labor arbitration, with a decision that reinstated her to her original position and paid two months compensation for the salary gap. When the company appealed the ruling to the courts, Shao reached out again to become more informed, visiting the Shanghai Municipal Trade Union legal aid office where she was redirected to ECUPL. She was also now alone as the "boy from the computer department" settled after management threatened him with retribution and another young receptionist gave up. At court, accompanied by a legal aid lawyer, Shao won again – believing that the court would uphold the original arbitration decision, the employer gave up the appeal. She notes ruefully how angry her boss was, *"the manager couldn't believe it, he was beside himself with anger."* Shao was reinstated into her former position and continued to go to work, but eventually the boss found an excuse to fire her. She returned to university legal aid again and began the process to initiate a second arbitration. However, this time Shao was tired of pursuing her legal claims and worried that her lawsuit would interfere with her daughter's preparation for the high school examination. Moreover, she knew that her contract would soon expire, leaving her with no compensation or employment regardless of any additional arbitration. So she went directly to the manager and negotiated a severance agreement with RMB 20,300 (USD 3222) in compensation. The matter was settled entirely privately, and without additional recourse to labor arbitration or any court proceedings.

Shao is realistic about the future. As an older worker facing discrimination and more powerful employers, she notes that employees have little protection from the legal system without these kinds of dogged fights and drawn-out procedures. She credits legal aid with giving her knowledge and confidence. *"I received new knowledge and education from legal aid. The strategy of how to sue was key. It's very comprehensive and really helps us. If I had problems again I would definitely use legal aid again...I used to believe that you must have done something wrong to have a lawsuit. Now I'm more mature, understand the process. I would definitely do it again. I got help; I'd get help again. It gives me more confidence."* However, Shao also gives details about everything that is wrong: how employers find loopholes in the law, underpay social insurance contributions, sign short term contracts to avoid the burdens of employment security. *"We really are exploited slaves. Men are more common than dogs. Bosses like people our age, 40–50 year olds, because we will be obedient, because we are scared."*

Pan (SH200426) was a woman in her mid-thirties, originally from outside Shanghai. She worked in an import-export Chinese–foreign (Hong Kong) joint venture, which suddenly fired her after the local management changed. Pan had previous experience with labor law from when she was terminated while pregnant a few years earlier. Pan regrets the outcome of that first case, as she gave up and took a small settlement after being diagnosed with gestational diabetes. *"I didn't want to sue while I was pregnant, running all over the place, from department to department, I've only one chance to have a child, I had to protect it...This time I didn't want to back down. It's better to get bosses to change their behavior."*

Her mobilization experience is quite typical – a mixture of frustrations and small victories. Pan begins by going to bookstores to read up on labor law. *"I just read the books at the bookstore, I didn't want to spend money on them. As soon as I left the bookstore, I called my employer to tell them that they would certainly lose the case."* She also reads the local labor news and watches a popular television show that features legal cases. However, Pan initially loses the case in arbitration, which she attends without legal representation. At the arbitration she meets a pregnant woman also involved in a labor dispute. Pan tells her about her own earlier settlement, encouraging the pregnant woman to sue her employer for violating her rights. The woman recommends the legal aid center at ECUPL to Pan. Pan then turns to legal aid for the court appeal of the arbitration decision that went against her.

Pan values the knowledge that she has acquired on her own and through the legal aid center as it gives her the confidence to face up to difficult legal experiences. *"When I first graduated, you would enter a company that you expected never to leave – you didn't care about the law. But now if you are switching from company to company every year, signing contracts all the time, of course you're going to start paying attention to the law. Now all the newspapers have information about the law, about how to negotiate, how to sign labor contracts."* Pan links the assistance of legal aid not only to professional assistance and advice, but also to mental health. *"At legal aid they should also give mental consultation. They help you with details and procedures. You can become very pessimistic, you need help to fight against the treatment at court and arbitration and ridicule by the managers. That's why so many people commit suicide and use violence."* But Pan herself is sanguine, even relishing the prospects of another lawsuit to teach employers how to behave. *"If it happened again, I would first negotiate, then go to court. I'd say 'See you in Court!' Of course I don't want it to happen again, but now I have more experience, once you do it you are no longer afraid."* Pan neatly sums up how her legal mobilization experience educated her on the faults in the system even while she gained personal confidence. *"The system doesn't work but it teaches you how it doesn't work."*

While many legal aid recipients displayed this mixture of cynical realism with heightened efficacy, they often valued legal aid for giving them the ability to play the game of law. Legal aid's contribution went beyond the mundane supply of substantive law and regulation or mastery of legal procedure but to more abstract notions of representation and stature within legal spaces. First, from an individual perspective, legal aid is credited with teaching people how to "talk," how to articulate themselves using specialized legal vocabulary in a legal context. Learning how to talk leads to increased confidence in bargaining and negotiation, which is important given the Chinese legal system's emphasis on mediation and compromise. Thus, even when people feel pressured to settle or compromise, they feel that their bargaining position is enhanced, both by the presence of legal aid representation and their increased fluency in "law talk." Second, the presence of legal aid, which represents both a public interest (workers' rights) and wields specialized knowledge, can be perceived to balance out the connections and corruption that are thought to be endemic to the operations of Chinese local government institutions. The litigators from the legal aid center capitalized on these dual identities by announcing openly in court that they are from ECUPL (the top law school in Shanghai) *and* representing the case for free. This grants them professional and moral stature: the university is highly respected and they are working in the public interest.

Hao (SH200419) was a middle-aged blue-collar dockworker who took a leave from her collectively-owned employer to work in South Korea as a factory worker.[1] After she returned to Shanghai the enterprise was in midst of restructuring and wanted to terminate her, ending twenty years of employment. While she had already given up her salary in order to look for work herself, she did not want to sever her ties to a public employer – which at the time were critical for her pension and retirement. She received advice from the ECUPL Legal Aid Center and went to arbitration without legal representation, whereupon the labor bureau refused to accept the case.[2] At court, with legal aid representation, she was pressured to submit to mediation and severance compensation of RMB 2–3,000 RMB, an exceedingly low amount for such long work tenure. Her legal aid lawyer refused the mediated offer and threatened to "*go to the media and let society decide.*" Eventually she settled for RMB 11,000 (USD 1746) through judicial mediation. Hao was not impressed with the court or the judge. "*They don't speak up for normal people. I wouldn't have been able to speak out if it hadn't been for Lawyer Lu, if she wasn't there to speak for me. When she addressed the court, she said she was from 'The Politics and Law University.' The judges are all graduated from there, so it*

---

[1] During the restructuring processes of the 1990s, many SOEs permitted their employees to find other full-time jobs in the private/foreign sector while keeping their formal position in the SOE (停薪留职). Some like Ms. Hao found subcontracted work overseas.

[2] At the time, Shanghai courts rarely accepted cases involving SOE layoffs. See Gallagher in (Gold 2009).

impressed them." Zheng (SH201307), a young migrant to Shanghai from Gansu Province in the far west of China, was burned by boiling water while on the job as a make-up artist. She sought out advice and representation from legal aid, but was at a disadvantage because she did not have a formal labor contract with her employer and was paid only in cash. In the end, she negotiated compensation from her boss directly. She noted that her lawyer *"taught me how to talk to the manager. I told him that I could also report him to the labor inspection bureau."*

Zhao (SH20044), an uneducated worker in a hotel laundry, was fired while on sick leave during the SARS epidemic, which shut down many Chinese cities for two months in 2003. While Zhao suspected she was fired because she was getting older and her employer took the opportunity of SARS to reduce the workforce, she fought back first through petitioning the government directly and then via the legal system. She credited receiving legal aid as a "turning point" in the case. Zhao went to arbitration on her own before receiving legal aid. She noted, *"At arbitration, I went on my own, with my relatives. Lawyer Lu didn't go. We couldn't speak or say anything. We had things to say and didn't know how to say them. We were in the right, but we couldn't speak clearly. But Lawyer Lu, she could repeat regulations over and over from memory. We really need more people like her, but she is too tired."*

Zhao credited legal aid with the power of legal articulation needed to be persuasive in court. She also credited the educative process of legal aid for her newfound role as a layman "expert" on labor law. *"We really need to expand legal aid for workers so that every worker can receive it. It strengthened our legal consciousness. Law is not advantageous to us, us weak groups. Once we began to use legal aid, the work unit spent much more energy finding ways to seek vengeance against us. Now friends and co-workers, many people, call us to ask us for advice. We have become experts, through this experience, we have really learned a lot – how to fight against the government departments."* While Zhao and her husband had become experts advising friends and colleagues, their own experiences left them with diminished hope and confidence. Zhao's case was ultimately unsuccessful; while she won on paper, the judicial decision was never implemented. Her husband's employer threatened him with dismissal unless Zhao gave up her lawsuit. This kind of "relational repression" is a common pressure tactic (Deng and O'Brien 2013).

Cases like Zhao's, apparent victories that aren't enforced, offer important opportunities to explore how legal aid plaintiffs interpret different kinds of failures and how failure is refracted by the assistance received via legal aid. The experiences of these plaintiffs demonstrate how legal representation facilitates a positive interpretation of events even in the context of procedural frustration, while also teaching plaintiffs about the power dynamics that often thwart the delivery of justice. When workers attribute failure to procedural issues that are partly attributable to their own lack of knowledge and preparation, they are more hopeful and optimistic about their own potential future iterations of legal mobilization. The potential attainment of further education and knowledge leads to renewed optimism that one can win at the game of law. However, when workers win outright on substantive decisions, but enforcement of those positive outcomes is stymied because of government corruption and "backdoor" connections, as was the case for Zhao, they are likely to reject wholesale the possibility of justice. While success or failure in a single case may seem like a simple thing to determine outright, a worker's interpretation of the experience of failure is more important in determining their post-dispute assessment. It matters whether you won or lost, but it also matters how the loss is interpreted, as a personal mistake or as a breakdown of the system. When Zhao and her husband gave up her lawsuit to save his job, they no longer believed in the legal system as a resource for normal people. A legal victory that cannot be enforced because of political power is not just a hollow victory, it is worse than failure. *"We are the weaker party, going to struggle against the work unit and the government. Ordinary people can't sue, it takes too much time, it is too much trouble... We are like eggs against a rock."*

Wei (SH200414), a Shanghai local born in 1969, was employed by a large foreign-invested (French) joint venture supermarket on a year-to-year contract. Wei worked about sixty hours per week with one-day off. After he inquired about overtime payment for these extra hours, he was suddenly informed that his contract would not be renewed. (Chinese law restricts overtime and mandates additional pay for it, which Wei had not received.) Upon learning of his imminent dismissal, Wei brought an arbitration claim for overtime compensation and holiday pay. When the employer negotiated some payment for holiday time, but refused to pay any overtime, Wei lost the case in arbitration based on insufficient evidence of overtime worked. His appeal in civil court was also unsuccessful. After his loss in the court proceedings, the company posted the court decision in the supermarket break room so that other workers would absorb the lesson of his loss. Wei felt *"like a bit of a fool."* He tried to get other former employees to join the lawsuit, but they were afraid it would hurt their chances to find other jobs. The company threatened to put his lawsuit information into his personnel dossier, which was held by the local government, but his legal aid lawyer assured him that this was just a scare tactic.[3]

Wei's interpretation of his failure focused on the procedural difficulties he faced in attaining the proper evidence for the initial arbitration. While he felt that *"he lost for nothing,"* he also noted that he would do it again if he could make sure that his evidence was sufficient even though companies try to hide evidence of their wrongdoing. His interpretation of the failure was not inaccurate nor naïve, as he correctly noted that the Labor Bureau tends to protect large employers like his own. He faced the typical difficulties of the "have-nots" in any legal system, but Wei focused on the procedural difficulties standing in the way of a successful case. Attempts to record his manager making self-incriminating statements were unsuccessful, as were requests to fellow colleagues to assist him in his case by serving as witnesses. Wei made many attempts to educate himself about the legal process through newspapers, the labor bureau's hotline, and the staff at the ECUPL legal-aid center. He focused on his own mistakes and on the ability of the employer to manipulate the legal system more successfully.

Jiang (SH200429) was born in 1948 and was a typical representative of China's "lost generation" of the Cultural Revolution. His formal education ended with middle school and in 1968 he was "sent down" [to the countryside] as were many Shanghai youth, to the border area near the Soviet Union in Heilongjiang province. He returned to Shanghai in 1979 and in 1985 he was allocated a job by the state in a local SOE producing airplane parts. Jiang's labor dispute with his company is intertwined with the state sector restructuring that occurred between 1998 and 2002, leaving more than thirty million state workers laid off and many more shunted into retirement or the private sector. While the case was pending, his designation as a "laid off worker" protected the enterprise from many legal and financial responsibilities and he eventually gave up his claim after the enterprise in negotiation with the legal aid lawyer increased his severance compensation from RMB 10,000 to RMB 21,000 (USD1587 to 3333). Jiang's wife was also laid off and he was then

---

[3] By Chinese law, the personnel dossier (档案) of foreign-invested enterprises (FIEs) employees cannot be housed at the FIE itself, or with the investor of the FIE. In those cases, it is filed at a PRC local government office, usually the labor bureau.

working in the informal sector, sometimes delivering water or trying to sell his paintings on the street.

Despite the increased severance payment, Jiang interpreted his engagement with the law as an abject failure because it failed to reinstate his permanent employment. He ridiculed the state's propaganda about law as a weapon, *"They say we have a weapon, what weapon? I pulled out this weapon and it was useless."* As an older, state-sector worker, Jiang wanted the law to protect him from the vagaries of market reform, which has eliminated permanent employment and allowed state employers to break long-standing relationships with their employees. But Jiang did not fully appreciate that the Labor Law itself was critical in achieving those market reforms. His labor relationship with his state employer was transformed into a contractual (legalized) form in the 1990s, making his dismissal perfectly legal. Jiang rejected the outcome as neither procedurally or substantively just. Substantively, his meager compensation could not provide long-term security for him nor make up for the opportunities he lost as an uneducated sent-down youth who worked for socialism until socialism was over. Procedurally, it was as if he was playing a game in which the rules changed midstream. *"The common people are very angry. I have been unfairly treated in comparison with treatment in other enterprises and even treatment in other workshops in my own enterprise. The leaders are corrupt whereas my wife and I have worked hard our whole life and have suffered much bitterness. ... My company asked me to make a sacrifice because I am older and an old comrade; they promised to take care of me, but they didn't care at all. I could be dead on the street."*

Jiang rejected law entirely while Wei critiqued its tendency to benefit employers over individual workers. The system failed them both, but their interpretations of the legal difficulties differed. Jiang rejected legal rules and relationships because they had replaced former socialist employment rules that guided his relationship with and expectations of his long-term state employer. Wei believed that legal procedures represented a barrier to justice because they were unnecessarily complex for individual workers to master. He was determined to place more emphasis on obtaining competent evidence in future engagements with the legal system while Jiang lost confidence more completely. Jiang noted at the end of the interview, *"My son also has a labor problem. I just told him to forget it. His enterprise is illegally withholding part of his salary, but I told him not to bother. Just switch jobs if you can."* Their differences captured an important generational divide between the old generation of socialist workers and new entrants to the labor market, including both young urban workers and rural migrants.

DISPUTANTS: A GENERATIONAL DIVIDE

The final comparison in this chapter focuses on this generational divide that emerged out of the reforms to China's socialist workplace. China's work unit (*danwei*) system of employment and the household registration system (*hukou*) protected and insulated urban workers. Together, they created a system that delivered stable and secure employment relations to most urban residents while excluding and marginalizing rural residents. With social welfare and benefits tied to the urban workplace, rural residents were also denied these benefits. The dismantling of the work unit and the relaxation in hukou policy were critical to the success of China's economic reform agenda, its transition to labor-intensive manufacturing and export-oriented industrialization, and its ambition to be a global economic superpower. As discussed in Chapter 3, the implementation of the labor contract system and the subsequent passage of the 1995 Labor Law were two important tools in this dismantling project. The gradual relaxation in the hukou policy and the expansion of the labor contract system and social insurance programs to migrants continue to be important for the construction of a new kind of workplace that is more open and meritocratic, but also much more competitive and unequal. These institutional changes had dramatic and varied effects on workers: stripping long-enjoyed entitlements and security away from older, urban state workers; opening up new employment opportunities for rural migrants and younger workers; and socializing a new generation of younger workers into a "marketized labor" economy, distinct from the previous system of a so-called "administrated labor" economy.

Unlike in the United States, where race, gender, and other ascriptive labels are most important in mediating people's experiences with the law (Nielsen 2000; Sun and Wu 2006), I attribute these differences within the group of legal aid plaintiffs as related to their different generational characteristics and experiences. During the reform era, the most privileged social group under socialism (older, urban public sector workers) became the least empowered and the least confident with respect to their legal institutions. This group's previously high social status and its access to superior social welfare and job security were undermined by China's rule of law project. On the other hand, young rural workers employed in the private and non-state sectors were emboldened by discourses of equality, fairness, and non-discrimination in legal settings (Lee 2007). These disputants are more likely to feel efficacious, seeking out legal knowledge and assistance and learning to use the law to press for their rights. These findings are similar to work by Diamant (2001) in research on Chinese rural women's mobilization of the marriage law and Upham's (1976) study of pollution victims in Japan. Both suggest that rural citizens will also avail themselves of the opportunity for legal mobilization. While I do not find that migrant workers are more likely to mobilize the law, I do find that they experience the law more positively than local residents.

In order to further explore this difference, I will first present some of the survey findings regarding differences across age cohorts and residential status, which indicate that younger workers and migrant workers (who are also overwhelmingly young) are more satisfied with the implementation of labor laws, more willing to initiate disputes, and more satisfied with the dispute process. While these differences are partially explained by the higher level of education of workers since the reform era began, as discussed in Chapter 4, these differences also reflect the more difficult demands of socialist workers who often ask for reinstatement and a return to the employment security of the pre-reform era. Moreover, given that these workers tend to be involved in disputes with SOEs closely tied to state actors, their claims may be frustrated by a greater degree of political interference.

I then turn to the dispute narratives to demonstrate why these general patterns exist, focusing on the different legal mobilization experiences of socialist workers compared to their younger counterparts. In these dispute narratives, all of the plaintiffs had access to legal representation, so we can focus more closely on other attributes that shape their experiences of engaging with the law and legal institutions. While I employ some of the survey data to show differences between generations, the goal of this analysis is not to demonstrate the relative importance of individual variables, but rather to show the collinearity of multiple variables in one group in contrast to the distinct characteristics of the other group. (See Table 5.2 below). While generation signifies a difference in age, the age differences are simply indicative of other differences in life experiences, educational opportunities, political socialization, and workplace practices that distinguish those socialized in the socialist workplace from those who entered the workplace under the new system of contract relations and labor markets. For example, age and education are closely related,

TABLE 5.2. *Generational Characteristics*

	Socialist Generation	Post-Socialist Generation
Age	Older	Younger
Education	Less educated	More educated
Employer	State/collective	Private/foreign
Mobilization target	State	Employer
Initial mobilization strategy	Petitioning	Law
Mobilization goal	Security	Compensation

with older workers far less educated than younger workers on average. (Table 5.3.) Older workers are also more likely to be employed by state or collectively-owned enterprises, which complicates their dispute experiences and opens up the dispute to more political interference.

The concept of political generations is a helpful way to conceptualize different patterns of political socialization in Chinese society. While it is used most often to differentiate between elites, the dramatic events in Chinese politics that followed the establishment of the PRC in 1949 also allow an extension of the concept to the citizenry. This is particularly the case for the generation most affected by the Cultural Revolution (1966–1976), or in popular terms, the "three old classes" (laosanjie) or "educated youth" (zhiqing) generation.[4] Young people who came of age during this ten-year period of political upheaval were affected across the board as they faced obstacles in educational opportunities, employment, and social mobility (Hung and Chiu 2003). It is this "lost generation," born between 1948 and 1957, that has had their lives most disrupted by shifting state and CCP policies, including early regime attempts to disrupt traditional patterns of social stratification, the closure of higher education during the Cultural Revolution, and the state enterprise reform of the 1990s, which coincided with this generation's later years of employment

---

[4] These terms indicate the early political experiences of this generation who were born around the time of the founding of the PRC and came of age during the Cultural Revolution. As educated, urban youth, they were sent down to the countryside after the Cultural Revolution turned violence. Many of them lost the chance to receive higher education and immediately entered the workforce upon their return to urban locations in the late 1970s or early 1980s. There are many popular jokes about the misfortunes of this particular generation, for example, that they first "xia-xiang" (went sent down to the countryside during the Cultural Revolution), then "xia-hai" in the reform era (tried to enter the "sea" of the market economy, only to be "xia-gang" in the late 1990s (laid off during the waves of SOE restructuring commencing in that period).

TABLE 5.3. *Bivariate Analysis of Age, Education, and Employment*

	AGE	SOE	FIE	GOV/PARTY	eduyr
AGE	1				
SOE	0.2930*	1			
FIE	−0.1278*	−0.1432*	1		
GOV/PARTY	0.0345*	−0.3727*	−0.0888*	1	
Edu year	−0.3210*	−0.1377*	0.0908*	0.2498*	1

*$p < 0.1$.
Source: LLMS 2005.

when they most wanted security but were least desirable in the burgeoning labor market.

These workers, socialized in the prior period of "work unit socialism" and "organized dependence," had enjoyed relative employment security and secure benefits (Walder 1988). Labor mobility until the 1980s was tightly curtailed so that most workers expected permanent employment. Even those workers who desired more mobility or greater advancement were usually thwarted because without a government sanctioned transfer, cutting ties with their employer threatened the extensive array of benefits and perquisites that the state delivered to urban workers via the work unit system. These distinctive characteristics of the socialist generation shaped their legal mobilization strategies and the dispute process in important ways. They also affected attitudes about the law as an adequate tool for workplace protection.

In the 2005 survey we find age is correlated with more negative views of litigation as an effective resolution strategy while in the 2010 CULS, age is negatively correlated with positive attitudes toward implementation (Gallagher et al. 2014). (Table 5.4). Younger workers also know more about the law and are more likely to initiate disputes. Finally, migrant workers are more satisfied with their dispute outcomes than residents with conforming hukou. Nearly 64 percent of such local residents are very unsatisfied or not very satisfied with the final resolution of their case, while only 37 percent are satisfied or very satisfied. Among migrants, the results are reversed: 72 percent of migrants are satisfied or very satisfied, with 28 percent very unsatisfied or not very satisfied. If we examine only the strongest category for dissatisfaction, 40 percent of residents with local hukou are very unsatisfied; but only 6.5 percent of migrants. (See Chart 5.3). These patterns in satisfaction reflect the different expectations of local residents and migrants, but they also represent the more complex outcomes desired

TABLE 5.4. *Age and Effectiveness (LLMS 2005)*

	Effectiveness			
Variables	(1)	(2)	(3)	(4)
Main Variables				
AGE	0.991***	0.992**	0.990***	0.996
	(0.003)	(0.003)	(0.004)	(0.004)
Born after 1980		1.047	1.043	1.086
		(0.140)	(0.144)	(0.156)
Female			0.937	0.931
			(0.063)	(0.067)
Contract			1.097	1.048
			(0.080)	(0.082)
SOE			1.086	1.086
			(0.091)	(0.096)
FIE			0.945	0.863
			(0.184)	(0.177)
Gov/party			1.325***	1.137
			(0.126)	(0.130)
Edu. groups				1.192***
				(0.062)
Migrant worker				0.964
				(0.146)
Dispute				0.502**
				(0.138)
Manu. & construct.				0.946
				(0.075)
Wuxi	0.928	0.928	0.922	0.949
	(0.084)	(0.084)	(0.087)	(0.095)
Chongqing	1.445***	1.443***	1.490***	1.517***
	(0.129)	(0.129)	(0.137)	(0.150)
Foshan	0.520***	0.521***	0.524***	0.545***
	(0.050)	(0.050)	(0.052)	(0.059)
Constant	0.962	0.934	0.915	0.561**
	(0.131)	(0.152)	(0.166)	(0.137)
Observations	4,112	4,112	3,913	3,497

Logit model is used. >1 = positive effect; <1 = negative effect.
Reported are odds ratios.
***$p < 0.01$, **$p < 0.05$.
Source: LLMS 2005.

in respect to residents' actions, especially older local residents. 69 percent of such residents reported that their disputes were either not solved or solved but not enforced. Among migrants, these figures were only 7 percent not solved and 1 percent solved but not implemented (Chart 5.4).

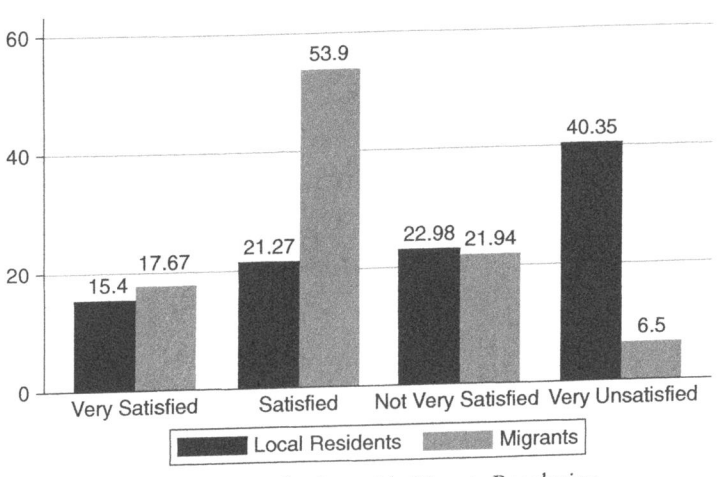

CHART 5.3. Satisfaction with Dispute Resolution.
Source: CULS 2010.

In multivariate analysis of views toward enforcement and levels of knowledge in the 2010 CULS, however, the role of education is more important than age in determining positive attitudes and higher levels of awareness (Gallagher et al 2014). The "lost generation" of state socialist

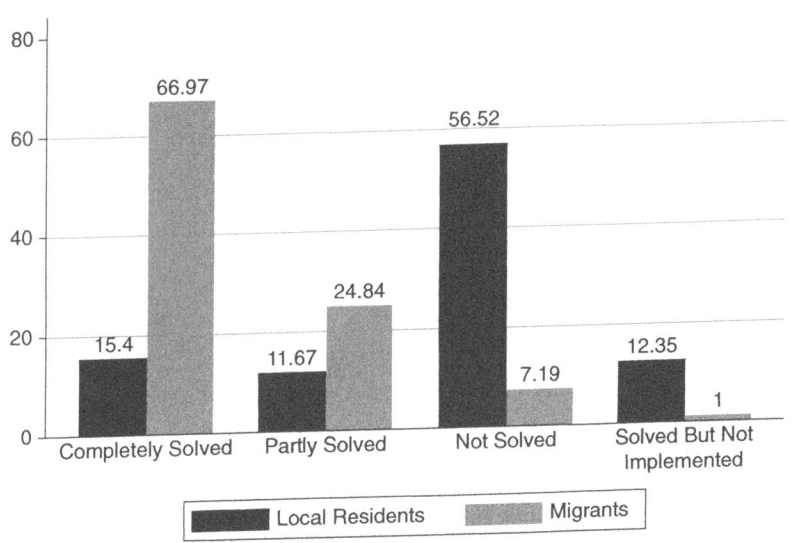

CHART 5.4. Labor Dispute Resolution Patterns.
Source: CULS 2010.

workers are as a group much less well educated than subsequent generations. The bad luck of being the first generation born in the PRC had ramifications for their educational opportunities, which in turn affected their attitudes toward new, reform-era institutions that demand significant individual knowledge and awareness to achieve rights protection.

Members of the socialist generation are also far more likely to be employed in the state sector, which has been ruthlessly downsized and restructured since the late 1990s. There are several reasons why this phenomenon reduces the possibility of successful legal mobilization for these workers. First, these workers are suing SOEs that are in most cases owned and managed by the same local government and/or party organizations that handle the dispute, whether through the local labor bureau or the local People's Courts. Second, the law itself was not written to protect the traditional "iron rice bowl" of SOE workers; on the contrary, it was written to destroy it. The law, with its emphasis on contractual labor relations and a labor market, is not well-suited to protect what these workers, in particular, wanted from the dispute process: reinstatement and employment security from a non-market actor until retirement. The Labor Law notably recognized just the opposite: the impermanence of employment and the right of employers under some circumstances to end employment relations. Also the restructuring process was largely implemented using top-down Pary directives, which often trump state law or governmental regulation in the Chinese setting. Thus, in many such cases where the claimants had a good "legal" (or regulatory) basis for their claims, the legal merits of the case were less important than internal Party or government decisions about restructuring. This particular phenomenon is demonstrated by the fact that many labor arbitration committees would refuse to hear cases regarding SOE layoffs (Gallagher 2009).

In addition to the adverse employment environment that tended to pit these older, less-educated workers against politically powerful state firms, socialist generation workers experienced the legal mobilization process as a second-best, inferior option to direct petitioning and negotiation with state officials (often through the hierarchy of the state firm and its bureaucratic counterpart in the local state and party organization). These workers often came to the law only after being redirected time and time again by state officials who rejected their particularistic appeals as "old comrades," "the sacrificed generation," or "workers as the ruling class of the nation." In a sense, the state pushed a more egalitarian and legalistic pathway of labor dispute resolution that disadvantaged them, precisely the group of workers that had previously benefitted from its close ties to the state. These workers wanted to go directly to the state and the party for resolution of their claims, but instead were pushed to the law as a second-best strategy, one that they knew would be unlikely to fulfill their expectations.

Finally, given their age, low education level, and lack of viable employment options, those in the socialist generation came to the legal system with hopes and expectations for job security, not monetary compensation. Often demanding reinstatement and long-term employment until retirement, these workers sought what the new legal system was most unable to give, especially during the period of state sector restructuring and massive layoffs. Their moral demands for the employment security and benefits of a prior era had to be recast under the new legal process into compensatory claims for severance termination. While legal aid representation could help make sense of this basic alteration and diminution of their claims, socialist workers were often unhappy with mere cash compensation (no matter the amount) and dissatisfied with results that may have looked like a victory on paper, but in reality still left them unemployed, unable to adjust to the labor markets of the reform era, and financially insecure.

Liu (SH20046) sat down to an interview without the plaintiff in the case, his wife, Mrs. Zhang, an accountant who became disabled after falling down a flight of stairs while attending a training program for accountants. Liu and Zhang were members of the Cultural Revolution generation. He was sent down to the countryside in 1970, coming back to Shanghai in 1981 and immediately entering a SOE in construction. At the time of the interview, Old Liu had just been laid off after working at the SOE for nearly a quarter of a century. His wife, Mrs. Zhang, had been a factory worker, but was also laid off through a designation called "xiebao,[5]" which required her previous employer to pay into her social insurance while allowing her to look for a new job in the non-state sector. Her new job as a bookkeeper in a state-owned management company

---

[5] "*Xiebao*" is shorthand for "an agreement (*xie*) to end employment but maintain social insurance (*bao*)." It was widely used in Shanghai and other cities during the SOE restructuring period to end employment of older workers and consisted of an arrangement in which the employer stopped paying salary but continued to make payments for social insurance (pension, medical, workers' compensation). This vastly improved the employability of older workers, as potential new employers could hire them on short-term contracts while avoiding the associated welfare burden. Several of the disputes discussed here involved workers on *xiebao* or workers who wanted *xiebao* instead of severance. See also (Gallagher 2009).

was relatively lucrative, paying a respectable salary of RMB 2,000–3,000 ($317–$476) per month. Zhang had made a successful transition from the iron rice bowl to the market until the day that she was injured. Her dispute then became a complex process of mutual blame and recrimination as each unit – her employer, her previous employer, and the school where the accident occurred – sought to absolve themselves of any responsibility for her health care costs or her long-term disability. As she recuperated in the hospital, the manager of her employer visited and terminated her employment. As Liu recounted it, *"we thought that her employer had a legal responsibility to help her, so we started to think about workers compensation. I'd never seen the labor law, didn't know much about it and had never studied it. But I just thought off the top of my head that this might be the case. I went to a bookstore to buy a copy of the Labor Law, but it was complicated, especially because she is 'xiebao.' The leader of her company was also the leader of the government department so there was no point in going there. We tried to negotiate directly with the management but it was no use. So we went to the local district labor bureau to qualify for workers compensation."*

Liu and Zhang's process of legal mobilization began with a search for legal representation, as they themselves felt too uneducated to understand the complexity of the case. Their one claim of occupational injury became instead 5–6 claims against multiple employers and an administrative lawsuit against the local labor bureau. While Mrs. Zhang won some compensation for illegal termination, none of the decisions were enforced and finally, the employer disappeared. While these cases dragged on for two years, Zhang did not receive any compensation and was unemployable due to her injury. Liu applied to receive the minimum income guarantee (*dibao*) of the city so that he could continue to finance the education of their twin sons, but worried about having enough to eat and his own health conditions. Liu ended his interview with an angry outburst about his experiences. *"The laws are written well, legislation is okay, but enforcement is not good. It needs to be more complete. These problems have to be solved quickly or we will starve to death. I don't have anything, nowhere to go for my livelihood. Where are my human rights? My right to life? My right to employment? I shouldn't have sued, I didn't have the experience. Law has no use so I'm very pessimistic. We've become an example that our rights can't be guaranteed. I wouldn't do it again. This has been my training, but I have no confidence. I wouldn't dare sue again…Media propaganda is just symbolic, it gives the ordinary people hope but it is too cruel...I feel like killing people, taking a machine gun out on the street, and just raking people down. Protection shouldn't just end with a document."*

Huang (SH200435) was born in 1957, and sent down to a farm in the countryside outside Shanghai from 1977 until 1984. Although she had a high school education, she entered a textile factory operated by a collectively-owned enterprise in 1986 making t-shirts. In 1994, this enterprise was absorbed into a Chinese–foreign (Swiss) joint venture when the factory assets were matched with "Swiss" cash investment. (Huang insists that the allegedly foreign capital component was actually just PRC money "round-tripped" abroad to allow the enterprise to take advantage of various preferences permitted for foreign companies). There were harsh working conditions at this factory: no overtime pay, long hours, and a low base salary. Huang watched over the years as rural migrants filled more and more positions. In 2001, the factory announced that the entire local workforce would be retired or laid off as the company restructured and switched to a migrant workforce. Workers with less than three years before retirement were offered RMB 445 (USD 54) per month until retirement and payment of social insurance. All other workers had to accept a severance package based on the years worked, but the enterprise would not factor in any of the years worked prior to the formation of the Chinese–foreign joint venture in 1994.

Huang and her colleagues began to protest these actions via the traditional methods of direct petitioning to government offices. They went to the district government, the city government, the labor bureau, the Shanghai Municipal Trade Union, the industrial sector trade union, and the women's federation. All of their attempts to negotiate directly with government departments ended in failure. *"They all just said that you had to sue. We cannot resolve this problem."* Huang was chosen to serve as the legal representative for all eight workers with such claims as her high school education set her apart from other, less-educated workers. Initially they tried to sue as a larger group of fifteen workers who did not qualify for the retirement package, but the enterprise offered seven people employment in the new company the day before the group was to meet to plan out their strategy. Huang noted that this strategy of "fragmentation" of aggrieved workers is very common. Huang also noted that initially these workers wanted to get their jobs back and to receive the *"xiebao"* designation that requires the previous employer to pay social insurance while you are free to go look for new employment in the market economy. (See supra note 3.) *"I wanted to have security, I only have seven or eight years before retirement, I could take my xiebao papers and find work."* The arbitration committee persuaded them to accept compensation in place of security and the group of workers mediated a settlement at arbitration with legal aid representation. Huang noted ruefully, *"We got RMB 14,000–15,000 (USD 1,707–1,829) in settlement, based on the RMB 445 (USD 54) laid off salary (that was then being paid to the retired workers). That's why the company delayed the process for so long so that we would all already be receiving the lower salary. We wanted RMB 30,000 (USD 3,658) because we knew the profits of the company were good! Our manager during this time went from riding a bike to work to an electric scooter, and finally to a car!* Huang was cynical about the outcome, but unlike Liu and Zhang, she was more optimistic about the future, realizing that law is now unavoidable though unfair. *"If I thought I was in the right, I would use the law again. First I would consult with legal aid and then decide, and of course try to negotiate first. Restructuring is not in favor of the workers."* Huang also believed that petitioning the state directly was a waste of time. *"They were all biased in favor of the enterprise. Of course the trade union favored the enterprise – it's the CCP's trade union! If it happened again, I wouldn't go to all these places; these places gave no help. In the end ordinary people shouldn't sue because we will always lose out to enterprises, all the government organizations favor them."*

Deng (SH200433) was born in 1959 and worked for twenty-seven years in a state-owned factory producing name-brand sewing machines. At its height, the factory employed more than 7,000 workers. During the restructuring process in the late 1990s there were several large-scale strikes as workers protested the downsizing and the loss of employment and security. Deng and two co-workers were skilled workers in a workshop that was kept operating longer than others. Portions of the factory's land were converted from allocated land to urban state-owned land, which allowed the enterprise to lease out land for real estate development as Shanghai's economy boomed and transitioned away from manufacturing and toward the financial sector, automotives, and high-tech. Although they were offered the opportunity to take *"xiebao,"* which would allow them to maintain social insurance but requires them to look for new employment, they resisted the loss of job security. The company retaliated by laying them off with a small stipend of just RMB 280 (USD 34) per month. After the assets including their workshop were made part of the restructuring, they were forcibly removed from their workplace and not permitted to return.

As with many in this generation, Deng and his two colleagues mobilized first in relation to the state itself, petitioning at the trade union, the city government, and the labor bureau. Although all of these places were, in their view, *"relatively fair,"* none could offer real remedies except to redirect them to the legal system. Deng noted that once the restructuring began they started to buy labor law books and consult with friends and colleagues. They read the *Labor Daily* at their housing units and they heard about legal aid on the radio and began to seek consultations there. However, Deng's interactions with the law and legal institutions only led to further disappointment and dejection. The labor arbitration committee rejected the case out of hand, while at the court they were encouraged by their legal aid-provided counsel to give up on any claim before the judiciary after their lawyer was pressured not to press this case given the employer's stature in the city and its political connections. Their murky status as long-term employees of a large and well-known company did not entitle them to many associated legal rights because the enterprise's restructuring process was approved by the local government despite irregularities in terms of how workers were treated during the process. Because Deng and his colleagues resisted the government-approved plan, they were reduced to the status of laid-off workers with meager stipends as salary substitutes that were eventually used as the basis for their termination packages. They came to believe that if they had taken the severance package offered at the start of the process, they would have been far better off; by attempting instead to vindicate their legally mandated rights, they lost out even more. Deng credited legal aid with helping them learn more, but lamented the impossible odds that they faced against their powerful employer. *"Legal aid helped by increasing our legal knowledge and consciousness, but the case itself was unwinnable. This is the most sorrowful point. Lawyer Lu also received pressure to give up the case. This country has no law. Out of thirteen workshops, we were the only ones who understood the law. The enterprise didn't want us to influence other people's cases. They tried to ensure that other people didn't find out ... It was also impossible to get any media coverage. We are three working class guys, at the lowest rungs of society. Now we can't find work. The first problem is our age; the second is that we have no connections and no background."*

Deng and other socialist generation workers like him faced difficult odds in the legal process. Their focus on unwinnable goals, such as employment security and a social safety net, came out of a sense of crisis that the state had forsaken them and the market rejected them. "*Right now the company is doing 'thought work' to get the rest of the employees to accept the severance. They are doing it to all the workers in this situation. We want security – we might get sick, we have kids in school, we can't find new jobs. It's not a question of being hardworking but a question of getting sicker as we get older. We worked for 27 years so it can't all disappear.*" While Deng's attachment to employment security is easy to understand given his age and future employability, their legal mobilization proved entirely unsuccessful.

Workers from the post-socialist generation, migrants and locals alike, tread a different path to legal mobilization. They have simpler cases, often less powerful employers, and lower expectations and demands. Their higher levels of education also make them more confident in their own abilities to navigate the legal system and the bureaucracy. Miss Chai (SH200439) was born in 1981 and worked for a private pharmaceutical company in Shanghai. She signed a one-year contract with the small firm, but was let go seven months later on the grounds that she had made a personal phone call from the office. When she refused to sign a statement of self-criticism, the employer terminated her labor relationship. Miss Chai immediately began to gather information on her rights. She visited a legal aid center for women at Fudan University, called the Municipal Labor Bureau's hotline (12333) to get advice, and finally read about the ECUPL legal aid center in the local evening paper. As she gained knowledge, she understood that the employer had violated her rights in a number of ways, including faulty calculation of her social insurance, non-payment of overtime, and underpayment of her salary. Her boss had demanded that she resign over the infraction and she also began to understand the difference between termination (with severance) and resignation (with no severance).

Chai's case was decided mostly in her favor at the initial labor arbitration, but the employer contested the arbitral award, so she also went to court. At the court appeal, she won again, but the company continued to appeal. Finally, at the second appeal at the Intermediate Court, the court issued a decision firmly on her side, which increased her compensation. She was satisfied and happy with the results, though she thought the process was inefficient and took too long, especially with the multiple appeal process. When asked about the impact of the suit on her life, Chai was nonplussed, "*No impact, nothing bad. I was just nervous and anxious when it was happening. Lawyer Lu had to do all the speaking in the court... Do it again? If I could negotiate the problem successfully, I would do that first. But if I couldn't, I'd go to the law."* She also notes that there are *"a lot of friends and relatives who need help understanding what they can get, what they can't. Now I help them."* Chai is also attentive to the specific problems faced by employees in the procurement of evidence. In her new position at a foreign-invested software company, she *"pays a lot of attention to labor laws."* On a one-year contract in her new position, Chai has no expectation of employment security and prepares for future disputes by paying attention to the media, promulgation of new laws, and collecting materials that might serve as evidence. She is matter of fact about the realities of the situation and while attentive to the problems does not condemn the system wholesale. Like many in her generation, she practices to get better at the law.

Dong (SH201309) was a middle-aged migrant from Anhui Province with a high school education and work experience in clothing factories as a skilled technician with a relatively high salary of RMB 8,000 (USD 1269). When his employer closed its Shanghai operations and prepared to move to a neighboring city, he negotiated a severance payment of RMB 24,400 (USD 3873) based on his three years of employment. Before he had received the severance, while looking for a new job, his former boss invited him to go to the new factory to work. Dong went for one day but decided against working there as the commute was too long. However, the boss then claimed that the severance compensation was no longer justified because Dong had in fact resigned. (No contract with the new factory had been signed.) Dong decided to try to protect his legal rights. He called telephone information and asked for *"a legal aid center in Changning District"* and was given the number of ECUPL. He began to receive legal aid and went to arbitration. During the arbitration proceedings, he refused the employer's settlement offer of RMB 12,000 (one half of the original agreement). *"I said at the time that I was willing to mediate. But I'm a laborer and that I was already willing to let two, three, or four thousand RMB go, it's already a big deal. I'm a laborer and he's the owner of a company. For me, two, three or four thousand RMB is already a lot of money, it's not a small figure. But the boss wasn't willing to mediate. He would only give half, RMB 12,000."* Dong was disparaging about bosses, noting that they constantly find ways to cheat workers. But he placed confidence in his own abilities to attend to the details of a successful case. *"I have a lot of knowledge now, at the start I didn't know much at all, my head was all muddled and I didn't understand... For example, now I understand about labor service contracts, about getting agreements with signatures. If I hadn't recorded that conversation, they wouldn't have recognized the evidence. At the time, I told the boss that they had to fix their chop on the agreement, but they said that the chop wasn't in the office."* (Dong showed recorded evidence of this conversation in court to demonstrate that an agreement had been signed, but not properly sealed.) While he fully credited legal aid with the assistance in training and education, he hoped to help other people like him. *"We are all just laborers and these kinds of bosses are really too many."*

These differences across two generations are indicative of the way in which law, delivered from above by a reformist state, has had disparate consequences for China's workers. The establishment of a legalized workplace did not work to the advantage of the generation that had existed and benefited from the prior non-legalized institutions and practices of traditional socialism. The same developments also expanded new rights and opportunities for migrants who had previously been marginalized members of the labor market, often shunted into the informal economy with dirty and dangerous working conditions and few if any legal rights. Given that the experiences of the socialist generation of workers are conditioned by a transitional period of market reforms, the experiences themselves will pass into history as these workers pass into retirement. While nostalgia for the Maoist period is stronger now than it was at the onset of reform and restructuring, and of the legal construction program, few members of the post-socialist generation seem to have hopes that the "iron rice bowl" that so defined the socialist era will return.

Conclusion

China's ongoing construction of legality at the workplace has empowered some, but disappointed many others. Other things being equal, experience with the law creates more realistic and cautious citizens. Law and litigation do not always deliver what is promised. For those with representation, however, the legal process is daunting, but not mysterious. Legal representation improves the outcomes of their cases, but also provides an entree into understanding how law works. This can lower expectations as well as educate them about their legal "mistakes" and how they might improve their chances the next time. Representation is integral to the durability of law, but it is sorely lacking for most aggrieved workers. While NGOs and legal aid organizations have expanded in China's larger cities, most disputants are unable to find affordable assistance. Finally, legality at the workplace diminished the privileges of socialist workers while offering new rights and securities to migrants. The labor contract system ended the "iron rice bowl" for one group of workers, even as it began to offer security and protection to another for the first time.

6

The Limits of Authoritarian Legality

> People crushed by law, have no hopes but from power. If laws are their enemies, they will be enemies to laws; and those who have much to hope and nothing to lose, will always be dangerous.
>
> Edmund Burke, Letter to Charles James Fox, 1777

> "I thought I would be able to scare the manager into signing the contract that I wanted, instead they called the police. You need to kill a couple of people before anyone will pay attention."
>
> (SH200410)

At the end of 2014, the Chinese Academy of Social Sciences (CASS) published a report that warned of a "rebound" in large-scale mass incidents of social contradiction and conflict, with labor grievances now outpacing other types of grievances in frequency (P. Li, Chen, and Zhang 2015, 12). The report noted that after several years of hard work in defusing conflicts and a gradual decline in their numbers, this trend was reversed in 2014 as "social contradictions conspicuously rebounded, with large scale mass incidents happening from time to time. Problems with rural land requisition, labor relations, environmental protection, and urban public safety and governance continued to be the major reasons for the frequent occurrence of social contradictions" (P. Li, Chen, and Zhang 2015, 13) The CASS report found that both formal labor disputes and strikes and street demonstrations were on the rise. In the first nine months of 2014, arbitrated labor disputes rose to 522,000 with over 721,000 people involved, an increase of 5.6 and 11.1 percent, respectively. In the same period, there were also fifty-two large-scale mass labor incidents (大规模群体性事件) involving over 1,000 workers. The key reasons for such intense worker frustration and anger were wage arrears, layoffs and severance compensation, and social insurance and welfare.[1] The report also noted that social media and public sentiment on the Internet were themselves becoming major factors in the evolution of social conflict, in some cases further inciting conflict and adding fuel to the fire of social grievances (P. Li, Chen, and Zhang 2015, 13).

The CASS report is an appropriate starting point to analyze the relationship between China's authoritarian legality and social conflict and mobilization. As a government think tank, the CASS interpretation of the recent spike in conflict reflects the government's belief that social mobilization and contention had been contained by direct government intervention and the "hard work" of taking an active role through grassroots mediation and other measures of state-led resolution and stability preservation. Conflict has suddenly "rebounded" as a consequence of the economic slowdown and more unpredictable social forces, such as social media and rights activists. The "new normal" of a Chinese economy, as it weans itself off a development model that has outlived its usefulness, is confronted with growing pains and necessary adjustments. The difficult economic situation has been exacerbated, moreover, by irresponsible Netizens who spread rumors online and feed the flames of popular passion against injustice and malfeasance. Government officials tasked with handling labor conflict share the CASS interpretation. They blame civil society actors, such as labor NGOs, for contributing to the "new" contentiousness. An official from the Ministry of Human Resources and Social Security commented informally on the problems.

In the media age, the conductivity of labor relations has strengthened. News about minor issues or news that is not correct can be easily spread. In Guangdong, a strike of a few hundred workers related to the housing provident fund, as soon as a Labor NGO got involved, it raised the alert all the way to the State Council ... The rights defense posturing of NGOs is getting stronger and stronger. The ACFTU and the Ministry are paying extremely close attention. Some lawyers and academics raise the flag of "rights defense" and increase the complexity of the government's handling. (BJ201501)

A labor bureau official from Guangdong was more pointed, "*in the governance of labor relations, labor NGOs are more and more active. We have to coordinate with public security on them.... We don't like labor*

---

[1] A fourth reason given was "disputes over the operation of the taxi industry." While strikes among transportation workers and other public sector workers, such as teachers, have been increasing over the past several years, they have been particularly frequent among taxi drivers with grievances against both employers and local governments

NGOs. Labor NGOs subsidize and support many petitioning workers." (BJ201504) Officials at the local level, tasked with the multiple and conflicting demands of enforcing labor laws, boosting employment, and maintaining social stability interpret the recent contentiousness of labor relations as further evidence of the necessity of direct government intervention. A Jiangsu labor official put it this way, *"the government has expanded its leading role in labor relations ... Within the tripartite system, the enterprise has the economic power of capital, it's very strong while the current state of the trade union is not worth mentioning; it's only the government who can take the lead role in the dialogue between labor and capital. I'm concurrently serving as the vice chairman of the provincial trade union, I know that the trade union doesn't penetrate into companies or society, only the government can intervene effectively."* (BJ201502)

In the aftermath of the CASS report, the contentiousness of labor relations and its potential threat to general social stability led the CCP's Central Committee and the State Council to release a joint statement on the importance of "harmonious" labor relations (中共中央国务院关于构建和谐劳动关系的意见 2015). This statement further advocated a "state-centric" approach to the management of labor relations, reiterating the views of these local officials that in the context of increased social mobilization, more active NGOs, and higher levels of contention, the state must increase its presence and "guiding" role. Thus, the first major proclamation of the Xi Jinping administration on labor politics invoked the key ideological term of its predecessor: "harmonious labor relations." The statement signaled that, in the realm of labor politics at least, the Xi administration was not diverging from the policies of the Hu Jintao era that put the government front and center in the management and containment of labor activism. Xi's solution to the continued unrest is to double down on the policies developed in the first five years of the Hu Jintao Administration (2003–2008), which promoted the notion of "harmonious society" through greater government intervention into dispute resolution and a turn away from formal legal processes for resolution toward government and CCP-led mediation and conciliation. By 2015, Xi's administration went even further in strengthening the government and Party's role in maintaining control over labor conflict. It unleashed an unprecedented wave of arrests of lawyers, social activists, and NGO leaders, including twenty five labor activists and labor NGO leaders, mainly concentrated in Guangdong Province (Mitchell and Hornby 2015). The experiments with greater NGO-led labor activism and trade union autonomy petered out as the crackdown signaled much less government tolerance, especially in the context of declining growth and economic volatility.

In this penultimate chapter, I present an argument that attributes the growing and unrelenting rise in labor conflict to the policies of the government to use law instrumentally as a tool for policy making and reform while thwarting the rise of necessary complementary institutions for the legal system to function effectively as a space for conflict resolution. Minzner's thesis is that the state's recourse to mediation and other extralegal forms of dispute resolution is a "turn against law" and a "top-down authoritarian political reaction to growing levels of social protest and conflict in the Chinese system" (Minzner 2011, 939).[2] While I agree with this insight, I add two points about law in the realm of labor relations. First, workers and the state have both turned against law. Second, the state's turn against law is *only one part* of a vicious circle that begins with the state's recourse to legality to pursue strategic goals and leads to workers' mobilization around these new legal rights. The state's incomplete adoption of legality feeds workers' disenchantment and radicalization. When legal mobilization ends in frustration and delay, hollow victories of unenforced judgments, and perceptions of bias and corruption, workers emboldened by both the promise of law and their own enhanced bargaining power, take to the streets, to the roofs, to the media, "to let society decide." The cycle ends with the state's reactive, post-hoc intervention to curtail protests, media agitation, and desperate petitioning by invoking both "harmonious" carrots like mediation and extra-legal compensation and the hard stick of repression.

The phrase "turn against law" is incomplete because the regime has not turned against law, especially in the labor realm where lawmaking and legislative activism have only increased during this period. The new laws passed since 2008 are critical elements of the government's goals to build more inclusive labor markets, increase urbanization, and enhance social protection. But the turn toward protective legislation and activist lawmaking was not complemented with adequate state-led enforcement of the minimum legal standards or sufficient representation and institutional support for an increasingly "rights conscious" workforce. Instead, the Chinese state relied on bottom-up mobilization by aggrieved workers to lodge claims for protection and demands for compliance. When mobilization led to defeat and frustration, the state reactively stepped in to

---

[2] See also Fu 2011.

"manage" instability. The increase in labor conflict and collective mobilization outside of the legal realm since then, workers' own "turn against law," is the product of this incomplete institutionalization of the dispute resolution process and the failure to structure a dispute resolution system that adequately represents workers' rights and interests, particularly as workers have become more adept in and emboldened to articulate their rights and interests collectively.

The chapter proceeds first with a brief description of the progression of labor conflict since the 2008 Labor Contract Law, including the unprecedented jump in disputes that occurred that year and the state's aggressive turn toward mediation and other extralegal forms of resolution. Rather than a recent "rebound" of labor conflict after the government's successful intervention in dispute resolution in the aftermath of the 2008 Labor Contract Law and Financial Crisis, I document that labor conflict has not abated, but continued to increase while the government's handling of labor conflict shifted to government intervention and mediation. Arbitrated disputes have moderately decreased because the mechanisms of resolution have shifted to emphasize pre-arbitration mediation and resolution, but the formal claims underlying disputes have only increased. In tandem with the unabated increase in formal claims, strikes and protests have also spiked. The chapter then moves to explain these trends – in particular the shift of some workers to collective mobilization and extra-legal modes of dispute resolution, including strikes, demonstrations, and informal collective bargaining. If the goal of the government's switch to mediation and extra-legal settlement was "harmonious labor relations," why do we see only less harmony and more conflict, with sustained increases in both formal labor disputes and labor protests? Why are the courts and the streets both under siege?

Although the overall context of China's labor markets explains some part of the increased bargaining power and confidence of Chinese workers to make claims at the workplace, it does not explain the greater recourse to extralegal mobilization and protest. Demographic shifts over the past few decades have led to labor shortages in key areas of the economy, including labor intensive manufacturing, emboldening workers to make claims against employers when they are confident of finding a new job elsewhere. The decline of the size of the working population relative to older workers has created structural shortages in the labor market while continued segmentation of workers by residential system further hampers integration (Cai and Wang 2012; Meng 2012; Yao 2011). At the same time, as detailed in Chapter 3, China's labor protections have strengthened over time while barriers to claim-making have fallen. To some degree, the increasing contentiousness of China's workers is no surprise as it reflects the changing labor market and more political and legal space for mobilization. On the other hand, given the state's emphasis on stability, harmony, and early resolution of disputes, it is surprising that labor conflict and instability only increases in tandem with formal claims. This chapter disentangles this puzzle by showing how the absence of representation thwarts individualized rights protection, radicalizing aggrieved workers and driving workers from the courts to the streets.

Using two case studies of collective mobilization, I argue that there are three main reasons for this vicious circle of legislation, mobilization, and state intervention. First, as the earlier chapters have discussed, this "fire-alarm" system of individual rights enforcement is extremely suboptimal for compliance with China's minimum legal standards, especially when the plaintiffs are poor, marginalized, and bereft of resources. When individualized legal mobilization is the main channel to solve endemic problems of basic compliance with minimum labor standards, not only will overall compliance be poor, individual litigants will be extremely frustrated and disappointed in the formal system. The government's dependence on workers themselves as the "firefighters" for enhanced compliance is insufficient and dangerous. Second, as workers' bargaining has increased due to labor shortages and more sympathetic media and government treatment, *some* workers' demands and expectations now regularly exceed the legal minimum guaranteed by labor legislation. Disputes over "interests" (higher wages, changes to working operations, better severance packages) are now endemic to developed coastal China. However, there are no institutionalized mechanisms to manage, much less prevent, conflict. Forcing interest disputes into the formal legal resolution process and limiting the ability of workers to represent themselves or be represented only further entrenches workers' impressions that the law is a dead end. Interest disputes require effective worker representation and a legal framework for collective bargaining and negotiation. Finally, as has been argued in analysis of social instability generally, the state's overwhelming focus on "stability preservation" and its allergy to organization and representation outside the Party has created incentives for protestors to target the government and to escalate strategically. If stability is the key goal of the government, then disputants must threaten the realization of that goal to elicit government response and conciliation (or repression). While this is a high-risk strategy for protestors, leading to either good results or arrest, it reflects the lack of any parameters or constraints once disputes have moved from the courts to the streets.

The two cases examined here highlight these basic problems of rights disputes regarding minimal compliance and interest disputes regarding demands above the minimum. The first dispute occurred in 2013 at a Guangzhou hospital affiliated to a local university when long-term migrant workers employed as nursing assistants began to demand legally-mandated social insurance. This "rights dispute" highlights the difficulty of achieving compliance with China's basic legal standards through the formal resolution system of arbitration and litigation. The second dispute occurred in 2014 at a Walmart store in Changde, Hubei. When the store was suddenly closed due to a national restructuring plan, the store workers, led by the store's trade union chairman, organized to demand better severance compensation. It highlights the growing trend of "interests" disputes in which workers' demands rise above the legal minimums set out by law. Both disputes demonstrate the limitations of the legal system and dispute resolution system and the logic of strategic escalation that drives workers from the courts to the streets.

LABOR CONFLICT AND THE PURSUIT OF A HARMONIOUS SOCIETY

Brought forth by Hu Jintao and Wen Jiabao at the seventeenth Party Congress of the CCP in 2007, the concept of "harmonious society" advocated placing goals of "social equity and justice" alongside the traditional reformist goals of growth and development. Just as Deng Xiaoping, the architect of China's early reform policies, advocated for the pursuit of a "well-off society," Hu Jintao's shift from a concept of economic well-being to one of societal well-being and balance marked the changing goalposts of China's reformist leaders. The pursuit of harmonious society was part of a strategy of the Hu-Wen government to re-orient central government policies away from a sole focus on growth and development and toward redistribution, reduction of inequality, and more social protection. Coined as "scientific development" and "putting people first," the central government advanced policies such as cancellation of the agricultural tax, new pension and health insurance programs for rural citizens, and the expansion of social welfare for impoverished urban citizens. "Harmonious society" and "scientific development" as the rallying cries of a new leadership did not mean that China cast law off as the main tool to manage the economy and to stipulate rights and obligations of social actors, such as firms, workers, and consumers. In a rather ironic way, pushing for harmony via social equity and justice led directly to the strong legislative push from the central government for more inclusive social protection, higher labor standards, and lower barriers to access legal institutions. The 2008 Labor Contract Law (LCL) focused on increasing formalization of labor relations through the written labor contract. It also has made it more difficult to employ workers continuously on short-term contracts. The 2008 Employment Promotion Law (EPL) strengthened restrictions on employment discrimination. The 2008 Labor Dispute Mediation and Arbitration Law (LDMAL) lowered the fee structure for labor dispute resolution and lengthened the statute of limitations. It also increased the evidentiary burdens of firms to the benefit of workers. The strengthened legal protections and the lower barriers to access promoted the bottom-up legal mobilization of workers as a mechanism to put greater pressure on local governments to enforce the law and on firms to comply with the law. In a very consequential way, the central government was delegating these important tasks of enforcement and compliance to workers themselves.

The subsequent "turn against law" by both workers and the state was a post-hoc necessary adjustment to the massive increase in rights-claiming that was sparked by these new central laws. During this critical time period, protective laws were continually advanced by the regime and the barriers to filling formal claims were lowered, but the modes of workers' representation and organization were not fundamentally reformed. Greater reliance on law and bottom-up legal mobilization led to an explosion of disputes, frustration and disappointment with resolution, protests and instability, and subsequent state intervention in the name of stability. Since 2008 labor relations have been anything but harmonious. Measured by either formal claims or street protests and strikes, labor conflict in China has continued to increase. The total number of disputes rose from 502,000 in 2007 to 1,512,000 in 2012 ("Statistical Analysis of 2012 Labor Disputes" 2013). Arbitrated disputes rose dramatically in 2008 as the response to the LCL, but then stabilized as the government pushed aggressively for mediation as the primary resolution channel. As Zhuang and Chen document, the government expanded the powers of local and grassroots bodies to do labor mediation, further incentivizing judges, local officials, and arbitrators to take part in mediation efforts, and to target large collective disputes (Zhuang and Chen 2015). Su and He's examination of the work of "stability preservation committees" and their role in the resolution of collective disputes also finds a strong emphasis on mediation and conciliation as replacements for formal resolution through arbitration and litigation (Su and He 2010). It's important to note, however, that the turn toward mediation and conciliation did not coincide with a decline in overall disputes. Arbitration committees and courts continued to be inundated with cases, though at a lower number than would have been the case if these new mediation channels had not been opened.

The rise in formal claims was matched by protests and strikes, as also discussed and documented in Chapter 3. China Labour Bulletin's strike data over the last few years corroborate this story of uninterrupted labor instability rather than a decline and recent rebound. In 2013 and 2014, according to their data, there were over 1,793 labor strikes, a substantial increase from 2011 and 2012 (Report on China's Workers Movement, 2013–2014, 2015). More than a quarter of these strikes occurred in Guangdong Province; Jiangsu ranked second with 120 strikes while Zhejiang ranked third with 106. Although 43 percent of all strikes occurred in the manufacturing sector, strikes in hospital, schools, transportation (bus and taxi drivers), and sanitation made up one third, with heightened dissatisfaction among public sector workers. Wage and salary disputes were most common, but disputes over social insurance followed closely behind. The CLB report notes that the aging migrant workforce in many areas is increasingly concerned with their long-term security and welfare. Moreover, local governments interested in boosting payments into the social insurance funds are putting more pressure on employers to pay into the social insurance funds, sometimes leading to disputes with workers when employers reduce overall compensation to the worker in order to pay into the funds. The CLB report also finds that strikes and protests most often occur after attempts at bargaining, conciliation, and legal redress have been attempted but failed (Report on China's Workers Movement, 2013–2014, 2015).

The push toward mediation and settlement is also obvious in the national and local trends of labor dispute resolution. The rates of mediation have increased substantially since 2008, with many more government and party units tasked with labor dispute mediation. These include neighborhood committees, large enterprises, and local government offices. In a 2012 official report, out of 1.5 million total disputes accepted by arbitration and mediation units, 46 percent were settled in mediation. Some localities with long experience in labor dispute resolution report even more impressive rates. A report from Huangpu District in central

Shanghai stated that in 2013 the district labor arbitration office accepted 3,701 disputes and successfully mediated 82 percent. It also found, however, that the number of disputes at the district people's court had also increased from 541 cases to 677.[3] The courts have not escaped the pressure to mediate or "settle" cases. Under the rubric of "grand mediation," Huangpu judges were encouraged to settle labor cases as much as possible. In 2013, Huangpu District judges settled over 40 percent of all labor cases (2013年黄浦区劳动人事争议调解仲裁与审判白皮书2014, 3).

Although not specific to labor disputes, but indicative of the general change in the government's approach, Lee and Zhang have documented the conciliatory and flexible response of the government in the wake of high levels of social conflict (Lee and Zhang 2013). Lee and Zhang also find that the law is not absent from the bargaining process between state officials tasked with preserving stability and unruly protestors threatening to disrupt it. As we see below in the two case studies, state officials use law and legal processes strategically to atomize and isolate mobilized citizens as well as to structure and limit demands. Wang and Minzner explore the fiscal, financial, and human resource side of the "security state," documenting the heavy costs of this approach, which requires very extensive coordination between state actors and deployment of state resources, both repressive and pecuniary (Wang and Minzner 2013).

TURNED AGAINST THE LAW

As the government developed these tactics of state-led intervention, mediation, and bargaining with aggrieved workers in the aftermath of the Labor Contract Law, a new movement of labor activists and lawyers was gaining strength in the Pearl River Delta[4]. Centered around law firms specializing in worker grievances and networks of labor NGOs that coordinate and cooperate, these activists used the vocabulary of law and rights to mobilize workers to avoid the law and the formal dispute resolution system.[5] Focusing on the shortcomings of the legal system – its duration and complexity, its tendency to fragment and atomize workers, and its

---

[3] In Shanghai, as in most places, the dispute process at both arbitration and litigation emphasized mediation and settlement. Shanghai was also experimenting with binding arbitration for some types of labor disputes and allowing some disputes to go directly to court, both of these changes were made possible by the Labor Dispute Mediation and Arbitration Law. The goals include more finality and a shorter appeal process.
[4] The larger network of labor activists and cause lawyers extends beyond the Pearl River Delta, but it began there and remains concentrated there.
[5] The disputes discussed in this chapter involve one law firm, "Labor Rights Law Firm" 劳维法律事务所).

lack of independence from local government influence – these lawyers and activists worked to harness the collective power of aggrieved workers to bargain directly with managers and bosses for better workplace conditions. Law was still important – as it set out the legal standards and the minimal protections that workers should but often did not enjoy – but these cause lawyers and activists rejected the strictures of the legal system and the ways in which it stripped workers of their unity and potential bargaining power. Often combined with strike actions, demonstrations, and moral pleas, labor activists redirected mobilization away from the law and toward society, the media, and the government.

Workers and activists' reluctance to use the legal system for rights protection mirrored the state's increasing dissatisfaction with the rise in litigation and social protest. Law was no longer a stabilizing force or an institutionalized "channel" to harness and placate aggrieved citizens as the NPC legislators believed. It had become part of a cycle of rights-mobilization and escalation through media attention, protests, threats of violence, and government intervention in the name of stability. Frustrated disputants found themselves bounced between various agencies with no clear path toward resolution. Employers used the long-drawn-out appeal process to weaken workers' resolve. Courts were often not powerful enough to enforce judgments. Litigants sometimes did not accept legal defeat when it violated other norms or expectations. Social mobilization and protest became necessary steps for better outcomes. The state's emphasis on social stability encouraged aggrieved citizens to threaten that stability in order to attract the state's attention and involvement in dispute resolution. The two cases below show how these dynamics play out as litigious workers and a beleaguered but feisty group of activists try to invoke the law without allowing the legal system to atomize and constrain them.

Rights Disputes and the Feedback Loop between Protest and Law

The dispute that occurred between workers at the Guangzhou Chinese Medicine Hospital began as a request from seven long-term nursing assistants for social insurance.[6] In this sense, it is a simple "rights" dispute. These employees requested that the employer comply with the legal standards, which require that employers pay into social insurance. The dispute transformed into a protracted fight between the hospital

---

[6] The information about this dispute is culled from interviews with participants during and after the strike, written reports and documents, media articles, and discussion at a workshop in May 2014 that focused on workers' strike activities and collective bargaining. For a more optimistic analysis of the significance of the Walmart strike, see Li and Liu 2016)

and over 120 workers, including nursing assistants, security guards, and stretcher-bearers, all low-level migrant workers from inland China and rural Guangdong Province with elementary to high school level education. Their road of rights-protection moved from dutifully following the procedural rules for arbitration and litigation to extended petitioning at government and trade union offices, to requests for collective bargaining directly with management, to peaceful sit-ins and demonstrations at the workplace, to a final "dare to die" rooftop protest that ended with twelve workers arrested on criminal charges.

The Guangzhou hospital case is not unusual. It typifies both the limitations of rights' defense and the growing power and organizational capacity of workers and activists to invoke the law for rights protection even while disavowing administrative and legal procedures that are to their disadvantage. The locus of the dispute, in a local hospital, a public organization, also captures a growing trend of labor disputes in China's public institutions, including schools, hospitals, and government institutions. As with the interest dispute discussed below, the government's reliance on law and the workers' inability to be represented collectively expose the limitations of an illiberal legality. It exemplifies the feedback loop between law and protest. Statutory rights in law offer hope and empowerment, but the legal process to make these statutory rights real often drives workers to despair.

In early 2012, Liang Huafen, who had worked for the hospital for over twenty years, heard from a fellow migrant worker that hospitals in Guangzhou were beginning to pay into social insurance for their lower level staff. Liang decided that she should avail herself of this benefit, as she had grown older and stayed in the city she was beginning to worry about her long-term security. In April 2012, she and a few co-workers approached the hospital with this request, but the hospital leadership refused. Liang proceeded to the district labor bureau to inquire about her rights. The district labor bureau informed her that without a formal written labor contract, it is not possible to receive social insurance. Liang needed to prove that she and her fellow workers had labor relations with the hospital. They began to compile the necessary evidence to demonstrate a relationship with the hospital, filing an arbitration claim against the hospital that requested recognition of formal labor relations and contributions to social insurance funds and the housing provident fund.

As they proceeded in the initial steps of legal mobilization and rights protection, Liang and some of her fellow nursing assistants were suddenly told by hospital management to "take a long vacation." Others found that their work positions were shifted to unfamiliar offices. A few months later, the hospital announced a restructuring, which included the employment termination of the entire nursing assistant staff of over 200 workers. When a reporter visited the hospital to inquire about the terminations, however, he found many still employed and working at their old positions. But they informed the reporter that they were paid only in cash, with no receipts and no proof of actual employment (Yuan 2013).

After six months of waiting for the initial arbitration ruling, the nurses received a ruling rejecting their central demands. The district labor arbitration committee only found evidence of labor relations between the nurses and the hospital for two years between 1999–2001 when the hospital directly managed the nursing assistants' wages and used direct deposit cards through a local bank for convenience. The arbitration committee accepted the hospital's defense that it had since switched the management of the nursing assistants to a third-party labor subcontractor, despite the fact that since 2008 the labor subcontracting company was a subsidiary of a company of which a hospital director was the chairman of the board and the legal representative. Ownership of the labor subcontracting company's stock was divided between this company, which owned 80 percent, and the committee of the education union affiliated to the hospital. In other words, while the labor arbitration committee rejected the claim that the hospital was the direct employer of the nursing assistants; the company that did directly employ them was owned by the hospital and led by hospital administrators. With the statute of limitations expired for the 1999–2001 period of employment, the arbitration committee denied their requests for social insurance.

Nurse Liang and her colleagues were dissatisfied with the arbitration ruling and immediately appealed the decision for a hearing at the Baiyun District Court. After another six months, in April 2013, the Baiyun Court came out with a judgment that favored the workers. The court ruled that since 2008, when the company owned by the hospital took over the subcontracting arrangement from an outside company, the hospital did have employment relations with the nurses and should retroactively contribute to five years of social insurance, 5600 RMB (USD 918) per nursing assistant. The hospital immediately appealed the ruling to the municipal level court for a second hearing. By the time the protests of the workers reached a crescendo in August 2013, the court had still not announced any decision in the second hearing.

As the nurses' claims progressed slowly through the procedures of arbitration and civil court appeal, the low-level workers of Guangzhou

Chinese Medicine University Hospital were beginning to come together over extended grievances involving not only social insurance, but also discriminatory compensation, overtime violations, and most viscerally, the retributive termination of the nursing staff who had first moved to protect their rights. Young guards and older nursing staff joined together in solidarity to fight for their growing number of grievances against the hospital. By this time, these low-level "rights-defenders" were receiving advice and strategic assistance from local labor activists and lawyers. At a large meeting in a local restaurant on May 12, a well-known labor lawyer advised the workers to elect representatives, to stick together, and to avoid violence. He emphasized time and time again to the workers to focus on collective bargaining and negotiation, not legal channels. The path to a just resolution of the dispute lay not in the law and in the courts, but in workers' solidarity and direct bargaining with management. The law would guide their demands but not dictate their path. The lawyer advised the workers to use collective mobilization to put pressure on hospital management to come to the negotiating table. On May 20th, after the unfavorable arbitral ruling had been released, over 120 workers convened a peaceful "sit in" within the hospital grounds. Four days later, more than eighty workers went out to petition at the provincial government office, but were apprehended along the way by police and sent directly to the public security bureau where their names were recorded.

The hospital management took advantage of the arbitral ruling against the nursing staff to offer the hospital guards a resolution to their dispute, which mainly involved different wage structures between subcontracted and directly hired guards, overtime pay, and salary increases. The guards were in a much more advantageous legal position than the nurses, with signed labor contracts and proof of employment, though they had yet to lodge a formal claim against the hospital. The resolution was relatively generous, offering each guard three months of salary for every year worked and an additional 5600 RMB (USD 918) in compensation for retroactive overtime pay, night work, and bonuses. The resolution had conditions of course: in order to take the compensation the guards had to sign an agreement that they would cease and desist any 'rights protection' activity. To accept the agreement, the guards would have to break with the nursing staff. The hospital clearly sought to break up and fragment the protesting workers by compromising with those most likely to win in court and isolating the nursing staff who had no proof of employment and had just failed in their arbitration claim.

The solidarity of the workers was hard to break, however. The guards rejected the resolution and informed the hospital that they would persevere with their collective rights' mobilization. The workers continued to stage a sit-in at the hospital while groups of workers petitioned at the Guangdong Provincial Trade Union, the Provincial Health Bureau, and the university affiliated with the hospital. The dispute began to be discussed in the media and on China's popular social media platforms. On July 10, conflict between the striking workers and hospital leaders became heated and physical. The workers took over the administrative offices and surrounded the hospital leaders. When the police arrived, they attempted to assist the hospital director and other managers in leaving the floor. Some of the older nursing assistants blocked them from leaving, grabbing their legs, and entreating them to sit down to negotiate. The police intervened and some of the nursing assistants were roughed up and dragged away. Many workers were detained at the local police station under the allegations that they had violated the leaders' physical freedom and disturbed social order.

Finally, on July 16, the workers entrusted a law firm to act as their bargaining agent and the hospital agreed to the first bargaining session. However, almost immediately, the hospital pulled out of the bargaining on the grounds that it was an internal hospital issue and should not involve any outside advisors or lawyers. Instead of bargaining with the whole group via legal representatives, the hospital management switched tactics, turning to the nursing assistants who were waiting for the municipal court to rule on the company's appeal of the judgment in April that had awarded the nurses each 5600 RMB for the last five years of social insurance. In early August, management enticed them with a settlement that significantly exceeded the Baiyun Court's ruling, 10,000 RMB for the last five years of social insurance and other related grievances and an additional 10,000 RMB (USD 1640) per worker as a "humanitarian economic subsidy" (人道主义经济补贴). The workers' solidarity began to break down. Some of the nursing staff accepted the agreement and took the compensation. Many left the hospital to look for new employment; others went home to their villages. A few stayed with the guards to support them in their continued attempts to reach an agreement with the hospital. However, when the guards indicated that they would be willing to accept the original resolution that the hospital had offered them in May, the hospital refused. On August 19th, the guards lost their patience, climbed to the top of the roof awning of the hospital's outpatient clinic, and unfurled large banners announcing a protest to the death. The main banner read "Guangzhou Chinese Medicine University Hospital Society of Defending Workers Rights to the Death." Two other banners highlighted their key demands: "Overtime Pay, Wage Increase, Decent Work" and "Strictly Respect the Law on Same Work, Same Pay." In the ensuing hours of protest, the police arrived under the cover of nightfall, climbed the awning and began to make arrests. In the end, twelve workers were arrested and charged with organizing to disrupt public order. After several months and a trial, nine workers were sent to prison to terms of 8–9 months; three were released.

During the dispute, the workers had petitioned many times to various branches of the ACFTU. The municipal trade union initially rejected their appeals with the reason that they did not have jurisdiction over the hospital. Given that the labor subcontracting company within the hospital was partially owned by the union branch (which was under the education department's union), the municipal union did not have the bureaucratic standing to intervene. When the workers petitioned the provincial trade union, the Guangdong Federation of Trade Unions (GFTU) in May and June, as the protests and sit-ins began, the initial response of the union was to persuade the workers to "use the law" and "use the proper channels" of arbitration and litigation to resolve the disputes. When the workers entreated GFTU to step into the dispute and represent the workers' collective interests after law firm representation had failed, there was no response. In early July, after the workers had petitioned five times to the provincial trade union, the GFTU used its official Weibo account to deliver a statement, which read:

The representatives of the guards and nursing assistants of the Guangzhou Chinese Medicine University Hospital have already petitioning the GFTU, which is handling it according to the regulations on petitioning. Until now the claims of the workers have still not been properly settled. Protecting the legal rights and interests of workers is the basic responsibility of the trade union, the GFTU leadership has already issued written comments and established a coordinating small group, it continues to pay attention to how things progress, urges the employer to fulfill its legal obligations, coordinates the functions of government departments, and promotes the settlement of this incident by law and regulation (CLB 2014).

During the scuffle between the police and the workers in mid-July, the GFTU sent a few legal aid officials to the police station but did not offer any concrete help to the workers. It continued to insist on legal procedures and it refused to represent the workers on the grounds that they were made up of more than one group. By the end of July, with the workers increasingly desperate, they made another entreaty to the GFTU to establish a small coordinating body to represent the workers in the dispute. The GFTU refused, saying that it would wait until August 2 (when the company would make an offer of compensation) before "resolving the demands of the workers within the confines of the law and regulation" (CLB 2014). On August 2, the company made a compensatory offer to the nurses while excluding the guards. The workers suspected that the GFTU and the hospital had already come to a jointly-agreed upon resolution that offered significant compensation to the nurses, far in excess of the court decision, with the goal of breaking the workers' unity, isolating the guards, and ending the dispute.

The Labor Defense Law Firm and the labor NGOs that worked with the striking workers from May had attempted to substitute for the trade union by representing the workers in collective negotiations. After the fracas of mid-July and increasing tensions between the workers and the police, the participation of the law firm and the NGOs were further complicated by the intervention of the State Security Bureau (SSB) and the Public Security Bureau (PSB). While the hospital had already rejected the law firm's participation on the grounds that the dispute was an "internal hospital issue," the SSB further limited the participation of these cause lawyers on the grounds that they were funded by foreign and Hong Kong-based organizations and that their motivations were shaped by external hostile forces. The law firm continued to represent the workers who were arrested and charged with criminal charges related to disrupting social order, but they were not able to successfully represent the workers in the settlement of the labor grievance. In the end, they were also not able to exonerate the guards who were arrested after the roof protest.

As a "rights-dispute" involving a key benefit of the labor laws, to enjoy social insurance via employment, this dispute showcases the extreme difficulties of marginalized workers in attaining their most basic rights. While Nursing Assistant Liang and her colleagues went exactly "by the book" in their initial strategy, they were thwarted at every juncture: a recalcitrant state-owned employer who flagrantly abuses the law while reaping the benefits of cheap, migrant labor, an uncooperative local labor bureaucracy that protects the local employer, a trade union that invokes "law and legal procedure" without ever taking on its mandated role as worker representative. This case also highlights my earlier argument that individualized legal mobilization as the main mode of compliance with labor laws results in suboptimal, market-conforming compliance. Workers with better resources, more skills, formal contracts, and market bargaining power might do okay in this system. Workers like Nursing Assistant Liang will not.

This case also demonstrates how aggrieved workers move from using law "as a weapon" to disappointment and frustration with the dispute resolution system. Extra-legal weapons such as demonstrations, sit-ins, and petitioning become necessary to raise the stakes and attract public sympathy and government attention.

Interest Disputes in an Institutional Vacuum

The Changde Walmart store closure case was a dispute about the proper procedures and compensation for workers following the implementation of a nation-wide restructuring plan of Walmart to close down stores not performing well and to open new stores in other areas.[7] Walmart's decision to close the Changde store, in northwestern Hunan Province, meant the unemployment or relocation of over 130 workers. When it was announced to the workforce in early March 2014, the workers were given two options: transfer to another Walmart Store (Yiyang and Changsha were both options in Hunan, with Yiyang about 100 kilometers away) or accept the severance compensation of "N + 1," one month of salary for every year worked plus one additional month. The workers were unhappy with both options and began to discuss strategies to improve the settlement plan. Then something historic happened. The Changde Walmart Store trade union chairman, Huang Xingguo, concurrently a manager in the administrative office but elected as the trade union chair three years earlier, decided to lead the workers in a "rights defense" movement. Meetings were held and documents were drawn up establishing a "rights defense small group," which was then entrusted with the representation of the seventy or so participating workers. The "rights defense small group" included nine members; three of which were selected as official bargaining representatives. The group also agreed that no one would individually bargain with management so as to ensure that the company could not buy out individuals with side deals. The workers began a campaign to stop Walmart officials and workers from other branches from taking inventory from the store. They set up a sit-in at the store loading dock with workers taking turns during the night shift, cooking for each other, and managing other parts of their lives. They also began to petition the

---

[7] The sources for this case include interviews with lawyers and activists involved in the case on both sides; the Walmart workers' blog, an extensive published interview between China Labour Bulletin (CLB) and the Walmart Trade Union chairman, Huang Xingguo, and a CLB research report on the strike as well as various media reports. I was also a participant in a workshop that included labor lawyers, activists, and academics in May 2014 that discussed the Walmart case in detail. The workshop included some of the participants in the strike and subsequent lawsuit. This case is also discussed in (C. Li and Liu, Mingwei 2016).

local city trade union for help and assistance in their bid for rights protection. The workers collectively drew up a list of fourteen demands that included both attention to how the store closure would affect their wages and benefits and other relatively minor details. Two of the demands were most significant: one, the workers demanded that the severance compensation be increased from N + 1 to 2(N + 1) (two months of salary for every year worked) on the grounds that the termination was in violation of the early notification required by law; two, the workers demanded the company pay the relocation costs of workers who agreed to relocate to other Walmart stores, including housing and education fees of workers' children.

One of the major arguments in this chapter is that the lack of effective representation of workers leads to frustration and disappointment with the formal dispute resolution system, including access to legal counsel and the right to freely form trade unions to bargain collectively with management. In this regard, the Walmart case is exceptional in that the workers, almost miraculously, had representation from their official trade union branch at the workplace. As the dispute progressed and drew significant media and social attention, the workers also received legal aid from the municipal trade union of Changde City and offers of legal representation from a Shenzhen labor law firm and a well-known industrial relations professor at Renmin University. However, even with very competent representation, the workers' struggle for a better severance package was dramatically unsuccessful, given the institutional context that constrains the trade union in its role as worker representative and that tends to redirect interest disputes to the legal system, which is structured to only offer protection for legal minimums in a highly individualistic setting. As with the Guangzhou hospital case above, the limits of the formal system encouraged workers to gain leverage by disrupting social stability. In this case, the workers focused on barricading the store's goods from removal, using their bodies to stop trucks from entering the loading docks, and appealing to public opinion through words, pictures, and videos on their blog and Weibo feed.

The workers' demands were framed in a legalistic way, alleging that the Walmart termination proceedings violated the Labor Law's clauses on layoffs for economic reasons, which require thirty days notice and notification of the trade union or worker representative committee. The severance compensation offered by Walmart of N + 1 is fairly standard for many termination procedures and is based on article 47 of the Labor Contract Law, which stipulates one month of salary for every year worked. The

Walmart compensation of one additional month salary was also specifically presented in the offer as additional compensation in lieu of notification. While there was some significant disagreement even among labor law experts in China whether Walmart's actions were in violation of the law, many lawyers agreed that Walmart had hewed to a narrow reading of the law and offered the legal minimum, or slightly above the legal minimum. Given that both the Labor Contract Law and the Labor Law do not have clearly delineated clauses on termination proceedings for dissolution (not bankruptcy), there was room for disagreement. In other words, it was possible, and in this case necessary, to turn the workers' dissatisfaction over the store's closure from an "interest dispute" into a "rights dispute," alleging illegal behavior by the employer. The need to look to the law and minimum standards, even during what is basically an interest disputes between workers about to lose their job and a large multinational corporation with big expansion plans for China (though not, unfortunately, in Changde), is absolutely necessary in the absence of any effective collective bargaining or contractual agreement between workers and employers. In this unusual case of a trade union chairman interested in "rights defense," the workers have no recourse to any collective agreement. As the trade union chair reported during the dispute, the collective wage agreements reached between the store and the employee union only guaranteed the workers the local legal minimum and wage increases that were even lower than the industry average. Moreover, the collective agreements did not speak to the issue of economic layoffs.

The trade union was also constrained in leveraging its power beyond the support it received from the workforce and the informal social and public support it received in the media. While part of the umbrella structure of the ACFTU, with union branches at the municipal (Changde) and provincial (Hunan) levels, the store trade union was increasingly isolated as Chairman Huang took his rights defense in an unprecedented direction. In the first few days of the dispute, the municipal trade union offered strong rhetorical support for the Changde Walmart trade union and also dispatched the head of the legal aid office, Director Zhang, to offer the workers legal advice and support. As the dispute began to involve higher levels of the Changde government and attract social attention nationally, the union's support disappeared. In an interview with a Hong Kong labor NGO, Chairman Huang described it this way:

Initially our upper level trade union's position, when we first started to petition, and found the related office, the head of the legal aid office, [he] was extremely indignant and very sympathetic. Moreover, his attitude and position were both very resolute. He really wasn't going to take it anymore and would certainly demand an explanation for us. But after the petitioning bureau got involved, his voice got smaller and smaller, until it finally just disappeared. (CLB audio transcript)

The trade union representatives at the municipal level were unable to offer institutional support to the Changde Walmart workers as the handling of the dispute extended to multiple government and party offices in charge of maintaining social stability. These offices convened several meetings in attempts to bring the workers and the employer to a mediated compromise. Participants included the Wuling government, the district government head, the district government general office director, an official from the labor bureau, the commerce bureau, the petitioning bureau, the labor inspection bureau, the police, and a coordinated office on public order in addition to representatives from Walmart and the store employees. Chairman Huang reported that these mediation sessions, of which three were convened, became like "big criticism sessions" of the workers as they were pressed to give up their claims and accept Walmart's termination proceedings as fully legal. In the absence of any other kind of agreement or contract between Walmart and its Changde workers, the workers were also unable to avail themselves of broader support within Walmart branch unions. Chairman Huang noted that there was no formal communication or coordination between the trade unions at different Walmart branches. While the rights' mobilization of the Changde Walmart trade union was impressive and unprecedented, it was also isolated.

As the Changde Walmart workers persevered in their rights' mobilization and store inventory blockade, on March 21, two weeks into the dispute, the provincial trade union, the Hunan Federation of Trade Unions (HFTU) also intervened in the dispute, castigating Chairman Huang for his pioneering attempts at rights defense. The HFTU instructed Chairman Huang to hew to legal means to protect the workers' rights and to use legal processes to solve their grievances. The upper level trade unions would provide no assistance to the Changde Walmart workers if their demands exceeded the legal standards. Ten days later, Walmart began to remove its inventory from the store. Chairman Huang was instructed by the municipal trade union to offer no resistance or to risk arrest. As the workers' blockade failed, they followed the upper level union's instruction to turn to the formal resolution system. Under Chairman Huang's leadership, and with legal representation from Renmin University's Professor Chang Kai and other labor law specialists, sixty-nine Changde workers filed individual claims at the city labor arbitration committee on April 25 alleging that Walmart did not abide by the legal regulations in terminating their labor contracts. As the arbitration proceedings began, Walmart offered the workers an additional RMB 3000 (USD 491) in a mediated settlement as compensation for their legal fees during the three month-long dispute. Local Changde officials visited the families of many workers to exhort them to accept the settlement and give up the arbitration claim. Fifty-one workers did so, but Chairman Huang and seventeen other workers waited for the arbitration decision. On June 26, 2014, those last remnants of the Changde Walmart rights defense small group lost their case in arbitration. The case result, by that time, was widely expected. When they attempted to appeal the arbitral ruling, the local court rejected the claim on the logic that an employer no longer existed as the Changde Walmart branch had already closed. The small group of workers, including Chairman Huang, then filed new arbitration claims against Walmart-Changsha. This last arbitration case was still winding its way through the appeal process in 2016, two years after the dispute began.

In addition to the individual claims, the Walmart Changde branch union filed a separate arbitration claim alleging violation of the collective agreement between the store trade union and the store. This was an unprecedented attempt, in the absence of a real collective contract, to invoke the power of the enterprise trade union against the unilateral decisions of the employer. This case lost in arbitration because the Changde branch trade union could not provide evidence of any agreement related to layoffs or store closure.[8]

Although the municipal and provincial level trade unions were not supportive of Chairman's Huang's attempt at "rights defense" above the legal standards, the municipal trade union did provide financial resources for these individualized legal claims to go forward. However, this narrow hewing to the legal minimums and the trade union's stern warning to the Changde workers to keep within the legal framework in making their demands underline the crux of the problem. There is no institutional space or mechanism, even within the official trade union system, for interest disputes to occur. Interest disputes can either be awkwardly shoehorned into the formal legal system or they can pour out into the streets and factory

---

[8] As with the vast majority of collective contracts or agreements, the Changde Walmart collective contract reflected the basic legal minimums. It did not reflect any bargaining between workers and the employer. As such, it could not show any evidence that the employer had violated the agreement.

yards to settle through worker unrest and state intervention. More often than not, both occur as frustrated workers find the legal system insufficient and unwelcoming, as it is not suited to manage demands that, while often reasonable, are not strictly guided by the legal minimum. Strategic escalation of the dispute through collective action and mobilization becomes necessary in the much more open-ended and flexible realm of government intervention in the name of "stability preservation."

THE LIMITS OF AUTHORITARIAN LEGALITY

Neither the Guangzhou Hospital workers nor the Changde Walmart workers were particularly violent or extreme in their protest actions. While both disputes did lead to the arrest of workers and in the Guangzhou case, to their imprisonment on criminal charges, it's very likely that the participation and consultative role of labor activists, cause lawyers, and academics had a stabilizing effect on the workers. For example, during the Guangzhou hospital strike, the nursing assistants took turns caring for their patients and participating in the sit-in. The lawyers and activists recommended that the workers use disruptive actions, such as the sit-in, to encourage hospital management to bargain with the workers as a collectivity, but not to disrupt their own work in caring for patients. In many other cases, workers' actions have been more extreme, including threats of suicide, kidnapping, and/or murder of managers, sabotage, and general rioting. Liebman labels the interaction between law and protest as "law in the shadow of violence," underlining the dynamics of settlement and conciliation in China (Liebman 2013). As the primary goal of the state is the maintenance of social stability, litigants use the threat of violence to improve their chances of a favorable settlement. Settlements are more flexible when reached via extralegal mechanisms just as grand mediation and state-directed negotiation. Unlike the medical malpractice disputes that Liebman examines, however, there is little evidence, in these cases or from the previous chapters, that the courts are compelled to reach decisions in labor disputes that exceed legal minimums in order to placate protesting workers. Instead, law and the legal process is used to break up workers' unity and divide up demands into individualistic claims based on the labor contract. Protests and demands for collective bargaining are strategies to avoid the law and the legal resolution process, which are perceived to be unfair and often unreliable given severe enforcement problems.

Many observers of Chinese society have noted this vicious circle between law and legal mobilization, protest, and state-led intervention and flexible settlement (Cai 2010; Chen 2014). As Chen notes, the stability preservation system "is inefficient at articulating interests and tends to encourage 'troublemaking' petitioning tactics. In the highly centralized power structure, only leaders can effectively addresses popular claims"(Chen 2013, 61). Both Liebman and Chen fault the state's failure to institutionalize, instead relying on Maoist traditions of flexibility and an ambivalent attitude toward political and legal institutions that emphasize autonomy and rule-bound decision making.

While the Xi Jinping administration appeared to signal a turn back toward law in initial reform proclamations at the Fourth Plenum in 2014, in the labor realm, the regime's fear of instability and the notion that government intervention is essential to maintain stability have thwarted any reformist breakthroughs or institutional reforms that might improve worker representation in the resolution of rights violations or interest disputes. Failure to reform these institutions would then require that the government maintain its reactive role in settlement of labor disputes. Although this approach is increasingly costly, it limits the political risks of a more independent trade union and more autonomous labor NGOs and maintains the CCP's political dominance over fragmented social actors.

This reactive approach will, however, complicate the broadly strategic goals of the protective legislation of recent years. If enforcement and compliance are left to workers themselves to demand, weak compliance will reinforce the existing inequalities of the labor market with the benefits of formal employment and social insurance accruing to the upper reaches of the labor market. However, the benefits of formal employment and a social safety net are no longer simply to improve the working conditions of individual employees. The Chinese state has a vested interest in improving compliance. The foundation of the large-scale urbanization plan developed by the Xi Jinping administration is granting migrating rural citizens access to urban social insurance and employment. As the Chinese urban welfare state is directly tied to formal employment, rural citizens are very unwilling to give up rural hukou status (and the land security that it has traditionally guaranteed) unless urban hukou status can offer substitutes for land security. These basic legal rights are critical to the new development model to which the government aspires, but the path to improved compliance is unlikely to be through individual workers lodging claims against recalcitrant employers in local courts.

On the other end of the spectrum lies the quandary of interest disputes, when workers demand more than the legal minimum. As the Chinese economy has matured, this problem has intensified and is particularly severe in wealthy coastal areas with sophisticated supply chains and production networks. Although the number of workplaces with a formal trade union presence has increased substantially since the 1990s, such presence does little to improve any sense of representation. As the Walmart case demonstrates by its unique characteristics, even a trade union leadership interested in representation will be hamstrung by the lack of institutional mechanisms and upper level trade union support. Aggrieved workers who turn to labor NGOs and cause lawyers to represent them during disputes and strikes are moving in a new, uncharted direction of interest representation as they are fundamentally searching for societal support to substitute for the ineffectual representation of the ACFTU.

Reliance on law as a mode of governance is difficult to realize if the complements of legislation and law-making are not provided. For China's minimum standards outlined in the labor legislation of the past three decades, litigious workers require greater assistance from the state to realize their legal rights. This might include a labor inspection system that could trump local government interests or administrative agencies with the power to file suit against employers who egregiously violate the law. While similar reforms are being tested in the realm of environmental protection, which also has severe compliance problems, the political sensitivities of the labor question have made the government much less willing to innovate. In the realm of interest disputes, the state would need to legislate more clearly the rights and responsibilities of the trade union in its representative role. The problem of representation will only intensify as the economy shifts to be more reliant on domestic demand. In a sense, the challenges facing the government are at both extremes of the labor market. Compliance with basic rights is necessary to integrate rural migrants as long-term citizens of urban China. Effective representation is needed at the other end as the expectations of highly-skilled and educated workers often exceed the law's minimum guarantees.

Epilogue

Requiem for the Labor Contract Law?

2007 was a turning point. From that year, wage increases exceeded labor productivity gains. 2007 was also the year in which the Labor Contract Law was discussed, and it was implemented in 2008. The Labor Contract Law has many shortcomings. Of course many people will disagree with me, but the law's shortcomings are mainly that it reduces labor market mobility and flexibility. Workers can fire their employers, but employers can't terminate workers. That's the reason why many investors have already left China...Promoting collective bargaining within enterprises is alright, but promoting sectoral or regional bargaining, that's just terrible, it's exactly the cause of Europe's labor market rigidity. In America, Detroit's automotive trade union is very powerful, salaries and benefits are very high...which in the end brought about the bankruptcy of the automotive industry.

– *Lou Jiwei, Minister of Finance, April 24, 2015 Speech at Tsinghua University*

Finance Minister Lou Jiwei's critical remarks regarding the Labor Contract Law (LCL) in 2015 signaled top-level dissatisfaction with the widening protections mandated by the legislative activism of the previous government under Hu Jintao and Wen Jiabao (*South China Morning Post* 2015; Lou 2015). Although most of the actual reforms proposed by Xi Jinping when he took office in 2013 have progressed slowly, the new emphasis on structural reforms, flexibility, and an expanded role for the market has filtered into the realm of labor and employment law. In a time of decelerating economic growth, these debates over the revisions to the LCL are to be expected as they reflect perennial debates regarding the best way to distribute the gains of economic growth and, more importantly for China now, how to distribute the pain of an economic slowdown. Restrictive labor protections that benefit current workers, which are often valued by workers and trade unions, are pitted against flexible labor reforms that might boost overall employment by reducing the cost of hiring. In China, as elsewhere, both sides profess to be serving the interests of workers. While the earlier administration under Hu and Wen opted for expanded protections, Xi's administration emphasizes "supply side" reforms that may strip away some of the newly bequeathed protections acquired in the 2008 LCL in exchange for more flexible labor markets, more autonomy for employers, and a revived economy.

Minister Lou was correct in noting the importance of the LCL as a turning point. The LCL, whatever its faults, promoted and expanded workers' legal mobilization. It enhanced workplace protections and, with other laws, reduced some of the important legal and financial barriers that restricted workers' claims. It marked a critical point in time when the central government's strategic goals to reduce inequality and improve social protections intersected with workers' growing bargaining power as labor shortages and generational shifts took hold. By 2015, however, the state was in retreat from its support for these protections and had far less enthusiasm for workers' feisty embrace of their role as the foot soldiers of China's rule of law project.

It would be a mistake to portray the debate over the LCL revisions as merely about the proper role of the state in the regulation of labor markets or how to determine the appropriate degree of labor protection over flexibility for China now. The revision of the LCL reflects a more fundamental hardening against the social consequences of the state's rule of law project: rights' activism, restive cause lawyers, and rising citizen expectations for an effective judiciary that is authoritative, if not independent. The LCL and the related 2008 Labor Dispute Mediation and Arbitration Law (LDMAL) are blamed for encouraging excessive mobilization of workers and threats to social and political stability (Unirule Institute 2016). The crackdown on labor NGOs and activists discussed in the last chapter is part of a much wider attack on cause lawyering and rights protection over the last few years, including sweeping arrests of hundreds of lawyers in July 2015 (Mitchell 2016; Mitchell and Hornby 2015). A move to weaken the LCL and to dramatically curtail labor activism via repression and arrests may signal the end of the CCP's experiment with progressive labor legislation, enhanced access to justice, and encouragement of popular legal awareness and mobilization.

In this brief conclusion, I relate the substantive debate about the revision of the LCL to the larger challenge that the CCP faces in trying to adopt "rule of law" institutions. The debate over the revisions of the law is important for demonstrating the contradiction between the government's need for law to structure labor relations and its fear that law, by delineating rights, spawns not just conflict and instability, but also encourages collective organization and representation. It is but one example of a larger quandary for the regime in its attempt to use democratic institutions to sustain and improve authoritarian rule. These institutions are deployed pragmatically to solve governance problems, but they often spawn unintended consequences that lead to their rollback.

However, a full-blown "turn against law" in the realm of labor and employment law will threaten the CCP's long-term developmental goals. Revisions to the LCL that remove key labor protections without adequate strengthening of enforcement and implementation will further entrench a system that protects those who need it least while leaving a growing stratum at the bottom with precious few protections and dwindling employment security. In other words, the governance problems of sub-optimal compliance and enforcement will remain and worsen if the law is weakened at the same time that bottom-up mobilization is curtailed. Repeal or significant revision of the LCL may not only affect workers, it will also impede the government's larger reformist goals of a changed development strategy and the rapid urbanization of its migratory and still marginalized rural workforce. If better compliance with labor laws has been largely driven by workers' own mobilization around the new rights of the LCL, what will be the new impetus for firm compliance and local government enforcement? What mechanisms will the government deploy to substitute for this bottom-up mobilization?

REQUIEM FOR THE LABOR CONTRACT LAW?

Ten years have passed since the period of public comment for the draft LCL led to an international furor. In 2006, comments poured in from workers, employers, and activists alike. Foreign business associations threatened to divest from China while international trade unions supported the ACFTU to an extent not seen in recent decades (Kuruvilla, Lee, and Gallagher 2011; Harper Ho and Huang 2014). With the law's passage in 2007, a decade long experiment began with workers' embracing the law to reverse the trend of declining employment security and greater labor market flexibility that began with the 1995 Labor Law and its departure from socialism. As this section details, the law has had a positive impact on some aspects of employment protection in China, while also leading to higher labor costs. However, two factors complicate the issue of higher labor costs. One, given the extensive non-compliance with the 1995 Labor Law, higher costs as a function of the LCL were unavoidable if the LCL's main goal of improved compliance was met. Second, it is difficult to parse out the impact of the LCL from structural issues, such as demographic change, that have also contributed to rising labor costs. I conclude by arguing that the debate is also incomplete, failing to examine enforcement and compliance problems of a relaxed law and avoiding other important factors that restrict labor market flexibility and raise costs, especially hukou restrictions.

With China's economic slowdown, the 2008 LCL has come under intense criticism for being too "pro-worker," for turning China's labor markets "inflexible," and for bringing back the "iron rice bowl" of the socialist era (Zhang 2008; *South China Morning Post 2015*; Dong et al. 2016). Up until this point, most criticism of Chinese labor law had been that it either didn't exist at all or was hardly implemented, today's criticism of the LCL is partially at least a vindication for those who take Chinese law seriously. In other words, the law MUST matter to have angered so many and to have caused such widespread disagreement. As has been shown in previous chapters and in the broader literature on the impact of the LCL, this imperfect law did bring about fundamental and important improvements to workplace conditions in China. Across numerous studies, using different data and methodologies, there has been a documented increase in the proportion of workers with written labor contracts, which is the key entry point to gain workplace protections and benefits. Using a more diverse city-based survey than the CULS examined in earlier chapters, the Rural-Urban Migration in China (RUMiC) survey found that nearly 66 percent of all migrants had labor contracts while over 90 percent of local workers did, a higher percentage than that found by the CULS (Cheng, Smyth, and Guo 2015). Li and Freeman, using firm-based migrant worker surveys in the Pearl River Delta, similarly found that this improvement extended to migrant workers in the region with the proportion of migrant workers with contracts increasing from about 43 percent in 2006 to 62 percent by 2009, a year after the law's implementation (X. Li and Freeman 2015).

Greater access to written labor contracts also led to better firm compliance with social insurance obligations. Migrant and urban workers' participation in the most important aspects of social insurance, pensions, and medical insurance, increased after the LCL, as shown both by the CULS and the migrant surveys in Li and Freeman. In the RUMiC study, done in 2008, participation in social insurance was higher among those urban and migrant workers who had signed a labor contract (Cheng, Smyth, and Guo 2015). Using a matching technique to rule out other factors that may determine what kinds of workers are offered contracts, Cheng et al also found that even among workers with similar characteristics, access to a written contract significantly improved access to employee benefits. While migrant workers' access to these benefits is still far lower than the participation rates of urban residents, the LCL and the 2011 Social Insurance Law were both important drivers of these improvements.

The benefits of the LCL have still tended to accrue to workers with higher levels of education, more skills, and local residency. As Cheng et al argue, this is to be expected in a highly segmented labor market with strong institutional barriers to labor mobility. It also conforms with the enforcement model analyzed in earlier chapters that is heavily dependent on workers themselves and handicaps the local labor bureaucracy through the decentralized system of governance. There is also ample evidence that the strict clauses on labor contracts and the heavier costs of termination have incentivized firms to evade formal employment via labor subcontracting, outsourcing, and even day laborers (Harney 2016; B. Wang 2012).

While the achievements of the LCL are important, many employers, government officials, and academics have complained bitterly that the LCL and other related laws have directly led to much larger costs to employers and negatively affected China's labor markets. First, employers charge that the law has increased the costs of hiring and firing workers due to its restrictions on short-term contracts and its requirement that companies pay severance costs even upon expiration of a labor contract (previously severance costs were required only upon early termination). Second, it has increased the costs of human resources management and compliance, fueling the rapid development of the human resources and employment law industry. Third, the LCL and related laws and regulations have led to rapid increases in wages, even when productivity has failed to keep pace, and larger social insurance burdens for firms.

Finally, both government officials and some employers have portrayed these laws as the engines behind the accelerated mobilization of Chinese workers, both in courtrooms and the streets. Thus the instability and extra-legal mobilization of workers discussed in Chapter 6 is portrayed as a negative effect of the law's "excessive" protection of workers and the incentive structure of the dispute resolution process amended in the LDMAL, with its reduced fee structure and longer statute of limitations (Dong et al. 2016; Unirule Institute 2016). Some have argued that employers have become targets of unreasonable litigation and bad-faith behavior by workers (Guo 2016). For example, workers may evade the employer's attempts to enter into a written labor contract in order to eventually sue the employer for double wages for its failure to sign a contract. The high level of disputes creates both additional financial costs while greater frequency of strikes and protests threaten the political and social stability highly valued by local governments and firms alike.

Proposed revisions to the law include general recommendations to increase employer autonomy over internal rule-making, including decisions about whether to enter into open-ended or term-limited contracts. The LCL requires that the employer enter into open-ended contracts once a worker has completed two term contracts or ten years of tenure. It also requires that companies carefully document their rules and regulations in an employee handbook, which restricts their decision-making capability and flexibility.

Many critics of the LCL have recommended differential treatment for high level managers or even that these top employees be excluded from the law's protection. Similarly, some propose differential treatment for small or start-up firms that are more adversely affected by the law's restrictions and associated costs. Some have also called for more adequate protection of workers in non-standard employment arrangements, such as part-time work, informal work, and independent contractors. These workers are often excluded from protection when they cannot demonstrate a formal "labor relationship" through a written contract.

Revisions to related laws and regulations have also been proposed, such as reduction in social insurance burdens, changes to the dispute resolution system, and tying mandated minimum wage increases to productivity gains (Lou 2015; Dong et al. 2016; SHUFE 2016; Unirule Institute 2016). Some changes have already occurred – not in formal law – but in the key implementing regulations and administrative rules. The fee structure of social insurance payments has been reduced for maternity, unemployment, and occupational injury and disease. The most recent 13th Five-Year Plan clearly indicated the central government's reduced enthusiasm for frequent minimum wage increases, noting that minimum wage increases should proceed more slowly and be tied to economic performance. In 2016, Guangdong froze its minimum wage for two years (Wong 2016; J. Wang and Wang 2016).

Higher Costs or a Red Herring?

In a period of global economic uncertainty and crisis, however, it is hard to disentangle the effect of the LCL and other recent laws from the effects of other trends. Empirical analysis of actual costs tends to show that the LCL had a moderate impact. Opinion surveys of managers, however, tend to show a larger impact. Firm managers as survey respondents may not be able to specify clearly the exact causes of the recent cost increases. Alternatively, they might strategically focus their blame on the LCL, which is amendable, over demographic changes, which are structural and long-term.

Recent research on the actual effects of the LCL shows modest increases in costs, especially for improved compliance with social insurance participation as a function of more inclusion into formal written labor contracts. Li and Freeman found a 4.6 percent increase in labor costs among firms in the Pearl River Delta (X. Li and Freeman 2015). Giles, Wang, and Park found that with improved social insurance compliance, the heavy burdens of social insurance also encouraged firms to push lower level workers into less secure work through labor subcontracting and outsourcing (Giles, Wang, and Park 2013). Gallagher, Giles, Park, and Wang found that in firm surveys, managers reported higher labor costs after the LCL, but that these cost increases did not seem to affect aggregate employment (Gallagher et al. 2014). A study using the same data also found that the effects of the LCL were stronger in cities with previous lax enforcement of the 1995 Labor Law, where there was a decrease in employment growth following the law's enactment (Park et al). However, in national trends, employment in China was not adversely affected by the initial passage of the LCL.

Some of the more negative effects, such as the limits on short-term contracts, could not be seen until several years after the law's passage when firms were mandated to extend open-term contracts to these employees. By 2015, many firms were indeed complaining about these long-term effects of the law on their hiring and firing practices. In recent surveys of Guangdong employers, labor costs were named as by far the most important barrier to firm development. Nearly 70 percent of the firms surveyed named labor costs as a large or prohibitive factor to their development (Park and Qian 2016). In the US–China Business Council annual surveys of its member companies, human resource issues and rising labor costs are perennially among the top concerns. However, these surveys do not reveal the precise effect of the legal and regulatory framework versus other factors that have contributed to rising labor costs, such as demographic changes and increased competition between inland and coastal regions for migrant labor (USCBC 2016).

As some labor lawyers have pointed, the LCL was bound to lead to increased costs because one of its main goals was to improve compliance with existing rules (in addition to mandating new protections in terms of employment security and workplace voice). For example, the 1995 Labor Law already required written labor contracts and compliance with social insurance obligations, but because it contained almost no punitive measures to compel firms to comply, many did not and thus their labor costs were lower. It bears noting that their labor costs were lower because they were violating *core* standards of the first 1995 Labor Law (Ma 2016).

To further confound the issue of "higher costs," the LCL was unfortunately timed with many other critically important events and trends that also had substantial impact on labor costs and workers' sense of empowerment and bargaining power. First and foremost, the Global Financial Crisis impacted the Chinese economy from late 2008 with a direct hit on the export-oriented manufacturing sector as China's key trading partners slid into recession. Migrant workers were laid off by the millions. Disputes skyrocketed as companies shut down often without paying workers due wages or severance. Many local governments passed temporary regulations to freeze social insurance contributions and reduce other burdens on firms. Second, even before the financial crisis hit firms, China's demographic dividend of a large working population proportionate to young and old dependents was ending. Wages began to rise in the manufacturing sector long before the LCL and were probably more strongly related to the labor shortages that began to appear in China's coastal developmental zones by 2004 than the LCL in 2008. Finally, workers' expectations were shifting as younger migrant workers were spending more time in cities and extending their time horizons and frames of reference away from the countryside and toward their urban brethren. This second generation of migrant workers expected to stay longer in cities and to develop into full urban citizens, if not in their temporary homes on the coast, then at least in inland cities closer to their rural hometowns. This created a pull back toward inland areas that further exacerbated coastal labor shortages and also gave workers higher expectations and more choice and bargaining power with employers everywhere.

If the LCL is significantly rolled back, there may be short-term improvements in the economy and labor markets though that is far from guaranteed given the many other factors that impact growth, such as overcapacity, recessions in other markets, and high levels of public debt. But combined with the clear crackdown on labor NGOs and collective mobilization of workers for better protection, a rollback of the law will significantly impact the long-term development goals of the government – to boost consumption, to improve access to social welfare, to reduce inequality, and in doing so to change China's model of growth to a more inclusive and sustainable one. The vibrant debate on the revision of the LCL neglected two critical issues. First, there was little discussion of how a weakened law will be implemented and enforced. There is no guarantee that local governments will even enforce a more flexible and employer-friendly law. If the enforcement system is not changed, relaxation of the LCL will only further diminish the gains made by those at the lower rungs of the labor market without the skill or education to enhance their own bargaining power with employers.

Second, the debate focused on the formal law with little recognition that one of the main barriers to greater labor market flexibility is not the LCL, but instead the institutional discrimination of the household registration system. If the hukou system was substantially relaxed and if migrant workers were extended the same treatment as local workers, this equality of treatment might compensate for reduced protections in a revised law while greatly enhancing labor market flexibility and mobility.

AUTHORITARIAN RULE AND ITS DISCONTENTS

China's development of rule of law, including reforms to the judiciary, the legal profession, and the legislation of an ever-expanding number of laws to regulate and govern society and the economy are part of the bundle of reforms undertaken since the 1980s to improve the CCP's ability to govern Chinese society and to manage its economic reforms. Many of these reforms attempt to use democratic institutions to strengthen and stabilize autocratic rule, such as grassroots elections, intraparty democracy, and the liberalization of the media. In all of these cases, institutions with democratic lineage, while aiding in the Party's governance project and enhancing its legitimacy, encouraged societal expectations and demands that exceeded the Party's limited and constrained version of these institutions. This in turn led the Party to repress and constrain social mobilization even when it was couched in the CCP's own legitimating discourse and invoked the very institutions that the government had constructed.

This pattern of state encouragement, societal response, and state repression reflects the CCP's ambivalence toward reforms that may serve some functional purpose, such as implementation of laws, better selection of leaders, and more transparent and reliable information, but have unintended consequences for politics, power, and organization. Examining the advancement of grassroots election in Chinese villages, for example, the CCP actively promoted democratic and competitive elections of village leaders from the 1980s as a mechanism to improve village leadership and increase villagers' trust in the leadership. When these reforms began to "creep" upward toward higher levels of government, however, the Party eventually stepped in to thwart any advancement of these elections beyond the most basic level of governance (L. Li 2002; Yuan 2011). They also put into place rules and restrictions that forbade basic practices of democratic elections, such as campaign platforms and the aggregation of policy positions, which they feared would morph into quasi-political parties (O'Brien and Han 2009).

Within the CCP, there have also been concerted attempts to improve the selection and appointment of Party leaders through intra-Party democracy, which included multi-candidate elections and greater competition between Party members for coveted leadership spots (Fewsmith 2013). However, reforms to advance inner-party democracy proceeded slowly and now seem to be in reverse. Zeng shows how the introduction of semi-competitive elections for internal Party positions increased uncertainty in the promotion and appointments to top leadership positions, such as the provincial Politburo Standing Committees and Party Congresses. Competitive selection of Party leaders by its members is carefully controlled to protect against "democratic accidents" – a term used to describe an election with an unexpected and unwelcome result (Zeng 2016). Li notes that "such experiments in intra-party democracy, however, have made little progress since 2009. The scope and scale of intra-Party competition have not increased much over the past two decades." (Li 2013, 45). In recent years, mainland scholars have noted that research on such reforms is now extremely sensitive and subject to much scrutiny if published in Chinese (SH201203).

In the 1990s, commercialization and liberalization of the media was touted as a means to improve transparency, to uncover corruption and malfeasance, and to advance the people's ability to supervise the government. However, the heady combination of media liberalization and technological change threatened the CCP's hold on public opinion and information control. In recent years, the regime has doubled down on efforts to manage and control information, tame social media, and target activists and public opinion leaders who are able to establish independent voices online. While some research has shown that the state calibrates its censorship efforts carefully to forestall collective mobilization while tolerating some kinds of critical discussion of the regime, the Xi Jinping administration has strengthened the Party's control of information considerably even when collective action is not a direct concern (Miller and Gallagher 2017). Social media outlets like Weibo have been restricted in favor of more manageable private discussion forums on WeChat.

It is, of course, not at all surprising that single-party regimes control the pace and extent of reforms that contain democratic elements. These reforms are inherently dangerous and potentially destabilizing. The benefits of improved governance and higher levels of legitimacy might be outweighed by the costs of easier coordination by societal groups or easier exchange of information between citizens. It is important to note, however, the ways in which control and repression happen and how this affects citizens' evaluation of these democratic experiments. In the legal realm, this book has shown how this cycle of law–mobilization–instability–repression affects those who attempt to use legal system to solve problems and resolve grievances. In grassroots election, Sun (2014) shows that once the state steps in to manage and control elections to their advantage, political trust declines among the population.

The Politics of the "Middle-Income" Trap

While Lou Jiwei's critical remarks on the LCL received significant media attention in China, the speech itself was a wide-ranging discussion of China's economic challenges, framed by his worry that China is in great danger of "falling into and getting stuck in the middle-income trap" (Lou 2015). Minister Lou's acrimony for the law is a red herring – seized on in the media because revisions of the law have been widely called for since it was first debated in 2006, and because out of all the challenges and problems discussed in the speech, revising the law would be relatively easy. In the rest of the speech he grapples with the far more consequential problems that face China's political economy, including the rapidly changing demographic structure, the institutional barriers of the hukou system, and the strictures of the current rural land system. The LCL and the other laws of the early 2000s did not cause these problems and their revision won't solve them. Quite the opposite, the LCL was intended to address them. By increasing the number of people in the formal sector, the LCL has improved inclusion into the social insurance system, even among young migrant workers. By hardening the penalties for failure to sign written contracts, the LCL has brought more migrant workers into formal urban employment, undoing some of the institutional discrimination of the hukou system. In giving workers enhanced access to dispute resolution and more time to lodge claims, the LDMAL gave marginalized workers more hope and greater expectations that justice will be done. The 2011 Social Insurance Law targeted greater portability of pensions and more inclusive coverage.

The law's impact was hamstrung, however, by the slow pace of other reforms. Institutional discrimination based on hukou continues to segment labor markets, restrict labor mobility, and deny migrant workers basic workplace protections. Social insurance participation among migrant workers remains low as local governments fear chasing away investment with high costs. Moreover, many migrant workers have little confidence that paying into the system will yield benefits later on. As the economy has slowed, local governments have no appetite to boost compliance with the law. As strikes and protests have grown more frequent, strictures on bottom-up mobilization have become more intense.

Minister Lou's remarks reveal the conundrum that China's leaders face. China's labor laws have never been (solely) about protecting workers. They have been levers for reform. The 1995 Labor Law smashed the iron rice bowl. The 2008 LCL was to hasten urbanization via formal employment and the exchange of land security for employment security. These laws, passed to protect workers and to widen social inclusion, are badly needed to achieve its long-term strategic goals. But they were not cost or risk-free; they brought new problems and pressures. Workers welcomed the promise of these new rights and they accepted the state's invitation to use them. A weakened LCL and a crackdown on bottom-up mobilization might diminish those demands or, as Chapter 6 suggests, they may drive workers to the streets instead. But a retreat on these laws (as vehicles for reform) will also endanger the central government's bid to push China's economy to a higher and more sustainable path. The "middle-income trap" that so worries Minister Lou is not merely a problem of *economic* stagnation; it is, more importantly, a political dilemma.

Bibliography

"2013 White Paper on Huangpu District Labor and Personnel Disputes Mediation, Arbitration and Litigation (2013 年黄浦区劳动人事争议调解仲裁与审判白皮书)." 2014. Shanghai: Huangpu District People's Court and Huangpu Human Resources and Social Security Bureau.

Acemoglu, Daron, Simon Johnson, James A. Robinson, and Pierre Yared. 2005. "From Education to Democracy." *The American Economic Review* 95 (2): 44–49.

Acemoglu, Daron, and James A. Robinson. 2006. *Economic Origins of Dictatorship and Democracy*. Cambridge; New York: Cambridge University Press.

Acemoglu, Daron, and James A. Robinson. 2012. *Why Nations Fail: The Origins of Power, Prosperity and Poverty*. 1st ed. New York: Crown Publishers.

ACFTU. 2010. "Research Report on the Living Conditions of the New Generation of Migrant Workers in Shenzhen." All-China Federation of Trade Unions. http://acftu.people.com.cn/GB/67582/12154737.html.

Albiston, Catherine R. 2005. "Bargaining in the Shadow of Social Institutions: Competing Discourses and Social Change in Workplace Mobilization of Civil Rights." *Law & Society Review* 39 (1): 11–50.

Andrew J. Nathan. 2009. "Authoritarian Impermanence." *Journal of Democracy* 20 (3): 37–40. doi:10.1353/jod.0.0097.

Ang, Yuen Yuen. 2016. *How China Escaped the Poverty Trap*. Cornell Studies in Political Economy. Ithaca: Cornell University Press.

Ang, Yuen Yuen, and Nan Jia. 2014. "Perverse Complementarity: Political Connections and the Use of Courts among Private Firms in China." *The Journal of Politics* 76 (02): 318–32. doi:10.1017/S0022381613001400.

Baker & McKenzie. 2016. "The Global Employer Magazine, 2015 Review and 2016 Preview." Baker & McKenzie.

Becker, J. 2012. "The Knowledge to Act: Chinese Migrant Labor Protests in Comparative Perspective." *Comparative Political Studies* 45 (11): 1379–404. doi:10.1177/0010414012437167.

Benesh, Sara C. 2006. "Understanding Public Confidence in American Courts." *Journal of Politics* 68 (3): 697–707.

Benney, Jonathan. 2013. *Defending Rights in Contemporary China*. Routledge/Asian Studies Association of Australia (ASAA) East Asian Series. London; New York: Routledge.

Biddulph, Sarah, Sean Cooney, and Ying Zhu. 2012. "Rule of Law with Chinese Characteristics: The Role of Campaigns in Lawmaking." *Law & Policy* 34 (4): 373–401.

Black, Donald J. 2010. *The Behavior of Law*.

Blaydes, Lisa. 2010. *Elections and Distributive Politics in Mubarak's Egypt*. New York: Cambridge University Press.

Boix, Carles. 2003. *Democracy and Redistribution*. Cambridge Studies in Comparative Politics. Cambridge, UK; New York: Cambridge University Press.

Boix, Carles, and Milan W. Svolik. 2013. "The Foundations of Limited Authoritarian Government: Institutions, Commitment, and Power-Sharing in Dictatorships." *The Journal of Politics* 75 (02): 300–16. doi:10.1017/S0022381613000029.

Brady, Henry E., Sidney Verba, and Kay Lehman Schlozman. 1995. "Beyond Ses: A Resource Model of Political Participation." *The American Political Science Review* 89 (2): 271. doi:10.2307/2082425.

Brinks, Daniel M., and Varun Gauri. 2014. "The Law's Majestic Equality? The Distributive Impact of Judicializing Social and Economic Rights." *Perspectives on Politics* 12 (02): 375–93. doi:10.1017/S1537592714000887.

Brown, Ronald C. 2015. "Collective Bargaining in China: Guangdong Regulation a Harbinger of National Model?" *China-EU Law Journal*, 4: 1–20.

Bučar, Bojko, Andrej Bukovnik, Ajda Čeledin, Tjaša Ivanc, Matjaž Jan, Rajko Knez, Peter Kos, et al. 2014. *The World Justice Project: Rule of Law Index 2014*. Washington, D.C.: The World Justice Project.

Bueno de Mesquita, Bruce, ed. 2003. *The Logic of Political Survival*. Cambridge, Mass.: MIT Press.

Bumiller, Kristin. 1988. *The Civil Rights Society: The Social Construction of Victims*. Baltimore: Johns Hopkins University Press.

Burns, N., K.L. Schlozman, and S. Verba. 2009. *The Private Roots of Public Action: Gender, Equality, and Political Participation*. Cambridge, Mass.: Harvard University Press. http://books.google.com/books?id=uW7sYFhAGr4C.

Cai, Yongshun. 2010. *Collective Resistance in China: Why Popular Protests Succeed or Fail*. Stanford: Stanford University Press.

Cai, Fang, Yang Du, and Meiyan Wang. 2009. "Migration and Labor Mobility in China." UNDP. Human Development Research Paper. United Nations.

Cai, Fang, and Meiyan Wang. 2012. "Labour Market Changes, Labour Disputes and Social Cohesion in China." www.oecd-ilibrary.org/development/labour-market-changes-labour-disputes-and-social-cohesion-in-china_5k9h5x9c8dwc-en.

Chang, Kai. 2007. "'Chang Kai Explains the Policy of the Draft Labor Contract Law.' (chang Kai Jieshi Laodong Hetongfa Caoan Zhengce." January 13. www.9ask.cn/blog/user/wr666/archives/2007/14953.html#top.

Chan, Kam Wing. 2010. "The Household Registration System and Migrant Labor in China: Notes on a Debate." *Population and Development Review* 36 (2): 357–64.

Chen, Christina. 2011. The Politics of Labor Protection in Authoritarian Systems: Evidence from Labor Law and Enforcement in Post-Reform China. The University of California, San Diego.

Chen, Feng. 2003. "Between the State and Labour: The Conflict of Chinese Trade Unions' Double Identity in Market Reform." *The China Quarterly* 176: 1006–28.

2007. "Individual Rights and Collective Rights: Labor's Predicament in China." *Communist and Post-Communist Studies* 40 (1): 59–79. doi:10.1016/j.postcomstud.2006.12.006.

Chen, Feng, and Xin Xu. 2012. "'Active Judiciary': Judicial Dismantling Of Workers' Collective Action in China." *China Journal*, 67: 87–108.

Chen, Xi. 2014. *Social Protest and Contentious Authoritarianism in China*. New York: Cambridge University Press.

Cheng, Joseph YS, Kinglun Ngok, and Wenjia Zhuang. 2010. "The Survival and Development Space for China's Labor NGOs: Informal Politics and Its Uncertainty." www.jstor.org/stable/10.1525/as.2010.50.6.1082.

Cheng, Z., R. Smyth, and F. Guo. 2015. "The Impact of China's New Labour Contract Law on Socioeconomic Outcomes for Migrant and Urban Workers." *Human Relations* 68 (3): 329–52. doi:10.1177/0018726714543480.

Chen, Xi. 2013. "The Rising Cost of Stability." *Journal of Democracy* 24 (1): 57–64.

China Labour Bulletin. 2010. "The Hard Road: Seeking Justice for Victims of Pneumoconiosis in China." Research Report. Hong Kong: China Labour Bulletin.

2015. "The Workers' Movement in China, 2013–2014 (中国工人运动观察报告, 2013–2014)." www.clb.org.hk/en/research-reports.

"China's Efforts and Achievements in Promoting the Rule of Law." 2008. White Paper. Beijing: State Council Information Office. www.china.org.cn/government/news/2008-02/28/content_11025486.htm.

Cho, Young Nam. 2006. "The Politics of Lawmaking in Chinese Local People's Congresses." *The China Quarterly* 187 (September): 592. doi:10.1017/S0305741006000397.

Clarke, Donald C. 2007. "Introduction: The Chinese Legal System Since 1995: Steady Development and Striking Continuities." *The China Quarterly* 191 (September). doi:10.1017/S0305741007001567.

2009. "Private Attorney-General in China: Potential and Pitfalls, The." *Wash. U. Global Stud. L. Rev.* 8: 241.

Collier, David, and Steven Levitsky. 1997. "Democracy with Adjectives: Conceptual Innovation in Comparative Research." *World Politics* 49 (03): 430–51.

Cooney, S. 2007. "China's Labour Law, Compliance and Flaws in Implementing Institutions." *Journal of Industrial Relations* 49 (5): 673–86. doi:10.1177/0022185607082215.

Cooney, Sean, Sarah Biddulph, and Ying Zhu. 2014. *Law and Fair Work in China*. London; New York: Routledge.

Davenport, Christian. 2015. *How Social Movements Die*. New York: Cambridge University Press.
Davis, Deborah, ed. 1995. *Urban Spaces in Contemporary China: The Potential for Autonomy and Community in Post-Mao China*. Woodrow Wilson Center Series. [Washington, D.C.]: Cambridge [England]; New York: Woodrow Wilson Center Press; Cambridge University Press.
de Mesquita, B. B., and A. Smith. 2008. "Political Survival and Endogenous Institutional Change." *Comparative Political Studies* 42 (2): 167–97. doi:10.1177/0010414008323330.
de Mesquita, Bruce Bueno, and Alastair Smith. 2010. "Leader Survival, Revolutions, and the Nature of Government Finance: LEADER SURVIVAL AND GOVERNMENT REVENUES." *American Journal of Political Science* 54 (4): 936–50. doi:10.1111/j.1540-5907.2010.00463.x.
Deng, Jiangxiu. 2007. "Labor Law Enforcment Faces a Crisis of Confidence [laodongzhifa Mianlin Xinren Weiji]." *Xin Xibu* 7: 70.
Deng, Liqun. 1985. "Speech at the National Legal Dissemination and Education Work Conference, June 15, 1985 [zai Quanguo Fazhi Xuanchuan Jiaoyu Gongzuo Huiyishang de Jiang Hua." In *China Legal Yearbook*, 665–70. Beijing.
Deng, Quheng, and Shi Li. 2012. "Low-Paid Workers in Urban China." *International Labour Review* 151 (3): 157–71.
Deng, Yanhua, and Kevin J. O'Brien. 2013. "Relational Repression in China: Using Social Ties to Demobilize Protesters." *The China Quarterly* 215: 533–52. doi:10.1017/S0305741013000714.
Development Research Center of the State Council, and World Bank. 2013. *China 2030: Building a Modern, Harmonious, and Creative Society*. The World Bank. http://documents.worldbank.org/curated/en/781101468239669951/China-2030-building-a-modern-harmonious-and-creative-society.
Diamant, Neil J. 2001. "Pursuing Rights and Getting Justice on China's Ethnic Frontier, 1949–1966." *Law and Society Review*, 799–840.
Diamant, Neil Jeffrey. 2000. *Revolutionizing the Family: Politics, Love, and Divorce in Urban and Rural China, 1949–1968*. Berkeley: University of California Press.
Diamant, Neil Jeffrey, Stanley B. Lubman, and Kevin J. O'Brien, eds. 2010. *Engaging the Law in China: State, Society, and Possibilities for Justice*. Nachdr. Stanford, Calif: Stanford University Press.
Diamond, Larry Jay. 2002. "Thinking About Hybrid Regimes." *Journal of Democracy* 13 (2): 21–35. doi:10.1353/jod.2002.0025.
Dong, Baohua, Kai Chang, Zhiping Liang, Jiangsong Wang, Bulei Chen, and Fangsheng Zhou. 2016. "Conceptual Adjustments and System Modifications in the Amendment of Labor Contract Law." Beijing: Unirule Institute. .
Dong, Baohua, and Gan Li. 2015. "To achieve 'rule of law' must overcome 'rights protection' vs. 'maintaining stability.' (yifazhiguo xu chaoyue 'weiquan' vs. 'weiwen')." *Explore and Contend (tansuo yu zhengming)*, no. 1.
Dongfang Jinbao. 2009. "In order to prove occupational disease, a worker insists on a thoracotomy." *Dongfang Jinbao*, July 10. http://news.sina.com.cn/s/2009-07-10/032718191682.shtml.

Du, Yang, and Wang Meiyan. 2010. "Discussions on Potential Bias and Implications of Lewis Turning Point." *China Economic Journal* 3 (2): 121–36. doi:10.1080/17538963.2010.511902.
Epp, Charles R. 1990. "Connecting Litigation Levels and Legal Mobilization: Explaining Interstate Variation in Employment Civil Rights Litigation." *Law and Society Review*, 145–63.
Erie, Matthew S. 2012. "Property Rights, Legal Consciousness and the New Media in China: The Hard Case of the 'toughest Nail-House in History.'" *China Information* 26 (1): 35–59.
Estlund, Cynthia. 2017. *A New Deal for China's Workers?* Cambridge, MA: Harvard University Press.
Ewick, Patricia. 1998. *The Common Place of Law: Stories from Everyday Life.* Language and Legal Discourse. Chicago: University of Chicago Press.
Exner, Mechthild. 1995. "The Convergence of Ideology and the Law: The Functions of the Legal Education Campaign in Building a Chinese Legal System." *Issues and Studies*, August, 31: 68–102.
Fan, Rong. 2011. "Investigative Report on Labor Dispatched Employees." *Gonghui Lilun Yanjiu*, 6: 21–25.
Felstiner, William LF, Richard L. Abel, and Austin Sarat. 1980. "The Emergence and Transformation of Disputes: Naming, Blaming, Claiming..." *Law and Society Review*, 15: 631–54.
Feng, Wang. 2011. "The Future of a Demographic Overachiever: Long-Term Implications of the Demographic Transition in China." *PoPulation and develoPment Review* 37 (s1): 173–90.
Fewsmith, Joseph. 2013. *The Logic and Limits of Political Reform in China.* Cambridge, [England]; New York: Cambridge University Press.
Forbath, William E. 1991. *Law and the Shaping of the American Labor Movement.* Cambridge, Mass.: Harvard University Press.
Frazier, Mark. 2010. *Socialist Insecurity: Pensions and the Politics of Uneven Development in China.* Ithaca: Cornell University Press.
Friedman, Eli. 2014. *Insurgency Trap: Labor Politics in Postsocialist China.* Ithaca; London: ILR Press, an imprint of Cornell University Press.
Fu, Hualing. 2011. "Challenging Authoritarianism Through Law: Potentials and LImit." *National Taiwan University Law Review* 6 (1): 339–65.
Fu, Hualing, and Richard Cullen. 2008. "Weiquan (rights Protection) Lawyering in an Authoritarian State: Building a Culture of Public-Interest Lawyering." *The China Journal*, 59: 111–27.
Fu, Yiqin. 2013. "China's Unfair College Admissions System." *The Atlantic*, June 19. www.theatlantic.com/china/archive/2013/06/chinas-unfair-college-admissions-system/276995/.
Galanter, Marc. 1974. "Why the 'Haves' Come out Ahead: Speculations on the Limits of Legal Change." *Law & Society Review* 9 (1): 95. doi:10.2307/3053023.
Gallagher, Mary E. 2005. "China in 2004: Stability above All." *Asian Survey* 45 (1): 21–32.
  2006. "Mobilizing the Law in China: 'Informed Disenchantment' and the Development of Legal Consciousness." *Law & Society Review* 40 (4): 783–816.

2009. "China's Older Workers: Between Law and Policy, Between Laid-Off and Unemployed." In *Laid-off Workers in a Workers' State: Unemployment with Chinese Characteristics*, 135–58. New York, N.Y: Palgrave Macmillan.

Gallagher, Mary E., and Jonathan K. Hanson. 2015. "Power Tool or Dull Blade? Selectorate Theory for Autocracies." *Annual Review of Political Science* 18 (1): 367–85. doi:10.1146/annurev-polisci-071213-041224.

Gallagher, Mary, and Yuhua Wang. 2011. "Users and Non-Users: Legal Experience and Its Effect on Legal Consciousness." In *Chinese Justice: Civil Dispute Resolution in Contemporary China*, 204–33. Cambridge; New York: Cambridge University Press.

Gallagher, M., J. Giles, A. Park, and M. Wang. 2014. "China's 2008 Labor Contract Law: Implementation and Implications for China's Workers." *Human Relations*, February. doi:10.1177/0018726713509418.

Gandhi, Jennifer. 2008. *Political Institutions under Dictatorship*. New York: Cambridge University Press.

Gandhi, Jennifer, and Ellen Lust-Okar. 2009. "Elections Under Authoritarianism." *Annual Review of Political Science* 12 (1): 403–22. doi:10.1146/annurev.polisci.11.060106.095434.

Gandhi, J., and A. Przeworski. 2007. "Authoritarian Institutions and the Survival of Autocrats." *Comparative Political Studies* 40 (11): 1279–1301. doi:10.1177/0010414007305817.

Garnaut, Ross, and Ligang Song, eds. 2006. *The Turning Point in China's Economic Development*. 1st ed. Canberra, ACT: ANU E Press: Asia Pacific Press.

Giles, John, Dewen Wang, and Albert Park. 2013. "Expanding Social Insurance Coverage in Urban China." *Research in Labor Economics* 37: 123–79.

Ginsburg, Tom, and Tamir Moustafa, eds. 2008. *Rule by Law: The Politics of Courts in Authoritarian Regimes*. Cambridge [UK]; New York: Cambridge University Press.

Gleeson, Shannon. 2009. "From Rights to Claims: The Role of Civil Society in Making Rights Real for Vulnerable Workers." *Law & Society Review* 43 (3): 669–700.

Gold, Thomas B., ed. 2009. *Laid-off Workers in a Workers' State: Unemployment with Chinese Characteristics*. 1st ed. New York, NY: Palgrave Macmillan.

Golley, Jane, and Xin Meng. 2011. "Has China Run out of Surplus Labour?" *China Economic Review* 22 (4): 555–72. doi:10.1016/j.chieco.2011.07.006.

Greene, Kenneth F. 2009. *Why Dominant Parties Lose: Mexico's Democratization in Comparative Perspective*. Cambridge New York: Cambridge University Press.

Guangdong Regulations on Collective Contracts. 2014.

Guo, Wenlong. 2016. "The Labor Contract Law Has Made Slackers into Stars." presented at the Unirule Institute Roundtable on the LCL and Supply Side Reform, Beijing, July 23. www.gegugu.com/2016/07/29/10719.html.

Halegua, Aaron. 2008. "Getting Paid: Processing the Labor Disputes of China's Migrant Workers." *Berkeley Journal of International Law* 26 (254).

Harney, Alexandra. 2016. "How Old-School Factories Stay Alive in China's South." *Reuters*, May 21. www.reuters.com/article/us-china-labour-idUSKCN0YD00L.

Harper Ho, Virginia, and Qiaoyan Huang. 2014. "The Recursivity of Reform: China's Amended Labor Contract Law." *Fordham International Law Journal* 37 (4).

Heilmann, Sebastian, and Elizabeth J. Perry, eds. 2011. *Mao's Invisible Hand: The Political Foundations of Adaptive Governance in China*. Harvard Contemporary China Series 17. Cambridge, Mass.: Harvard University Asia Center: Distributed by Harvard University Press.

Hess, Steve. 2013. *Authoritarian Landscapes: Popular Mobilization and the Institutional Sources of Resilience in Nondemocracies*. New York: Springer.

He, Xin. 2014. "Maintaining Stability by Law: Protest-Supported Housing Demolition Litigation and Social Change in China." *Law & Social Inquiry* 39 (4): 849–73.

Holliday, Ian. 2000. "Productivist Welfare Capitalism: Social Policy in East Asia." *Political Studies* 48 (4): 706–23.

Hornby, Lucy. 2015. "China Migration: Dying for Land." *The Financial Times*, August 6. www.ft.com/content/33ae0866-3098-11e5-91ac-a5e17d9b4cff.

Ho, Virginia Harper. 2003. *Labor Dispute Resolution in China: Implications for Labor Rights and Legal Reform*. China Research Monograph 59. Berkeley, Calif: Institute of East Asian Studies, University of California – Berkeley.

Hualing, Fu, and Richard Cullen. 2011. "Climbing the Weiquan Ladder: A Radicalizing Process for Rights-Protection Lawyers." *The China Quarterly* 205 (March): 40–59. doi:10.1017/S0305741010001384.

Hung, Eva P.W., and Stephen W.K. Chiu. 2003. "The Lost Generation: Life Course Dynamics and Xiagang in China." *Modern China* 29 (2): 204–36. doi:10.1177/0097700402250740.

Hung, Ho-Fung. 2011. *Protest with Chinese Characteristics*. New York: Columbia University Press.

Hurst, William. 2012. *The Chinese Worker after Socialism*. Cambridge: Cambridge University Press.

Hurst, William, and Kevin J. O'Brien. 2002. "China's Contentious Pensioners." *The China Quarterly* 170: 345–60.

"Investigative Report on the Collective Rights Defense of the Hospital of the Guangzhou Traditional Chinese Medicine University (广州中医药大学第一附属医院集体维权案调查报告)." 2014. Hong Kong: China Labour Bulletin.

Jennings, M. Kent. 1997. "Political Participation in the Chinese Countryside." *American Political Science Review*, 91: 361–72.

Jiang, Jin, and Ruone Li. 2015. "广东省劳动争议大数据报告." Guangdong: Guangdong MoreKing Law Firm. http://chuansong.me/n/1590202.

Jiang, Shanhe, and Yuning Wu. 2015. "Chinese People's Intended and Actual Use of the Court to Resolve Grievance/dispute." *Social Science Research* 49 (January): 42–52. doi:10.1016/j.ssresearch.2014.07.009.

Kagan, Robert, Bryant Garth, and Austin Sarat. 2002. "Facilitating and Domesticating Change: Democracy, Capitalism, and Law's Double Role in the Twentieth Century." In *Looking Back at Law's Century*, 1–34. Ithaca and London: Cornell University Press.

Kamo, Tomoki, and Hiroki Takeuchi. 2013. "Representation and Local People's Congresses in China: A Case Study of the Yangzhou Municipal

People's Congress." *Journal of Chinese Political Science* 18 (1): 41–60. doi:10.1007/s11366-012-9226-y.

Kim, Wonik, and Jennifer Gandhi. 2010. "Coopting Workers under Dictatorship." *The Journal of Politics* 72 (03): 646–58. doi:10.1017/S0022381610000071.

Kinkley, Jeffrey C. 2000. *Chinese Justice, the Fiction: Law and Literature in Modern China*. Stanford, Calif: Stanford University Press.

Knight, J., and L. Yueh. 2008. "Segmentation or Competition in China's Urban Labour Market?" *Cambridge Journal of Economics* 33 (1): 79–94. doi:10.1093/cje/ben025.

Kuruvilla, Sarosh, Ching Kwan Lee, and Mary Elizabeth Gallagher, eds. 2011. *From Iron Rice Bowl to Informalization: Markets, Workers, and the State in a Changing China*. Frank W. Pierce Memorial Lectureship and Conference Series, no. 14. Ithaca [N.Y.]: ILR Press.

Labor Daily. 2013. "Don't Constantly Force Workers to Sue," May 25.

Landry, Pierre Francois. 2008. *Decentralized Authoritarianism in China: The Communist Party's Control of Local Elites in the Post-Mao Era*. Cambridge: Cambridge Univ. Press.

Lan, Tu, John Pickles, and Shengjun Zhu. 2015. "State Regulation, Economic Reform and Worker Rights: The Contingent Effects of China's Labour Contract Law." *Journal of Contemporary Asia* 45 (2): 266–93. doi:10.1080/00472336.2014.940592.

Lee, Ching Kwan. 2002. "From the Specter of Mao to the Spirit of the Law: Labor Insurgency in China." *Theory and Society* 31 (2): 189–228.

——— 2007. *Against the Law: Labor Protests in China's Rustbelt and Sunbelt*. Berkeley: University of California Press.

Lee, Ching Kwan, and Yonghong Zhang. 2013. "The Power of Instability: Unraveling the Microfoundations of Bargained Authoritarianism in China 1." *American Journal of Sociology* 118 (6): 1475–1508. doi:10.1086/670802.

Lee, Sang-Heon, Deirdre M. McCann, and Jon C. Messenger. 2007. *Working Time around the World: Trends in Working Hours, Laws and Policies in a Global Comparative Perspective*. Routledge Studies in the Modern World Economy. London; New York: Geneva: Routledge; ILO.

Levitsky, Steven. 2010. *Competitive Authoritarianism: Hybrid Regimes after the Cold War*. Problems of International Politics. New York: Cambridge University Press.

Levitsky, Steven, and Lucan Way. 2002. "The Rise of Competitive Authoritarianism." *Journal of Democracy* 13 (2): 51–65.

Lewis, W. Arthur. 1954. "Economic Development with Unlimited Supplies of Labour." *The Manchester School* 22 (2): 139–91. doi:10.1111/j.1467-9957.1954.tb00021.x.

Li, Cheng. 2013. "Top-Level Reform or Bottom-up Revolution?" *Journal of Democracy* 24 (1): 41–48.

Lichtenstein, Nelson. 2003. "The Rights Revolution." *New Labor Forum* 12 (1): 61–73.

Li, Chunyun, and Liu, Mingwei. 2016. "A Pathway to a Vital Labour Movement in China? A Case Study of a Union-Led Protest against Walmart." In *China at Work: A Labour Process Perspective on the Transformation of Work and Employment in China*, 281–311. Palgrave Macmillan.

Lieberthal, Kenneth. 2004. *Governing China: From Revolution through Reform.* 2nd ed. New York: W. W. Norton.

Liebman, Benjamin L. 2011a. "A Return to Populist Legality: Historical Legacies and Legal Reform." In *Mao's Invisible Hand: The Political Foundations of Adaptive Governance in China*, 165–200. Cambridge MA and London: Harvard University Asia Center.

2011b. "The Media and the Courts: Towards Competitive Supervision?" *The China Quarterly* 208 (December): 833–50. doi:10.1017/S0305741011001020.

2013. "Malpractice Mobs: Medical Dispute Resolution in China." *Columbia Law Review*, 113: 181–264.

2014. "Legal Reform: China's Law-Stability Paradox." *Daedalus* 143 (2): 96–109. doi:10.1162/DAED_a_00275.

Li, Hongbin, and Li-An Zhou. 2005. "Political Turnover and Economic Performance: The Incentive Role of Personnel Control in China." *Journal of Public Economics* 89 (9–10): 1743–62. doi:10.1016/j.jpubeco.2004.06.009.

Li, L. 2013. "The Magnitude and Resilience of Trust in the Center: Evidence from Interviews with Petitioners in Beijing and a Local Survey in Rural China." *Modern China* 39 (1): 3–36. doi:10.1177/0097700412450661.

Li, Lianjiang. 2002. "The Politics of Introducing Direct Township Elections in China." *The China Quarterly* 171: 704–23. doi:10.1017/S0009443902000438.

2016. "Reassessing Trust in the Central Government: Evidence from Five National Surveys." *The China Quarterly* 225: 100–121. doi:10.1017/S0305741015001629.

Lin, Jia. 2007. "Ten Big New Concepts in Labor Contract Law Legislation (laodonghetongfa Lifa Shidaxinyi)." *Legal Daily*, August 19.

Li, Peilin, Guangjin Chen, and Yi Zhang. 2015. *Analysis and Forecast of Chinese Society (2015)*. Beijing: Chinese Academy of Social Sciences Publishing House.

Lipset, Seymour Martin. 1959. "Some Social Requisites of Democracy: Economic Development and Political Legitimacy." *American Political Science Review* 53 (01): 69–105. doi:10.2307/1951731.

Liu, Mingwei. 2010. "Union Organizing in China: Still a Monolithic Labor Movement?" *Industrial and Labor Relations Review*, 55: 30–52.

2014. "The Future of Chinese Labor Relations." *Members-Only Library*. http://50.87.169.168/OJS/ojs-2.4.4-1/index.php/LERAMR/article/view/1144.

Liu, Sida. 2011. "With or Without the Law: The Changing Meaning of Ordinary Legal Work in China, 1979–2003." In *Chinese Justice: Civil Dispute Resolution in Contemporary China*, 234–66. New York: Cambridge University Press.

Liu, Yu, and Dingding Chen. 2012. "Why China Will Democratize." *The Washington Quarterly* 35 (1): 41–63. doi:10.1080/0163660X.2012.641918.

Li, Xiaoying, and Richard B. Freeman. 2015. "How Does China's New Labour Contract Law Affect Floating Workers?: China's New Labour Contract Law." *British Journal of Industrial Relations* 53 (4): 711–35. doi:10.1111/bjir.12056.

Locke, Richard M. 2013. *The Promise and Limits of Private Power*. New York: Cambridge University Press.
Lorentzen, Peter L. 2013. "Regularizing Rioting: Permitting Public Protest in an Authoritarian Regime." *Quarterly Journal of Political Science* 8 (2): 127–58. doi:10.1561/100.00012051.
Lorentzen, Peter, Pierre Landry, and John Yasuda. 2014. "Undermining Authoritarian Innovation: The Power of China's Industrial Giants." *The Journal of Politics* 76 (01): 182–94.
Lou, Jiwei. 2015. "Full Text of Minister of Finance Lou Ji Wei Speech at Tsinghua University Business School (caizhengbuzhang loujiwei zai qinghua jingguan xueyuan yanjiang quanwen)."
Luo, Wangshu, and Zhu Jin. 2013. "Move to Change Gaokao Rules Spark Heated Debate." *China Daily*, January 24. http://africa.chinadaily.com.cn/china/2013-01/24/content_16167521.htm.
Magaloni, B. 2008. "Credible Power-Sharing and the Longevity of Authoritarian Rule." *Comparative Political Studies* 41 (4–5): 715–41. doi:10.1177/0010414007313124.
Magaloni, Beatriz. 2008. *Voting for Autocracy: Hegemonic Party Survival and Its Demise in Mexico*. Cambridge; New York: Cambridge University Press.
Magaloni, Beatriz, and Ruth Kricheli. 2010. "Political Order and One-Party Rule." *Annual Review of Political Science* 13 (1): 123–43. doi:10.1146/annurev.polisci.031908.220529.
Ma, Jianjun. 2016. "The Influence of Supply-Side Reform on the LCL." April 1. www.linkedin.com/pulse/%E9%A9%AC%E5%BB%BA%E5%86%9B%E4%BE%9B%E7%BB%99%E4%BE%A7%E6%94%B9%E9%9D%A9%E5%AF%B9%E5%8A%B3%E5%8A%A8%E5%90%88E5%90%8C%E6%B3%95%E7%9A%84%E5%BD%B1%E5%93%8D-margaret-fung.
Manion, M. 2014. "'Good Types' in Authoritarian Elections: The Selectoral Connection in Chinese Local Congresses." *Comparative Political Studies*, June. doi:10.1177/0010414014537027.
Manion, Melanie. 1996. "The Electoral Connection in the Chinese Countryside." *The American Political Science Review* 90 (4): 736. doi:10.2307/2945839.
   2014. "Authoritarian Parochialism: Local Congressional Representation in China." *The China Quarterly* 218 (June): 311–38. doi:10.1017/S0305741014000319.
McCann, Michael W. 1994. *Rights at Work: Pay Equity Reform and the Politics of Legal Mobilization*. Language and Legal Discourse. Chicago: University of Chicago Press.
McCubbins, Mathew D., and Thomas Schwartz. 1984. "Congressional Oversight Overlooked: Police Patrols versus Fire Alarms." *American Journal of Political Science* 28 (1): 165. doi:10.2307/2110792.
Meng, Xin. 2012. "Labor Market Outcomes and Reforms in China." *Journal of Economic Perspectives* 26 (4): 75–102. doi:10.1257/jep.26.4.75.
Michelson, Ethan. 2006. "The Practice of Law as an Obstacle to Justice: Chinese Lawyers at Work." *Law & Society Review* 40 (1): 1–38. doi:10.1111/j.1540-5893.2006.00257.x.

2007. "Climbing the Dispute Pagoda: Grievances and Appeals to the Official Justice System in Rural China." *American Sociological Review* 72 (3): 459–85.

2008. "Dear Lawyer Bao: Everyday Problems, Legal Advice, and State Power in China." *Social Problems* 55 (1): 43–71. doi:10.1525/sp.2008.55.1.43.

Miller, Blake and Mary Gallagher. 2017. "Can the Chinese Government really control the internet? We found cracks in the Great Firewall." *The Washington Post*, February 21. https://www.washingtonpost.com/news/monkey-cage/wp/2017/02/21/can-the-chinese-government-really-control-the-internet-we-found-cracks-in-the-great-firewall/?utm_term=.7f824a33e8c9.

Miller, Richard E., and Austin Sarat. 1980. "Grievances, Claims, and Disputes: Assessing the Adversary Culture." *Law and Society Review*, 15: 525–66.

Minzner, Carl F. 2006. "Xinfang: An Alternative to Formal Chinese Legal Institutions." *Stanford Journal of International Law* 42: 103.

2011. "China's Turn Against Law." *American Journal of Comparative Law* 59 (4): 935–84. doi:10.5131/AJCL.2011.0006.

Mitchell, Tom. 2015. "Chinese Factory Workers Strike over Benefits." *Financial Times*, March 18. www.ft.com/content/c46252d0-cd48-11e4-9144-00144feab7de.

2016. "Xi's China: Smothering Dissent." *The Financial Times*, July 27. www.ft.com/content/ccd94b46-4db5-11e6-88c5-db83e98a590a.

Mitchell, Tom, and Lucy Hornby. 2015. "China Lawyer Trial Begins amid Crackdown on Labour Rights Groups." *The Financial Times*, December 14. www.ft.com/content/a67e3882-a183-11e5-8d70-42b68cfae6e4.

Mok, Ka Ho, and John Hudson. 2014. "Managing Social Change and Social Policy in Greater China: Welfare Regimes in Transition?" *Social Policy and Society* 13 (02): 235–38. doi:10.1017/S1474746413000596.

Montinola, Gabriella, Yingyi Qian, and Barry R. Weingast. 1995. "Federalism, Chinese Style: The Political Basis for Economic Success in China." *World Politics* 48 (1): 50–81. doi:10.2307/25053952.

Moustafa, Tamir. 2009. *The Struggle for Constitutional Power: Law, Politics, and Economic Development in Egypt*. Cambridge: Cambridge University Press.

Nathan, Andrew J. 2003. "Authoritarian Resilience." *Journal of Democracy* 14 (1): 6–17.

National Bureau of Statistics. Various Years. *Labor Statistical Yearbook (zhongguo Laodong Tongji Nianjian)*. Beijing: China Statistics Press.

Ngai, Pun, and Huilin Lu. 2010. "A Culture of Violence: The Labor Subcontracting System and Collective Action by Construction Workers in Post-Socialist China." *The China Journal*, 64: 143–58.

Ngok, Kinglun. 2008. "The Changes of Chinese Labor Policy and Labor Legislation in the Context of Market Transition." *International Labor and Working Class History* 73 (01): 45–64.

Nielsen, Laura Beth. 2000. "Situating Legal Consciousness: Experiences and Attitudes of Ordinary Citizens about Law and Street Harassment." *Law & Society Review* 34 (4): 1055. doi:10.2307/3115131.

O'Brien, Kevin J. 1996. "Rightful Resistance." *World Politics* 49 (01): 31–55.

2013. "Rightful Resistance Revisited." *Journal of Peasant Studies* 40 (6): 1051–62. doi:10.1080/03066150.2013.821466.

O'Brien, Kevin J., and Yanhua Deng. 2015. "Repression Backfires: Tactical Radicalization and Protest Spectacle in Rural China." *Journal of Contemporary China* 24 (93): 457–70.

O'Brien, Kevin J., and Rongbin Han. 2009. "Path to Democracy? Assessing Village Elections in China." *Journal of Contemporary China* 18 (60): 359–78. doi:10.1080/10670560902770206.

O'Brien, Kevin J., and Lianjiang Li. 2006. *Rightful Resistance in Rural China*. Cambridge Studies in Contentious Politics. Cambridge; New York: Cambridge University Press.

O'Brien, K.J., and L. Li. 2006. *Rightful Resistance in Rural China*. Cambridge University Press. http://books.google.com/books?id=ZEcgOgqQoKUC.

Ong, Lynette H. 2014. "State-Led Urbanization in China: Skyscrapers, Land Revenue and 'Concentrated Villages.'" *The China Quarterly* 217 (March): 162–79. doi:10.1017/S0305741014000010.

Orren, Karen. 1991. *Belated Feudalism: Labor, the Law, and Liberal Development in the United States*. Cambridge [England]; New York: Cambridge University Press.

Paler, Laura. 2005. "China's Legislation Law and the Making of a More Orderly and Representative Legislative System." *The China Quarterly* 182: 301–18.

Pan, Wei. 2003. "Toward a Consultative Rule of Law Regime in China." *Journal of Contemporary China* 12 (34): 3–43.

Park, Albert, and Xuechao Qian. 2016. "How Are Chinese Manufacturing Firms Coping with Rising Labor Costs: Preliminary Evidence from Employer-Employee Surveys in Guangdong." HKUST.

Party School Research Group. 2009. "An Investigation into Ma'an Shan City's Implementation of the Labor Contract Law [duiwoshi Guanche Shishi Laodonghetongfa Qingkuang de Diaocha Yu Sikao." *JIangdong Luntan* 97.

Peerenboom. Randall; He, Xin. 2009. "Dispute Resolution in China: Patterns, Causes and Prognosis." *E. Asia L. Rev.* 4: 1.

Pei, Minxin. 1997. "Citizens v. Mandarins: Administrative Litigation in China." *The China Quarterly* 152: 832–62.

Peng, Dongyu. 2008. "三法实施将对和谐社会建设产生深远影响." *Zhongguo Renda*, April, 18–20.

Perry, Elizabeth J. 2008. "Chinese Conceptions of 'Rights': From Mencius to Mao—and Now." *Perspectives on Politics* 6 (01). doi:10.1017/S1537592708080055.

——— 2010. "Popular Protest: Playing by the Rules." In *China Today, China Tomorrow: Domestic Politics, Economy, and Society*, 11–28. Rowman & Littlefield Publishers.

Perry, Elizabeth J., and Merle Goldman, eds. 2007. *Grassroots Political Reform in Contemporary China*. Harvard Contemporary China Series 14. Cambridge, Mass.: Harvard University Press.

Pope, James Gray. 1997. "Labor's Constitution of Freedom." *Yale Law Journal*, 106: 941–1031.

Pringle, Tim. 2013. *Trade Unions in China: The Challenge of Labour Unrest*. [S.l.]: Oxford UK and New York, NY: Routledge.

Pringle, Tim, and Simon Clarke. 2011. *The Challenge of Transition: Trade Unions in Russia, China and Vietnam*. Non-Governmental Public Action Series. New York: Palgrave Macmillan.
Pun, N., and J. Chan. 2013. "The Spatial Politics of Labor in China: Life, Labor, and a New Generation of Migrant Workers." *South Atlantic Quarterly* 112 (1): 179–90. doi:10.1215/00382876-1891332.
Qiu, Jie. 2014. "The Paradox of China's Collective Consultation (集体协商的中国悖论)." *Gonghui Lilun Yanjjie*, 14: 8–14.
Rajah, Jothie. 2012. *Authoritarian Rule of Law: Legislation, Discourse, and Legitimacy in Singapore*. Cambridge Studies in Law and Society. Cambridge; New York: Cambridge University Press.
Relis, Tamara. 2002. "Civil Litigation from Litigants' Perspectives: What We Know and What We Don't Know about the Litigation Experience of Individual Litigants." In *Studies in Law, Politics, and Society*, 25:151–212. Elsevier.
"Report on China's Workers Movement, 2013–2014 (中国工人运动观察报告, 2013–2014." 2015. 24. Hong Kong: China Labour Bulletin.
Rickne, Johanna. 2012. "Labor Market Conditions and Social Insurance in China." 924. IFN Working Paper. Research Institute of Industrial Economics.
Rithmire, Meg. 2013. "Land Politics and Local State Capacities: The Political Economy of Urban Change in China." *The China Quarterly* 216 (December): 872–95. doi:10.1017/S0305741013001033.
Rooij, Benjamin van. 2006. *Regulating Land and Pollution in China: Lawmaking, Compliance, and Enforcement; Theory and Cases*. Leiden: Leiden University Press.
Schedler, Andreas, ed. 2006. *Electoral Authoritarianism: The Dynamics of Unfree Competition*. Boulder, Colo: L. Rienner Publishers, Inc.
SFTU. 2010. "Report on the Investigation of Shenzhen's New Generation of Migrant Workers Living Conditions." Shenzhen Federation of Trade Unions. http://acftu.people.com.cn/GB/67582/12154737.html.
Shi, Tianjian. 1997. *Political Participation in Beijing*. Cambridge, Mass: Harvard University Press.
SHUFE. 2016. "Shanghai University of Finance and Economics Convenes Symposium on LCL Revision." Shanghai: SHUFE. http://law.shufe.edu.cn/show.aspx?info_lb=12&flag=12&info_id=2980.
Silbey, Susan S. 2005. "AFTER LEGAL CONSCIOUSNESS." *Annual Review of Law and Social Science* 1 (1): 323–68. doi:10.1146/annurev.lawsocsci.1.041604.115938.
Silver, Beverly J. 2003. *Forces of Labor: Workers' Movements and Globalization since 1870*. Cambridge Studies in Comparative Politics. Cambridge; New York: Cambridge University Press.
Siu, Kaxton. 2015. "Continuity and Change in the Everyday Lives of Chinese Migrant Factory Workers." *China Journal*, 74: 43–65.
Slater, Dan. 2010. *Ordering Power: Contentious Politics and Authoritarian Leviathans in Southeast Asia*. New York: Cambridge University Press.
Smith, A. 2009. "Political Groups, Leader Change, and the Pattern of International Cooperation." *Journal of Conflict Resolution* 53 (6): 853–77. doi:10.1177/0022002709344419.

Solinger, Dorothy J. 1999. *Contesting Citizenship in Urban China: Peasant Migrants, the State, and the Logic of the Market.* Studies of the East Asian Institute, Columbia University. Berkeley: University of California Press.

Song, Ligang, Ross Garnaut, and Cai Cai, eds. 2014. *Deepening Reform for China's Long-Term Growth and Development.* China Update Book Series. Canberra: ANU Press [u.a.].

Sorace, Christian, and William Hurst. 2016. "China's Phantom Urbanisation and the Pathology of Ghost Cities." *Journal of Contemporary Asia* 46 (2): 304–22. doi:10.1080/00472336.2015.1115532.

South China Morning Post. 2015. "Top China Official's Criticism of Labour Policy Sparks Controversy," May 3. www.scmp.com/news/china/policies-politics/article/1784530/top-china-officials-criticism-labour-policy-sparks.

"Speech Excerpts: Group Deliberation on the Draft Labor Contract Law (1)." 2005. Beijing: National People's Congress.

Spires, Anthony J. 2011. "Contingent Symbiosis and Civil Society in an Authoritarian State: Understanding the Survival of China's Grassroots NGOs 1." *American Journal of Sociology* 117 (1): 1–45. doi:10.1086/660741.

Spires, Anthony J., Lin Tao, and Kin-man Chan. 2014. "Societal Support for China's Grass-Roots NGOs: Evidence from Yunnan, Guangdong and Beijing." *China Journal*, no. 71: 65–90.

"Statistical Analysis of 2012 Labor Disputes (2012年全国劳动人事争议处理情况统计数据分析)." 2013.

Stern, Rachel E. 2014. *Environmental Litigation in China: A Study in Political Ambivalence.* [Place of publication not identified]: Cambridge University Press.

Stockmann, D., and M. E. Gallagher. 2011. "Remote Control: How the Media Sustain Authoritarian Rule in China." *Comparative Political Studies* 44 (4): 436–67. doi:10.1177/0010414010394773.

"Strikes Continue Unabated in China during First Half of the Year." 2016. Hong Kong: China Labour Bulletin. www.clb.org.hk/content/strikes-continue-unabated-china-during-first-half-year.

Sun, Ivan Y., and Yuning Wu. 2006. "Citizens' Perceptions of the Courts: The Impact of Race, Gender, and Recent Experience." *Journal of Criminal Justice* 34 (5): 457–67. doi:10.1016/j.jcrimjus.2006.09.001.

Sun, Xin. 2014. "Autocrats' Dilemma: The Dual Impacts of Village Elections on Public Opinion in China." *China Journal*, no. 71: 109–31.

Su, Yang, and Xin He. 2010. "Street as Courtroom: State Accommodation of Labor Protest in South China." *Law & Society Review* 44 (1): 157–84.

Su, Yihui. 2010. "Student Workers in the Foxconn Empire: The Commodification of Education and Labor in China." *Journal of Workplace Rights* 15 (3): 341–62.

Tang, W. 2005. *Public Opinion and Political Change in China.* Stanford University Press. http://books.google.com/books?id=VGA9OONVhtcC.

Tang, Wenfang. 2009. "Rule of Law and Dispute Resolution in China: Evidence from Survey Data." *China Review*, 73–96.

2016. *Populist Authoritarianism: Chinese Political Culture and Regime Sustainability.* New York, NY: Oxford University Press.

Tang, Wenfang, and Qing Yang. 2008. "The Chinese Urban Caste System in Transition." *The China Quarterly* 196 (December): 759. doi:10.1017/S0305741008001112.

Taylor, Bill. 2000. "Trade Unions and Social Capital in Transitional Communist States: The Case of China." *Policy Sciences* 33 (3–4): 341–54.

Taylor, Bill, Chang Chang, and Li Li. 2003. *Industrial Relations in China*. Cheltenham: Elgar.

Traub-Merz, Rudolf., International Labour Office., and Global Labour University (Germany). 2011. *All China Federation of Trade Unions: Structure, Functions and the Challenge of Collective Bargaining*. Geneva: ILO.

Trejo, Guillermo. 2012. *Popular Movements in Autocracies*. New York: Cambridge University Press.

Troyer, R.J., J.P. Clark, and D.G. Rojek. 1989. *Social Control in the People's Republic of China*. New York: Praeger Publishing Group.

Tsai, Kellee S. 2006. "Adaptive Informal Institutions and Endogenous Institutional Change in China." *World Politics* 59 (01): 116–41. doi:10.1353/wp.2007.0018.

Tsai, Lily L. 2007. "Solidary Groups, Informal Accountability, and Local Public Goods Provision in Rural China." *American Political Science Review* 101 (02): 355–72.

Unirule Institute. 2016. "Unirule Institute Symposium on the Labor Contract Law and Supply Side Reform." Beijing, July 27.

Upham, Frank K. 1976. "Litigation and Moral Consciousness in Japan: An Interpretive Analysis of Four Japanese Pollution Suits." *Law and Society Review*, 10: 579–619.

USCBC. 2016. "2015 USCBC Member Survey Report: Growth Continues Amidst Economic Slowdown, Rising Competition, Policy Uncertainty." Washington, D.C: The US-China Business Council.

Venn, Danielle. 2009. *Legislation, Collective Bargaining and Enforcement: Updating the OECD Employment Protection Indicators*. OECD Paris. www.oecd.org/employment/emp/43116624.pdf.

Walder, Andrew George. 1988. *Communist Neo-Traditionalism: Work and Authority in Chinese Industry*. Berkeley, Calif.: University of California Press.

Wallace, Jeremy L. 2014. *Cities and Stability: Urbanization, Redistribution, & Regime Survival in China*. New York: Oxford University Press.

Wang, Biqiang. 2012. "'Build a Hedge' Labor Dispatch." *Caijing*, May 21.

Wang, Fei-Ling. 2005. *Organizing through Division and Exclusion: China's Hukou System*. Stanford, Calif: Stanford University Press.

Wang, Jing, and Yanyan Wang. 2016. "Guangdong Freezes Worker Salaries to 'Help Manufacturers.'" *Caixin Online*, March 3. www.caixinglobal.com/2016-03-03/101011829.html.

Wang, Quanxing. 2007. "Options to Overcome the Phenomenon of Short-Term Contractualization (kefu Laodonghetong Duanqihua Xianxiang de Mubiao Xuanze." *China Social Security Daily*, April 3.

Wang, Yuhua. 2014. *Tying the Autocrat's Hands: The Rise of the Rule of Law in China*. New York, NY: Cambridge University Press.

Wang, Yuhua, and Carl F. Minzner. 2013. "The Rise of the Security State." Available at SSRN 2365624. http://papers.ssrn.com/sol3/papers.cfm?abstract_id=2365624.

Weil, David. 2004. "Individual Rights and Collective Agents. The Role of Old and New Workplace Institutions in the Regulation of Labor Markets." In *Emerging Labor Market Institutions for the Twenty-First Century*, 13–44. University of Chicago Press. www.nber.org/chapters/c9948.pdf.

Weil, David. 2014. *The Fissured Workplace*. Cambridge, MA: Harvard University Press.

White, Gordon. 1987. "The Politics of Economic Reform in Chinese Industry: The Introduction of the Labour Contract System." *The China Quarterly*, 111 (September): 365–89.

Whiting, S. 2011. "Values in Land: Fiscal Pressures, Land Disputes and Justice Claims in Rural and Peri-Urban China." *Urban Studies* 48 (3): 569–87. doi:10.1177/0042098010390242.

Whiting, Susan. 2006. "The Cadre Evaluation System at the Grassroots: The Paradox of Party Rule." In *Holding China Together: Diversity and National Integration in the Post-Deng Era*. New York and London: Cambridge University Press.

Whyte, Martin King, ed. 2010. *One Country, Two Societies: Rural-Urban Inequality in Contemporary China*. Harvard Contemporary China Series 16. Cambridge, Mass.: Harvard University Press.

Wilentz, Sean. 1984. "Against Exceptionalism: Class Consciousness and the American Labor Movement, 1790–1920." *International Labor and Working-Class History* 26: 1–24.

Wing Chan, Kam, and Will Buckingham. 2008. "Is China Abolishing the Hukou System?" *The China Quarterly* 195 (September). doi:10.1017/S0305741008000787.

Wintrobe, Ronald. 2000. *The Political Economy of Dictatorship*. Cambridge, UK; New York, NY: Cambridge University Press.

Wong, Chun Han. 2016. "China May Rein in Wage Increases to Boost Economy." *The Wall Street Journal*, March 10. www.wsj.com/articles/china-may-rein-in-wage-rises-to-boost-economy-1457616686.

World Bank. 2014. *Urban China: Toward Efficient, Inclusive, and Sustainable Urbanization*. The World Bank. www.worldbank.org/en/country/china/publication/urban-china-toward-efficient-inclusive-sustainable-urbanization.

Wright, Erik Olin. 2000. "Working-Class Power, Capitalist-Class Interests, and Class Compromise." *American Journal of Sociology*, 957–1002.

Xinhua News Online. 2006. "The Draft Labor Contract Law Public Solicitation for Opinions Yields 191,849." (laodong Hetongfa Caoan Gongkai Zhengqiu Yijian Jiangong 191,849," April 21.

⸻ 2016. "Xinhua Insight: China's Finance Minister Criticizes Law on Live TV," March 7. http://news.xinhuanet.com/english/2016-03/07/c_135164575.htm.

Yang, G., and C. Calhoun. 2007. "Media, Civil Society, and the Rise of a Green Public Sphere in China." *China Information* 21 (2): 211–36. doi:10.1177/0920203X07079644.

Yang, Yi. 2014. "Highlights of Communique of 4th Plenary Session of CPC Central Committee." *Xinhua News Online*, October 23. http://news.xinhuanet.com/english/china/2014-10/23/c_133737957.htm.

Yan, Xiaojun. 2011. "Regime Inclusion and the Resilience of Authoritarianism: The Local People's Political Consultative Conference in Post-Mao Chinese Politics." *The China Journal*, 66: 53–75.

Yan, Yunxiang. 2010. "The Chinese Path to Individualization: The Chinese Path to Individualization." *The British Journal of Sociology* 61 (3): 489–512. doi:10.1111/j.1468-4446.2010.01323.x.

Yao, Yang. 2011. "The Relationship between China's Export-Led Growth and Its Double Transition of Demographic Change and Industrialization*." *Asian Economic Papers* 10 (2): 52–76.

Yao, Yang, and Ninghua Zhong. 2013. "Unions and Workers' Welfare in Chinese Firms." *Journal of Labor Economics* 31 (3): 633–67. doi:10.1086/669819.

Yuan, Jianzhang. 2013. "'I've Been a Nursing Assistant for Twenty Years, How Could I Not Have Relations with the Hospital' (做了20年护工, 怎么就和医院没关系)." *Information Times (信息时报)*, April 13. http://chuansong.me/n/1044380852453.

Yuan, Zaijun. 2011. "Independent Candidates in China's Local People's Congress Elections." *Journal of Chinese Political Science* 16 (4): 389–405. doi:10.1007/s11366-011-9167-x.

Zemans, Frances Kahn. 1983. "Legal Mobilization: The Neglected Role of the Law in the Political System." *The American Political Science Review* 77 (3): 690. doi:10.2307/1957268.

Zeng, Qingjie. 2016. "Democratic Procedures in the CCP's Cadre Selection Process: Implementation and Consequences." *The China Quarterly* 225: 73–99.

Zhang, Li. 2001. *Strangers in the City: Reconfigurations of Space, Power, and Social Networks within China's Floating Population*. Stanford, Calif: Stanford University Press.

Zhang, Wuchang. 2008. "Another Discussion of the New Labor Law." *Zhang Wuchang de Boke*. January 9. http://blog.sina.com.cn/zhangwuchang.

Zheng, Dongliang. 2008. "Expert Discussion on the Implementation of the Labor Contract Law (laodonghetongfa shishi zhuanjia tan)." *China Labor (zhongguolaodong)*, 1: 6–14.

Zhuang, Wenjia, and Feng Chen. 2015. "'Mediate First': The Revival of Mediation in Labour Dispute Resolution in China." *The China Quarterly* 222: 380–402.

Zhuang, Wenjia, and Kinglun Ngok. 2014. "Labour Inspection in Contemporary China: Like the Anglo-Saxon Model, but Different." *International Labour Review* 153 (4): 561–85.

Zhu, Zhe. 2007. "Legislation to Focus on Social Issues." *China Daily*, March 12.

"中共中央国务院关于构建和谐劳动关系的意见 (Central Party and the State Council Opinion on the Construction of Harmonious Labor Relations)." 2015. http://baike.baidu.com/item/中共中央国务院关于构建和谐劳动关系的意见.

朱建新, and 王新阳. 2004. *HELP 生活诉讼丛书*,. 南京: 江苏人民出版社.

董保华, and 杨杰. 2003. *外地来沪就为人员法律知识 200 问*. 上海: 上海交通大学出版社.

许淑红. 2008. *劳动合同法案例讲堂*. 北京: 中国法制出版社.

黄健, 黄雷, and 章琼怡. 2008. *企业常输的劳动官司 = Navigating Labor Suits Made Easy*. 上海: 百家出版社.

Index

All-China Federation of Trade Unions (ACFTU), 5, 71–77, 86
arbitration in labor disputes, 86–89
authoritarian legality
  bottom-up mobilization of workers, 30–32
  Chinese situation compared to theory, 38–43
  comparative perspective on China, 36–50
  constraints on, 50
  encouragement of citizen engagement with the law, 48–50
  limits of, 213–15
  market conforming nature in China, 34–36
  motivations for, 30–32
  politically restrained nature in China, 34–36
  quasi-democratic nature in China, 30–32
authoritarian regimes
  ambivalence towards reforms, 224–26
  resilience in China, 43–46
  resilience theories, 46–50
  use of democratic institutions to strengthen and stabilize, 224–26
authoritarianism
  theories of regime survival, 38–43

Beijing
  restricted educational opportunities for migrant children, 11–12
bottom-up legal mobilization of workers
  as means of building hierarchical trust, 33–34
  government motivations for, 30–32
  pressures on local government, 32–33
Burke, Edmund, 191

cadre evaluation system, 32
Changde Walmart
  interest dispute, 208–13
China
  factors in rapid economic growth, 6
China Urban Labor Survey (CULS), 16, 95–96
Chinese Academy of Social Sciences (CASS), 16
  report on the scale of labor grievances, 191–93
Chinese Communist Party (CCP), 30, 45, 72
  deployment of rule of law, 31–32
Chinese Enterprise Management Association, 86
Chinese government
  constrained and reactive enforcement of labor laws, 102–8
  difficulties of managing at local level, 32–33
  effects of removal of socialist system entitlements, 34–36
  high standards of workplace protections, 27–28

247

Chinese government (*cont.*)
    incomplete institutionalization of the dispute resolution system, 194–95
    labor dispute resolution system, 29
    labor market reforms to promote urbanization, 4
    labor reform enforcement and compliance mechanisms, 4–5
    legal dissemination campaigns, 28–29
    legislation enforcement and compliance model, 13–14
    legislation to formalize employment relations, 4
    promotion of workplace rights, 4–5
    strategic aims of labor law reform, 149–52
    strategic motivation for workplace reforms, 5–6
    turn against the law, 200–01
citizen engagement with the law, 48–50
collective land ownership system, 9
collective mobilization
    as a result of government policy, 194–95
    Changde Walmart interest dispute, 208–13
    Guangzhou Chinese Medicine Hospital, 201–08
collective representation and bargaining limitations on, 71–77
Cultural Revolution, 130, 137, 146, 152

demographic dividend
    benefits to China, 6–9
    effects of changing demographics, 6–9
demographic structure
    new model of development in China, 8–9
Deng Liqun, 79
Deng Xiaoping, 73, 79, 81, 197
development
    transition to a new model in China, 50–51
dictatorship
    nature of, 39
disputants
    generational divide, 175–89
dispute resolution system. *See* labor dispute resolution system

East China University of Politics and Law (ECUPL) Legal Aid Center for Workers, 14

economic development
    factors in rapid growth in China, 6
    middle-income trap, 226–27
    necessity of a new model for China, 8–9
education
    claiming rights, 122–25
    comparing legal theory and practice, 125–29
    consequences of expansion in China, 50–51
    experiential knowledge from using the law, 113–14
    higher education and effective use of the law, 112–13
    impact of the Cultural Revolution, 130
    importance in legal mobilization, 118–19
    knowing and naming rights, 119–22
    restricted opportunities for migrant children, 11–12
    role in legal mobilization, 112–14, 146–48
    self-education about the law, 113. *See also* learning narratives
Egypt
    Mubarak autocracy, 44
employment
    formal employment contracts, 2–3
    legislation to promote formal employment relations, 4
Employment Promotion Law (2008), 16, 67, 198
Employment Protection Index (OECD)
    China's ranking, 27–28
equality challenge
    migrant workers as urban citizens, 11–12
experience of the law
    comparing theory and practice, 125–29
    rates of dissatisfaction, 125–29
experiential learning
    disenchantment with legal processes, 141–46
    from using the law, 113–14

Feng Chen, 72
fire-alarm mechanism for workplace regulation, 108–11
firm compliance
    effects of workplace legal reforms, 94–102
foreign-invested enterprises (FIEs), 121, 153

formal employment contracts
  link with social welfare access, 2

'ghost city' developments, 10
Global Financial Crisis (2008), 68, 89
Guangdong
  disputes and strikes over social insurance, 9
Guangdong Federation of Trade Unions (GFTU), 206
Guangzhou Chinese Medicine Hospital
  collective mobilization, 201–08

harmonious labor relations policy, 193–94
harmonious society concept
  and labor conflict, 197–200
Heilmann, Sebastian, 46–47
Heilongjiang
  disputes and strikes over social insurance, 9
hierarchical trust
  legal mobilization as means of building, 33–34
Hong Kong, 14
household registration system, 12–14, 175
Hu Jintao, 10, 23, 67, 81, 193, 197, 217
Huang Xingguo, 208
hukou system, 175
  restrictions on labor supply, 8
  rights and benefits based on *hukou* status, 2
  rural-urban inequalities, 12–14
Hunan Federation of Trade Unions (HFTU), 211

individualistic rights mobilization
  strategic use by the Chinese state, 55–62
industrialization
  and the Lewis turning point, 7–8
  and urbanization, 2
informed disenchantment, 113
  consequence of legal experience, 152–61
Institute of Population and Labor Economics (IPLE), 16
institutional context of China's rights mobilization, 62–89
institutional reform
  strategic aims of the government, 149–52
  summary of reforms and effects, 54
  transition from the socialist system, 52–54

institutions
  failings exposed by legal mobilization of workers, 113–14
  role in authoritarian resilience, 46–50
interest disputes
  in an institutional vacuum, 208–13
internet
  spread of social grievances, 192

Jiangsu
  disputes and strikes over social insurance, 9

labor activists, 17, 73, 200
Labor Arbitration Committees (LACs), 24, 86
labor conflict
  and pursuit of a harmonious society, 197–200
  arbitration, 86–89
  as a result of government policy, 194–95
  increase after 2008, 197–200
  increase in strikes, 199–200
  labor dispute resolution process, 85–89
  turn against the law, 200–01
Labor Contract Law (2008), 8, 16, 29, 35, 88, 198
  debate over revision and weakening of the law, 218–21
  formalization of employment relations, 4
  legal mobilization effect, 153
  purpose and development, 67–70
  research on the effects of, 221–24
  severance compensation, 209
  shortcomings of the law, 216–18
  turn against the law, 216–18
Labor Daily, 84–85
Labor Defense Law Firm, 207
Labor Dispute Mediation and Arbitration Law (2008), 16, 29, 67, 87–89, 198
  legal mobilization effect, 153
labor dispute resolution system, 85–89
  effects on firm compliance, 94–102
  incomplete institutionalization, 194–95
  individualized nature, 29, 34–36
  introduction and rates of usage, 29
labor disputes
  fire-alarm mechanism for workplace regulation, 108–11
  generational differences in disputants, 175–89

labor disputes (*cont.*)
  importance of legal aid and
    representation, 162–75
  lack of affordable legal assistance for
    disputants, 189–90
  view of users and non-users of the law,
    150, 151
labor grievances
  CASS report on the scale of, 191–93
labor inspection
  constrained and reactive enforcement,
    102–08
labor institutions
  role in China's changing workplace
    relations, 1
Labor Law (1995), 7, 26–27, 29, 35, 61
  inclusiveness and protection, 64–67
  labor dispute resolution, 85
  purpose and development, 63–64
Labor Law Mobilization Survey (2005),
  15, 95
labor lawyers, 200
labor legislation
  challenges of introduction and
    implementation, 1–2
  constrained and reactive enforcement by
    government, 102–08
  development of, 63–64
  inclusion and protection, 64–70
  individualized focus, 70–77
  strategic purpose, 63–64
  transformation of the Chinese socialist
    system, 26–30
labor market
  legislation to promote urbanization,
    4
labor NGOs, 17, 73–74, 192, 193, 200,
  207
labor supply
  effects of *hukou* restrictions, 8
land development
  consequences of the drive for, 9–10
  creation of landless peasants, 10–11
land ownership
  collective land ownership system, 9
  exchange for employment, 2–3
  security challenge of exchanging for
    work, 9–11
law
  encouragement of citizen engagement
    with, 48–50

learning narratives, 129–30
  disenchantment following experience of
    legal processes, 141–46
  experiential knowledge of the law,
    141–46
  from petitioner to citizen representative,
    137–41
  law and formal education, 131–34
  leadership through legal and formal
    education, 134–37
  petitioning, 137–39
  role of education in legal mobilization,
    146–48
  self-education in the law, 137–41
Lee, C.K., 56–57
legal advice
  sources available to workers, 83–85
legal dissemination campaigns
  Chinese government campaigns, 28–29
  control and mobilization, 78–85
legal experience
  and informed disenchantment, 152–61
legal mobilization
  as political participation, 114, 115–18
  awareness of rights, 119–22
  benefits of higher education, 112–13
  claiming rights, 122–25
  comparing legal theory with practice,
    125–29
  constitutive interpretation, 55–62
  effects of reactive government in China,
    108–11
  effects on firm compliance, 94–102
  fire-alarm mechanism for workplace
    regulation, 108–11
  forms in the United States, 115
  generational differences, 150–51, 152,
    175–89
  importance of education, 118–19
  importance of legal aid and
    representation, 150, 151, 162–75
  individualized nature in China, 34–36
  lack of affordable legal assistance,
    189–90
  likelihood of naming a problem and
    making a claim, 152–61
  negative effects of experiences of using
    the law, 113–14
  political generations in China, 175–89
  rates of dissatisfaction with the legal
    process, 125–29

role of education, 112–14, 146–48
self-education about the law, 113
strategic aims of the government, 149–52
surge in labor disputes after 2008, 89–94
view of user and non-user disputants, 150, 151
legal representation
  importance for disputants, 162–75
Lewis, Arthur, 7–8
Li Keqiang, 77
local governments
  consequences of the land development drive, 9–10
  diverging incentives, 32–33
Lou Jiwei, 68, 216, 226, 227

Mao Zedong, 38, 73, 175
market economy
  China's transition to, 1–2
Marriage Law (1950), 48
Marxist-Leninism, 73
middle-income trap
  as a political dilemma, 226–27

Nathan, Andrew, 46, 47
National New Type of Urbanization plan (2014–2020), 3
New People Evening News, 84

O'Brien, Kevin J. and Lianjiang Li, 34, 58, 79

peasants
  loss of land security, 10–11
People's Daily, 79
Perry, Elizabeth, 46–47, 55–56
petitioning, 137–39
political generations in China, 175–89
political participation
  legal mobilization as, 114, 115–18
principal–agent problem
  pressures on local government, 32–33
Public Security Bureau, 207

research data and methodology, 14–17
rightful resistance model of state–society relations, 58–59
rights
  awareness of, 119–22
rights consciousness
  United States, 59–62

rights disputes
  Changde Walmart, 208–13
  feedback loop between protest and the law, 201–08
  use of extra-legal measures, 201–08
rights mobilization
  constitutive interpretation, 55–62
  experience of marginalized groups, 56–57
  focus on individualistic rights, 55–62
  implications of rules consciousness in China, 55–56
Rule of Law Index (World Justice Project), 82–83
rules consciousness in China
  implications for rights mobilization, 55–56
rural migrant children
  restricted educational opportunities in cities, 11–12
rural migrants
  access to urban social welfare, 2–3
  equality challenge as urban citizens, 11–12
  exchange of land ownership for employement, 2–3
  inequality and discrimination in cities, 2
  institutional barriers faced by, 7–8
  process of becoming urbanized, 2

security challenge
  exchanging land for work, 9–11
self-education about the law, 113
Shanghai
  restricted educational opportunities for migrant children, 11–12
social conflict and mobilization
  CASS report, 191–93
social divisions
  use of the law to exploit, 49–50
social insurance
  disputes and strikes over, 9
Social Insurance Law (2011), 8, 9, 16, 67, 227
social welfare
  access to, 2–3
  link to formal employment, 2–3
state-led urbanization, 2–3
State Security Bureau, 207
strikes
  increase in, 199–200

Tullock, Gordon, 21
turn against the law
　shortcomings of the Labor Contract Law (2008), 216–18
　workers and the state, 200–01

United States
　Congressional oversight mechanisms, 108–09
　Equal Employment Opportunity Commission (EEOC), 61
　Fair Labor Standards Act (1939), 59
　history of workplace rights and protections, 59–62
　National Labor Relations Act (1935) (Wagner Act), 59
　nature of legal mobilization, 115
　nature of political participation, 115
　rights consciousness, 59–62
urban social welfare
　access to, 2–3
urbanization
　and industrialization, 2
　challenge of workplace rights, 12–14
　exchange of rural land ownership for employment, 2–3
　extent and rapidity in China, 1
　labor market reforms to promote, 4
　National New Type of Urbanization plan (2014–2020), 3
　state-led, 2–3

traditional process based on *hukou* status, 2

WeChat, 226
Weibo, 226
Wen Jiabao, 10, 67, 197, 217
work unit (*danwei*) system of employment, 175
worker legal mobilization. *See* bottom-up legal mobilization of workers; legal mobilization
workers
　sources of legal advice and support, 83–85
　turn against the law, 200–01
workplace reforms
　strategic motivations of the Chinese state, 5–6
workplace rights
　awareness of, 119–22
　challenge of urbanization, 12–14
　claiming rights, 122–25
　determined by *hukou* status, 2
　inequality between urban and rural citizens, 11–12
　influence of the *hukou* system, 12–14
　promotion by the Chinese state, 4–5
　workers' methods of pursuing, 4–5
World Bank Doing Business Index, 66

Xi Jinping, 23, 193, 214, 216, 217, 225
Xin Chunying, 88, 89, 94